GAMES
TO PLAY

This book was devised and produced by
Dunestyle (Publishing) Limited

First published in 1988 by
Michael Joseph Limited

Published by the Penguin Group
27 Wrights Lane, London W8 5TZ, England
Viking Penguin Inc., 40 West 23rd Street,
New York, New York 10010, USA
Penguin Books Australia Ltd, Ringwood,
Victoria, Australia
Penguin Books Canada Ltd, 2801 John Street,
Markham, Ontario, Canada L3R IB4
Penguin Books (NZ) Ltd, 182-190 Wairau Road,
Auckland 10, New Zealand
Penguin Books Ltd,
Registered Offices: Harmondsworth,
Middlesex, England

A CIP catalogue record for this book
is available from the British Library

Text © _____ R. C. Bell
Pictures © _____ Dunestyle (Publishing) Limited
Edited by_____ Linda Doeser
Editorial Director_ Megra Mitchell
Art Director_____ John Strange
Photography_____ Kirsty McLaren
Copyright © _____ Dunestyle Publishing Limited
                    25 West Cottages, West End Lane,
                    London NW6 1RJ
Design_____ Strange Design Associates (London)
Typesetting_____ O'Reilly Clark (London)
Origination_____ J. Film Process Company Limited,
                    Bangkok, Thailand
Printed by_____ Lito Roberto Terrazzi, Italy
ISBN _____ 0 7181 2993 8

This edition published 1988 by
Guild Publishing by arrangement with
Michael Joseph Ltd   CN 5854

Half title page
Pottery figurine of the
'Card Players' c.1970.

Title page
Six pieces from a Spanish bone
'Pulpit' chess set. 18th Century.

BOARD
AND TABLE
GAMES FOR ALL
THE FAMILY

GAMES
TO PLAY

R.C. BELL

Introduction————————————————————————Page 6

Chapter 1————————Race Games————————————— Page 8

Nyout • Pachisi • Ludo • The Snake Game • The Royal Game of Goose
Geographical Game Thro' Europe • The Game of Race • Snakes and Ladders
Tau • Senat • Duodecim Scriptorum • Backgammon • Tavli • The Snail Game

Chapter 2————————War Games—————————————Page 23

Ludus Latrunculorum • Seega • High Jump • Hnefatafl • Halatafl • Asalto
Sixteen Soldiers • Cows and Leopards • Tablan • Chaturanga • Shatranj • Chess
Four-Handed Chess • Maharajah and Sepoys • Alquerque • Fanorona
Quadruple Alquerque • Ratti-Chitti-Bakri • Draughts and variants • Tams
L'Attaque • Dover Patrol • Aviation • Tri-Tactics • Hasami Shogi II • Yoté
Konane • Ming Mang • German Tactics • Siege of Paris • Stockade

Chapter 3————————Games of Position————————————Page 45

Tic-Tac-Toe • Achi • Nine Men's Morris • Dara • Go-moku • Hasami Shogi I
Four Balls • 3-D Three-in-a-Row • Five Field Kono • Halma • Chinese Checkers
Reversi • Pong Hau K'i • Mu Torere • Go • Pasang • Star of David • Solitaire
Lam Turki

Chapter 4————————Mancala Games—————————————Page 54

Sunka • Pallanguli • Tamilnadi • Olinda Keliya • Abalala'e • Baré • Wari

Chapter 5————————Dice and Spinners————————————Page 62

Thirty-six • Aces in the Pot • Rotation • The Game of the Pedlar • Martinetti
Indian Dice • Sequences • Aces • Shut the Box • Crown and Anchor • Poker Dice
Liar Dice • Put and Take • Dreidel • Roulette • Hoca • Roly Poly
Jeu de Courses • Electric Derby • Four Numbers • Hoo Hey How

Chapter 6————————Playable Games————————————Page 73

Royal Game of Goose • Nine Men's Morris • Aphelion • Continental Draughts
Ups and Downs • Ludus Latrunculorum • The Royal Hurdle Race Game
Siege of Paris • Lam Turki • Lau Kati Kata • Cows and Leopards
Officers and Sepoys • The Sumerian Game • Race to the Gold Diggings • Go
Crossroads to Conquerors Castle • The Snake Game • Blackjack
South Sea Adventures • Sunka • Halma • Poch

Chapter 7 ——— Dominoes ——— Page 116

The Block Game • Two-Handed Block Game • All Fives • Domino Pool
The Matador Game • Cyprus • Tiddle-a-Wink • Chinese Dominoes
Disputing Tens • Mah-jongg • Tops • Rummikub • Tri-Ominos

Chapter 8 ——— Card Games ——— Page 132
Requiring Boards or Markers

Cribbage • Pope Joan • Poch • Le Nain Jaune • Bonanza • Blackjack
The Royal Hurdle Race Game

Chapter 9 ——— Games ——— Page 139
Requiring Manual Dexterity

Shove Ha'penny • Squails • Carroms • Brother Jonathan • Bagatelle
Table Ten-Pins • Skittles • Table Skittles • Table Quoits • Blow Football
Ping-Pong • Rings • One Hundred and Fifty-One • Twice Round the Board
Eighty-One • Darts • Three Hundred and One • Round the Clock
Carpet Bowls • Royal Game of Billiard Bowls • Trench Football • Ti Rakau

Chapter 10 ——— North American ——— Page 150
Indian Games

Slahal • The Dice Game • The Bowl Game • The Stave Game • Patolli
Gambling Sticks

Chapter 11 ——— Fortune Telling ——— Page 156

Chi Chi Sticks • The Telepathic Spirit Communicator • Tarot Cards
Fortune Telling Bagatelle • The Fortune Teller
Talismen, Charms and Good Luck Symbols

Chapter 12 — Making a Games Collection ——— Page 160

——— Glossary ——— Page 188

——— Index ——— Page 189

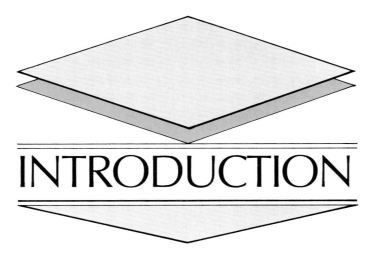

INTRODUCTION

'One day Charlot, having nothing else to do, invited young Baldwin to play at chess. The lad willingly consented, ran for the chessboard, all of solid gold, inlaid with silver, got out the ivory pieces, and the game began.

Charlot prided himself on his skill at chess; but, to tell the truth, it was not great, and he soon found that he had met more than his match. The boy Baldwin moved his pieces so skilfully that before long he had taken a knight and given check to Charlot, who began to lose his temper.

'Aha, my lord, you are going to be checkmated!' cried the boy, clapping his hands and laughing.

'Have done with your laughing, young sir, or you will repent it,' replied Charlot with a frown.

'Why should I not laugh? The game is worth nothing without laughing.'

'Do you mean to mock me, you little knave?'

'No, but to beat you.'

'Charlot castled his king, and saw his second knight taken. Hastily, then, he moved his queen, which was at once taken by a bishop. He played wildly at random, growing too angry to think what he was doing. When after a few more moves, he found himself checkmated, he started up from the table, seized the golden chessboard with both hands, and struck the boy over the forehead with it so violently that he fell dead on the marble pavement.'

As can be seen in this extract from the medieval story of Ogier the Dane (translated by A. R. Hope Moncrieff), games can arouse deepfelt passion on the part of the participants. Although most of us would now thankfully refrain from physically berating a victorious opponent, we must all be well aware that the playing of games is fundamentally a ritualized microcosm of our daily battle for life. For as Marshall McLuhan states, in games we create 'a sort of artificial paradise... By which we interpret and complete the daily meaning of our lives. In games we devise a means of nonspecialized participation in the larger drama of our time.'

The need for competitive play in man is endemic and as a consequence questions such as What was the first game? When did it come about? are essentially spurious. All one can ultimately do is to seek to find the origins of specific game formats.

The basic components of play, a patch of earth, some stones or twigs or bits of bone, have an existence older than man's, requiring only his presence to be transmuted into formalized symbols of his own actions. The Australian aborigines, for example, would use a bone which was thrown into the centre of a circle around which the tribe was gathered to determine who among them was causing unrest. Many of the earliest known games can be shown to have had a religious significance, logical byproducts of man's animism, by means of which every object was seen as an independent living entity capable of affecting and moulding the course of his life. Indeed, man sought by means of games to explain his own origins. Thus, the ancient Egyptians explained the advent of the 365 day calendar (hitherto only 360 days) as a by-product of a dice game between Thoth the god of night and the moon. So too the ancient Greeks, who explained the equitable division of the earth between Zeus, Poseidon and Hades as the result of their casting lots.

Chance has always been seen as a vital force in the determining of daily events. By its nature it cannot be predicted, but it can seemingly be used to predict. Being determined by an unknown entity, it partakes of the hand of God, free from intrapersonal relationships, and thereby is found to be infinitely more acceptable. Chance as a consequence plays a part in the vast majority of games; even a game as skilful as chess makes use of chance for determining which of the two players makes the first move.

Although chance can never be entirely disposed of in the playing of any game, its importance to the outcome of a game can, of course, be varied. In this respect, it is of significance to note that of all the many thousands of different games invented over the ages, whether they take on, for example, the form of a race, a battle or an attempt at territorial domination, can all be encompassed in one of only three interrelated categories. These are:
1. Where chance predominates and the player (ESP aside) has no direct influence as the outcome.
2. In which skill predominates. The opposing sides being given no particular advantage, mastery of the game is achieved solely by the skill of the participant.
3. A combination of varying proportions of both the previous elements.

As we have noted, games may take many different forms, although they are all ultimately concerned with success, the success more often than not of the individual. They all set up a challenge, like some cerebral initiation ceremony, the object of which is to succeed, to achieve a complex task or to defeat the other participants thereby proving or reinforcing the individual's feeling of ultimate worth. They are like a ritualized combat by means of which all participants can live to fight again, but only one emerges the victor. As Erving Goffman notes in his sociological study entitled *Fun in Games*: 'Games give the players an opportunity to exhibit attributes valued in the wider social world, such as dexterity, knowledge, intelligence, courage and self-control. Externally relevant attributes thus obtain official expression within the milieu of an encounter. These attributes could even be earned within the encounter, to be claimed later outside it.'

Kurt Riezler, in his study *Play and Seriousness* notes: 'We play games such as chess or bridge. They have rules the players agree to observe. These rules are not the rules of the "real" world or of "ordinary" life. Chess has its king

and queen, knights and pawns, its space, its geometry, its laws of motion, its demands and its goal. The queen is not a real queen, nor is she a piece of wood or ivory. She is an entity in the game defined by the movements the game allows her. The game is the context within which the queen is what she is. The context is not the context of the real world or of ordinary life. The game is a little cosmos of its own.' Yet as we have seen in our opening extract the 'little cosmos' a game represents is intimately linked to the macrocosm of our daily lives.

Nicholas Costa

Early weighted Staunton chess set and fine English mahogany board with inlaid squares of ebony and ivory, both c.1840.

CHAPTER 1

RACE GAMES

In the earliest board games players' pieces probably
raced around a track under the control of chance.
Such games may have been used to foretell the future
rather than for pleasure — a request to the gods for advice
before an important undertaking with the enquirer playing
against a priest. If the enquirer won, the gods looked
with favour on the enterprise, but if he lost, urgent
reappraisal was indicated.

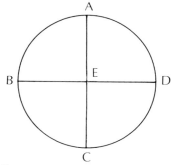

Fig. 1.

NYOUT (Korea)

The kingdom of Korea was founded in 1122 BC and one
of its games, *Nyout (1)*, still played there today, is an
example of a Cross and Circle game surviving unchanged
for many centuries. Two, three or four players take part
using a diagram scratched on the ground or drawn on a
piece of paper around which they move pieces representing
racehorses. Fig. 1.

The board consists of twenty-nine marks, with those at
the four quarters and the centre larger than the others. The
mark at the top is the Chinese character *ch'ut* meaning
'EXIT'.

The movements of the horses are controlled by the
scores of the four two-sided dice known as *pam-nyout*, each
being about 1 inch long (2.5cm), flat on one side and
convex on the other. To prevent unfair throws using sleight
of hand the *pam-nyout* are often thrown through a ring
about 2 inches (5cm) in diameter fastened to the end of a
stick about a foot (30cm) above the ground.

The throws of the *pam-nyout* score:

Four flat sides up, called *nyout*	4
Four curved sides up, called *mo*	5
Three flat sides up, called *kel*	3
Two flat sides up, called *kai*	2
One flat side up, called *to*	1

If a block falls upright, it counts as a curved side up.
A throw of *nyout* or *mo* wins another throw, which is made
before the piece is moved.

First move in a game is decided by the players throwing
the *pam-nyout* in turn, the highest scorer starting first and
the lowest playing last.

The horses are entered on the mark to the left of the
EXIT and move anticlockwise around the board. The
object of the game is to be the first player to move an
agreed number of horses, from one to four, as may be
decided at the beginning of the game, around the track and
out at the EXIT with throws carrying the horses beyond

(1) Reproduction *Nyout* board
with *pam-nyout* and *mal* (horses).

this mark. With two players one, two or four horses may be moved around the course, with three players each has three horses and when four play, two partners play against two opponents and the winning team must get four horses round and off the board.

If a throw brings a horse to a space occupied by another of the same colour they may double up and move as a single piece, but will count again as two at the end of the game. Three or four horses may be linked in this way and move as a single horse.

If a player moves a horse on to a space occupied by an opponent's horse, the latter is sent off the board to start again. When a player removes an opponent's horse he wins an extra turn for himself.

When a player throws a 4 or a 5 and earns another throw, whatever it may be, he may divide the two parts of the score between two horses. In a four-handed game a player may move his partner's pieces instead of his own.

If a horse lands on one of the larger spaces, it changes direction, and at B, C, and E it takes the shorter route, (BEA, CEA) but if it lands on D, it must take the longer route. (DEA).

In Korean cities *Nyout* is played for money, especially in public houses. Parents forbid their children to play the game and *pam-nyout* are confiscated by teachers when found at school.

On 15th January *pam-nyout* are used for divination. A small book on sale in Seoul is used with the *pam-nyout*, the players throwing them three times, noting the numbers scored for each throw. This series of numbers is then checked in the book which lists the various possible permutations of numbers and their significance.

Nyout is an excellent game for playing on a holiday beach; the board is marked out on the sand, contrasting pebbles will serve as horses and shells for *pam-nyout* convex surface up being 'curved' and concave surface up 'flat'. *Nyout* was the prototype of a large number of Cross and Circle race games played throughout the world, including *Pachisi*, the national game of India.

PACHISI (India)

In this Hindu game *(3)* for four players the *Nyout* circle has been invaginated against the sides of the cross, making a cross three spaces wide. Each player has four markers made of wood, bone or ivory, distinguished by their colours — red, green, yellow and black — symbolic of the four directions. Their movements are controlled by the casting of six cowrie shells.

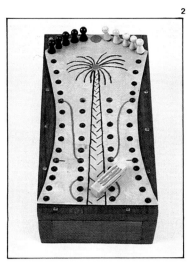

(2) Reproduction of the Palm Tree Game from Thebes. (Also known as Dogs and Jackals.) Original, *c*.1700 BC. Five pegs for each player and a long die.

(3) *Pachisi* board. Made of cloth and embroidered, this board originally belonged to a monk at a temple in Lucknow.

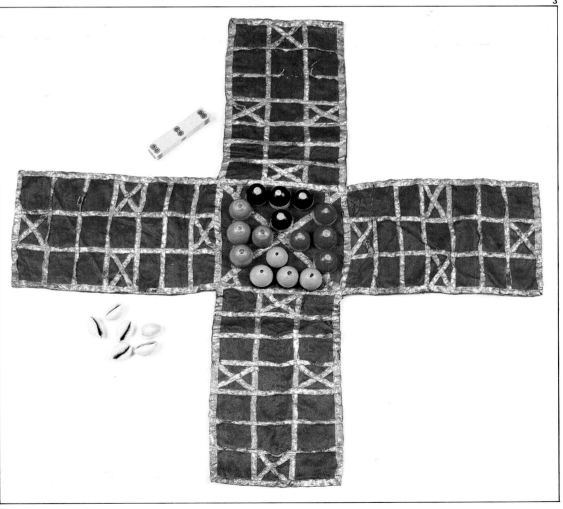

Scoring:

Two cowries with mouths up	2
Three cowries with mouths up	3
Four cowries with mouths up	4
Five cowries with mouths up	5
Six cowries with mouths up	6 and another throw
One cowrie with mouth up	10 and another throw
No mouths up	25 and another throw

The last throw, called *pachisi*, or twenty-five, gives the game its name.

Pachisi is played in cafés, zennas and palaces alike. The Emperor Akbar had courtyards laid out in marble squares, with a dais four feet high in the centre on which he and his courtiers sat, while sixteen slaves from the harem, wearing saris of the appropriate colours, moved on to the red and white areas of the board as directed by the casts of the players' cowries. Remains of these boards are still visible at Allahabad and Agra.

Modern boards are usually made of cloth cut into the shape of a cross and then embroidered. The example illustrated *(3)* is about forty years old and once belonged to a monk in a temple in Lucknow. The marked squares represent castles on which any resting piece is free from attack and capture. A castle occupied by a player's piece is open to his partner's pieces, but closed to both opponents.

The players sitting opposite each other are partners yellow and black playing against red and green. Each player has four pieces of his own colour and each piece enters the game from the central space known as the *Char-koni*. On arriving back at the middle row of his own arm of the cross the player's pieces are turned on their sides to show that they have completed the circuit. They can only reach home with an exact throw.

Rules

1. The cowries are thrown from the hands. On finishing a turn the player moves his pieces before the next player casts the cowries.
2. Each throw allows the player to move a piece by the indicated number of spaces and if he throws more than once in a turn, the different throws can be used to move different pieces, but a single throw cannot be split.
3. A capture is made by a player moving a piece on to a plain square occupied by an enemy piece, the latter is removed from the board and must re-enter the *Char-koni* with a score of 6, 10, or 25. A player making a capture has another throw.
4. At the beginning of the game a player's first piece may enter the board with any throw; thereafter pieces can only be entered on throwing 6, 10, or 25.
5. The pieces move anticlockwise around the board.
6. A player may pass when it is his turn or he can throw and then refuse to move. This may be to avoid the risk of

capture, or to help his partner.
7. On reaching the castle at the end of the third limb a player may hold a piece there in safety until throwing a 25 and then move out in the one throw.
8. Pieces may 'double-up' on any square, and then move on as a single piece. However, doubled men can be sent back to the start again if they are hit by an equal or larger unit of men belonging to the opponents.
9. The partners first returning all their pieces to the *Char-koni* win the game. Both partners win or lose together, and if one rushes ahead and out of the game, the other partner is at a disadvantage as he has only one throw to the opponents' two. They may keep pieces just behind him hoping to make a capturing throw and send him back to the start again. Sometimes a leading player reaching his own home arm will continue around on another circuit of the board to support his partner instead of turning his piece on to its side and moving up the central column to the *Char-koni*.

LUDO (England)

This familiar British game *(4)*, a modified form of *Pachisi*, was introduced into England about 1896, patent 14636. The cowrie shells were replaced by a cubic die and the players' pieces started from squares set into the angles of the cross. The *Char-koni* became HOME. In the Royal Navy and Merchant Navy, Ludo is known as Ucca and this board *(5)* is made of mahogany inlaid with exotic woods. Note the brass loop for hanging on a wardroom wall.

(4) Ludo board and pieces used in the television programme *Points North*, 18th December 1959 and signed by the studio team.

(5) Ucca board in inlaid woods with dice, counters, and pre-1971 halfpennies.

(6) Two reproduction boards for the Snake Game. (Originals pre-dynastic Egypt, c. 3000 BC.)

THE SNAKE GAME (Ancient Egypt)

The Snake Game (6), another member of the race game family, was popular in early dynastic Egypt. The boards were flat discs with a snake carved on the upper surface, its head in the centre and its tail along the rim. The body was divided by cross lines into segments. These varied from as few as twenty-nine to over five hundred, the more segments to travel over the longer the game lasted. Illustrated here is a replica in holly with a mahogany stem and base made by the author. There is a very beautiful alabaster Snake Game board in the Fitzwilliam Museum, Cambridge. Although no description of how to play the game has survived a suggestion is offered on page 104 where the board has been reproduced to playable size.

THE ROYAL GAME OF GOOSE (Italy)

Guioco Dell'Oca (The Game of Goose) was invented in Florence under Francesco de Medici (1574-87) who sent it to Phillip II of Spain. The game spread rapidly to other parts of Europe, reaching England in 1597 when John Wolfe entered '…the Newe and Most Pleasant Game of the Goose' in the Stationers' Register 16th June, 1597.

The game is played on a spiral course of sixty-three spaces, numbered consecutively, set out on an oblong board. Any number can play, each with a single piece which is entered on space 1 and borne off from space 63, the moves being controlled by throws of two dice. There are no captures; when a piece reaches a space which is already occupied by another piece, they exchange places.

This uncoloured print of the Royal and most Pleasant Game of the Goose, *(7)*, was found in a Northumberland farmhouse in 1958 between the pages of a large atlas published by F.Senex in 1720. The board is undated but the portrait in the upper right-hand corner 'JACK SHEPHERD *drawn from life*' shows him in handcuffs. Shepherd was born in Stepney in December 1702 and was brought up in a Bishopsgate workhouse. He was apprenticed to a carpenter, but in 1723 he ran away and took to crime. He escaped from jail twice in the first half of 1724 and was responsible for almost daily robberies in the London area. He was captured, tried and condemned to death in July but escaped. He was re-arrested and, on 16th November 1724, was hanged at Tyburn shortly before his twenty-second birthday.

The upper left hand corner shows 'JONATHAN WILD, *Thief-taker General of Great Britain*'. Wild was born about 1682 in Wolverhampton and became a receiver of stolen goods. He also arranged robberies and then claimed a reward for the recovery of the property. He betrayed several thieves, including Shepherd who had refused to work for him, and in return for this help Jonathan's activities were tolerated by the authorities for a time, but he was eventually arrested for receiving a piece of stolen lace, tried at the Old Bailey and hanged at Tyburn on 24th May 1725.

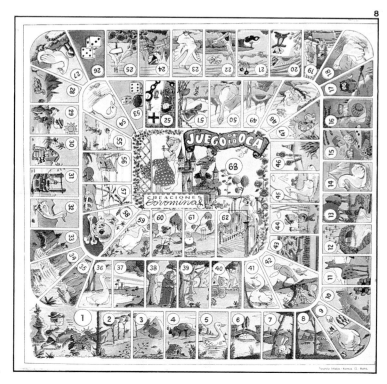

(8) *Juego do la Oca* The Game of Goose. A Spanish board bought in Spain in 1978 showing little change in the game in four hundred years.

(7) Board for the Royal Game of Goose.

This engraving was apparently made after Shepherd's death in 1724, but before Wild's fall from grace and execution at Tyburn in 1725. The rules are printed in the central panel and beneath is the inscription, LONDON. Printed for and sold by John Bowles & Son at the Black Horse in Cornhill. Invented at the Consistory *(Sic)* in Rome.

Reproduced to playable size on page 74 is another version of the game under the title *Laurie's New and Entertaining Game of the Golden Goose*. It was published by Richard Holmes Laurie of 53 Fleet Street, London on 22nd November 1831.

Such spiral race games of pure amusement were soon followed by many others designed to teach children history, geography, architecture, botany and astronomy. Many were handcoloured printed sections mounted on canvas and housed in slip cases or between boards *(9 & 10)*.

The 'New Game of Aphelion or the Race to Sun' was issued by F.H. Ayres in the late Victorian era and there is little difference between this game and the Royal Game of Goose published some 150 years earlier. *Aphelion* is mentioned to show the frequent dressing up of old ideas in new clothing and for the blurb introducing the rules printed on two sheets of paper. These can be seen on page 78 where the board has been reproduced to playable size.

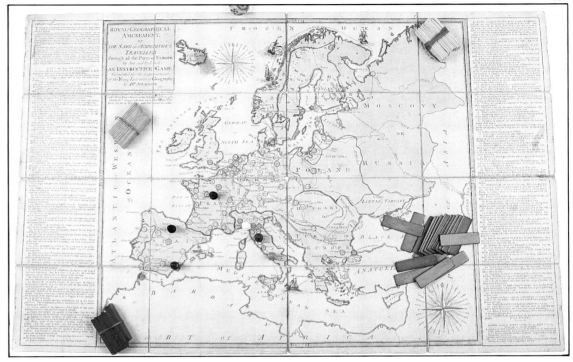

(9) The Jubilee (of George III) 1810, with slip case, book of rules, pillars, teetotum and Regency gaming box, published on 1st January, 1810.

(10) Royal Geographical Amusement with pillars, bone counters and teetotum, 1787.

GEOGRAPHICAL GAME THRO' EUROPE (England)

Of more use for teaching purposes was Robert Sayer's Geographical Game *(10)* published in 1787. The instructions were printed at the sides of the board and there was a short note about every town or city visited. The travellers' moves were controlled by the spinning of a totum. A few of the comments may be of interest.

'7. *St Malo*, a seaport of Brittany. If it is late when you arrive, take care of the twelve bulldogs who guard its avenues in the night time.

17. LISBON, the capital of Portugal. For fear of earthquakes, *autos da fe*, and Portuguese ministers, stay here as short as you can, and go directly to *Seville*, the next number.

32. *Lyons*, the second city of France. Stay one turn to see its silk manufacture, the first in Europe, and in which 100,000 persons are employed.

(11) Paper *Sugoruku* board for a children's game played in Japan at the New Year. The game is similar to Snakes and Ladders.

(12) A child's Snakes and Ladders board *c.*1960.

(13) The Game of the Race, *c.*1850.

71. WARSAW, the capital of Poland, a large city and dirty city. On account of the Three Powers that lately divided Poland, come back to Ratisbon, No. 66, to complain to the Imperial Diet.
99. ANTWERP or ANVERS a fine city in the Austrian or Gothic Netherlands, on the river Escaut. Stay one turn to see Ruben's paintings in the several churches.
103. LONDON, the capital of England, and metropolis of the British Empire.'

THE GAME OF THE RACE (England)

Each player had a little lead horse ridden by a jockey wearing colours of well-known racing stables. The obstacles along the course of the race were also of lead fences, waterjumps, etc. *(13)*. Complete sets of horses and obstacles are becoming rare and the little horses are collectors' items, sought after by the racing fraternity, the colours worn by the jockeys recalling famous stables of the past. Note that the jockeys sit in the middle of the horses' backs and ride with straight legs, whereas today jockeys sit further forward and rise with their legs bent. The horses are shown galloping in a 'rocking-horse' position. The real action of a galloping horse was only understood with the use of high-speed photography.

To return to the game, the horses' progress in the steeplechase was controlled by the throw of a cubic die. Along the course were hazards. At 11 the horse bolted, at 24 he fell into a stream, at 38 the horse balked at a high wall, at 54 the rider was thrown, at 67 the horse fell, and at 88 horse and rider lost their way.

One board in the author's collection (*c.*1880) is made of heavy cardboard covered with a thin skiver and folds into four portions. On the reverse, the central two panels form a backgammon board and the outer two panels fold over it to meet in the centre making a chess or draughts board.

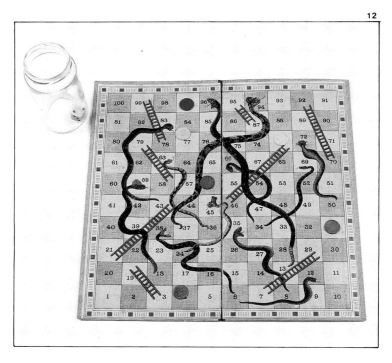

SNAKES AND LADDERS (India)

This simple race game on a square board *(12)* is popular with children as it depends purely on luck and they meet their elders on equal terms. Any number can play, each having their own distinctive marker which is entered on the board only with a throw of 6 on the cubic die. A player throwing a 6 has another turn, otherwise after a throw the die is passed clockwise to the next player. The markers move on the number of squares indicated by the upturned face of the die and if the marker lands on a square supporting the foot of a ladder, the marker moves to the top rung, while a marker landing on the head of a snake descends to the tip of its tail. If a marker lands on a square occupied by another marker, the latter is sent back to the START square. The first player to reach HOME wins the game and the other players continue playing to determine places. The last player left on the board may pay a forfeit.

Snakes and Ladders is based on a game called *Moksha-Patamu*, once used in India for religious instruction.

According to Hindu sages, virtuous acts, represented by ladders, shorten the soul's journey through a number of incarnations to *Nirvana*, the state of ultimate perfection. Sin, symbolized by the head of a snake, leads to reincarnation in a lower animal form and delays the individual's ultimate achievement of *Nirvana*. Snakes and Ladders was thus originally a symbolic moral journey through life to heaven.

Ups and Downs is a variation of Snakes and Ladders and is reproduced on page 82 to playable size with the rules.

GAMES OF THE BACKGAMMON GROUP

This important family of race games dates back to *c*.3000 BC and examples have been found in the Royal Tombs of Ur.

In 1929 Sir Leonard Woolley excavated several tombs in the Royal cemetery at Ur and found in them four gaming boards of the same type. The most elaborate is now in the British Museum, London and a few years ago the Trustees put a photographic reproduction on sale in the museum's shop *(14)*. The coloured print was mounted on a cardboard box, with a sheet of devised rules and a set of wooden pieces. Unfortunately a cubic die was provided instead of the fascinating pyramidal dice found with the original board *(15)*. A board has been reproduced to playable size on page 94, together with the rules.

TAU (Ancient Egypt)

Fifteen hundred years later the Ancient Egyptians were using gaming boards which appear to have been derived from those of Ur. The group of squares at the smaller end of the Sumerian boards have been unfolded into a straight tail, but the rosettes were retained and the game may have been played in a similar way. The Egyptian boards were usually made as a box with a drawer to house the pieces and dice or throwing sticks. This game was called *Tau* (Robbers). The under surface of the box was often marked out for another game known as *Senat* with 3 x 10 or 3 x 12 squares.

Several *Tau* boards have been found in tombs of the 'Empire' age about 1580 BC. A reproduction of one of these boards for the game known to archeologists as 'The Game of Twenty Squares' *(Tau)* is illustrated here *(16)*. The board and die are reproductions, but the clay gaming pieces are original and were found by Prof. Flinders Petrie in tombs dating from the Thirteenth to Fourteenth Dynasties. (*c*.1567-525 BC)

The finest *Tau/Senat* board *(17)* illustrated on a post card on sale during the Tutankamun exhibition at the British

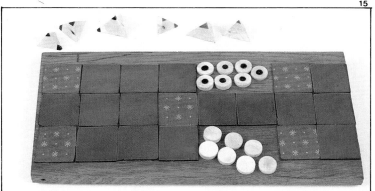

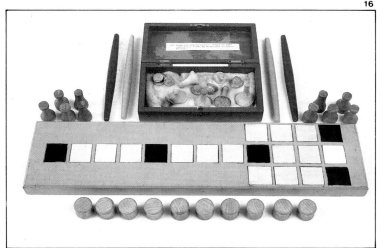

(14) Commercial reproduction of Royal Game of Ur on sale at the British Museum about 1976. Original *c*.2500-3000 BC.

(15) Reproduction board Royal Game of Ur. Note pyramidal dice.

(16) Reproduction *Tau* board with ten pieces on each side and four throwing sticks. The pieces in the box are originals, Thirteenth to Fourteenth Dynasties, found by Prof. Flinders Petrie.

(17) A page from the author's small collection of games postcards showing a stone ninepins game *c*.3200 BC found in a child's grave at Nagada, Egypt. Now in the Ashmolean Museum, Oxford.

Museum, was one of the four boards found in the king's tomb by Howard Carter in the Valley of the Kings in 1923. To quote from Volume III of his monumental work *The Tomb of Tut-Ankhamen*, 1933:

'Plate LXXV. A gambling-board and "Throwing sticks".

A. A set of four "Throwing sticks" having backs of ebony and underparts of ivory, which by the manner of their fall, denote the moves upon the gaming board.

B. A reversible gaming-board of ebony and ivory having on the top a game of three by ten squares, and on the bottom a game of three by four with an approach of eight squares.'

Discussing the objects found in the annexe of the tomb Carter wrote, 'Gaming-boxes for the diversion with their playing-pieces were scattered far and wide about this room, even some of their parts were discovered in the antechamber, where they have been thrown during the dynastic plundering. They are of three different sizes — large, medium and quite small for the house, and of a portable form for the pocket. The latter size, small and made of plain ivory, came from the knick-knack chest previously described.'

'Their presence in the tomb is apparently justified by some mythical precedent, which the deceased hoped to enjoy in the life to come. (c.f. *The Book of the Dead*, Ch. XVIII). However, the smaller specimens, at least, seem to be chattels of an everyday pastime. The largest and most important of the games, 21 by 11 by 7 inches (54.5 by 28 by 18cm) overall, rests upon a neat black ebony sledge, having the "cushions" and "claws" of the feet embellished with gold.

'They were played according to set rules but were decided by luck, and although they involved little or no skill, they nevertheless afforded an amusing and an exciting past-time. I would even go so far as to say that the modern games of skill like *seega* or draughts, and chess, were in all probability evolved from games of hazard, such as we find from time to time in ancient Egyptian tombs, and so well represented in this burial.'

Reference: Carter, H. *The Tomb of Tutankhamun* Vol.III, Cassell & Co. 1933, pps. 130-2.

SENAT (Ancient Egypt)

In 1986 the city of Vancouver hosted Expo '86 along the shore of False Creek, an inlet off Vancouver harbour. At the extreme end of the site the Egyptian pavilion simulated an ancient Egyptian temple and inside was an exhibition of sixty-seven items from the Cairo museum illustrating life in the time of Ramses II (1290-1224 BC). Among them was the painted wooden door of a burial chamber from Thebes. The illustration *(18)* shows a photocopy of the design on the inside of the door, which was on sale in the pavilion shop. (The catalogue reference of this door in the Cairo museum is 27,303). The measurements of the panel are recorded as: height 3ft 10in (1.17m), width 2ft 6in (0.78m). Further details given: 'Made of stuccoed painted wood with a yellow background. Provenance: Western Thebes, Deir el-Medina, Tomb No. 1 of Sennudjem dating from the first half of the reign of Ramses II, shown with his wife Lyneferty and his daughter Irunefer'.

The panel contains eleven lines of text and above a representation of the deceased Sennudjem and his wife playing *Senat* against an invisible opponent. Quoting from the exhibition catalogue:

'In front of them is a well-laden offering table where ovoid vessels and round breads, fruit baskets, figs, vegetables and cucumbers are heaped on a papyrus mat. Below, four cabbage lettuces and two bottles of milk complete the more-or-less symbolic food. The deceased and his wife are on seats recalling those found in the family burial chamber. Their wigs are still more voluminous than on the other side of the door. (This is a view of Sennudjem and Lyneferty appearing before the enthroned god, Osiris). The woman entwines a shoulder and an arm of her husband with her own arms. Sennudjem holds a long ceremonial handkerchief in one hand and rests the other on one of the ten pawns of the game which are alternately white and red and of different shapes. At the foot of the stool is a large knucklebone used to play the game.' The knucklebone or astragal often served as a four-sided die instead of the four throwing sticks already described on page 15.

The Ancient Egyptians seem to have enjoyed playing

(18) Poster showing the door of Sennudjem's tomb in Deir-el-Medina, Western Thebes, showing him supported by his wife Lyneferty playing *Senat* against the invisible Osiris. Note the large astragal at the foot of the stool used as a die in the game.

(19) Plaster plaque of Queen Nefertari playing *Senat* against an invisible Osiris. On sale in Cairo Museum, 1986. Original c.1250 BC.

(20) Commercially produced *Senat* game with dicing sticks and counters, c.1970.

(21) A board for *Duodecim Scriptorum* scratched into the pavement outside Hadrianic baths at Aphrodisias in Anatolia, Turkey, *R.C. Bell.*

(22) Reproduction *Senat* board. Lion and jackal pieces with long die. Astragals and throwing sticks also used. The original lion pieces each had a cartouche of Queen Hatshepsut, c.1498-1483 BC.

Senat as a social pastime but the game also had a funerary use and skill in playing was essential to the deceased in their quest for admittance to eternity. On the panel Sennudjem is shown playing against an invisible god and must win from him passage into eternal life. The text shown under the picture consists of the last paragraph of Chapter 72 and the first paragraph of Chapter 17 of the *Book of the Dead*.

The painted plaster cast of Queen Nefertari playing *Senat (19)* was bought in the shop of the Cairo Museum in 1986.

Reference: *Catalogue of the Great Pharoah Ramses and his Times.* Expo '86. 2nd May-13th October, 1986. ©1985.

DUODECIM SCRIPTORUM

This game for two *(21)* was popular throughout the Roman World in the first and second centuries and the illustration shows a board scratched into the pavement outside Hadrianic baths at Aphrodisias in Anatolio, Turkey. This was one of five boards seen there by the author during a visit in 1985. Most boards consist of three rows of twelve spaces, each row separated in some way into halves of six spaces. A board, found in Ostia, the port of Rome, may hold a clue to the direction in which the pieces were entered on to and moved along the board as the spaces were marked with the letters. See fig.5.

This suggests that the players entered their pieces at either end of the central line and moved along the board from A spaces to B spaces to C spaces to D spaces to E spaces and then off the board. The first player to bear all his pieces off won the game. Movement seems to have been in the same direction with a safe area of entry on half the middle row for each player. Presumably, if a piece landed on a space occupied by an opponent's piece the latter was sent back to start again, while if a player had two or more pieces on the same space, they were safe from attack.

Spaces were marked in many ways as squares, circles, vertical bars, letters, leaves, crosses, monographs or crescents. Often the groups of letters formed words and the whole series, a sentence. A copy of one such board *(23)* was reproduced from an original found in Timgad, North Africa. See fig.6.

N.I.Lanciani, writing in 1892, said that more than a hundred *ludus scriptorum* boards have been found in Rome alone during his lifetime, indicating the popularity this game once enjoyed. Each player had fifteen pieces, the moves of which were controlled by the throws of three cubic dice, the players throwing them alternately. The throws could be used singly or combined, but could not be divided and a throw of doublets or triplets does not seem to have earned a second throw. Single men on a space

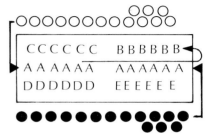

Fig. 5.

VENARI LAVARI
LVDERE RIDERE
OCCEST VIVERE

ROUGH TRANSLATION

TO HUNT   TO WASH
TO PLAY   TO LAFF
THIS IS   TO LIVE

Fig. 6.

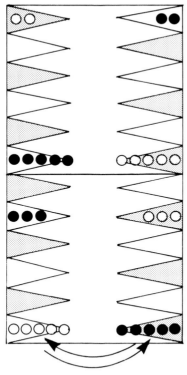

Fig. 7.

(23) Reproduction *Ludus Duodecim Scriptorum* board. Original from Timgad, *c*.AD 250.

(24) Reproduction Roman *fritillum* and five ivory dice. Originals found at Qustul, Egypt, *c*.AD 350.

23

(*blots* in backgammon) were called *vagi* and could be sent off the board to start again if an enemy piece landed on the same space. A player could pile any number of his men on to any space; piled men were called *ordinarii* and were safe from capture. Pieces that could not be moved by any throw of the dice were called *inciti*. The rule permitting piling introduced the use of flat discs instead of the pawn-shaped pieces of the Egyptian games, evidence that the latter permitted only one piece on each space.

W. B. Emery found a very fine *duodecim scriptorum* board during excavations at Qustul, a little north of the second cataract on the Nile. It was recovered from the tomb of a Blemye noble and was made from a single piece of wood 2ft 6in long by 1ft 2in wide (77.5 by 37cm). The border was framed and the corners strengthened with silver brackets. The points were marked by small squares of filigree ivory. Found with the board were thirty pieces, fifteen of ivory and fifteen of ebony with five cubic dice and a leather bag in which they were kept. With them were fragments of a *pyrgus* or dicing tower down which they were thrown to prevent sleight of hand *(24)*. The tomb dates from between the beginning of the fourth century and the end of the sixth.

Three-rank *Duodecim Scriptorum* was replaced by Alea with only two rows of spaces and thus a shortening of the track. The Emperor Claudius (AD 41-58) had an Alea board fixed to his carriage for playing during journeys and according to Suetonius he also wrote a book on the game. Alea became so popular that it acquired a second name, *tabula*, taken from the name of the board. *Tabula* provided the medieval name of the game Tables. In turn, Tables became the *Tric-trac* of France and the Middle East and Backgammon of Britain and America.

Reference: Emery, W.B. Nubian Treasure, London, 1948 p.46 & pl.32.

BACKGAMMON

Backgammon must be a strong contender for the title of 'the best race-game'. It can be played for pleasure, gambling or both. The board is divided into two pairs of tables by a partition known as the BAR. Each table consists of six points. By custom the side of the board nearest to the light source window or lamp is called the *inner table* and that away from the light is the *outer table*. Most of the important play takes place in the inner table and in the days before electric light it was important to have this area well illuminated. Each player has his own outer and inner table, the latter also being known as his home table. The position of the pieces at the start of a game and their direction of movement is shown in fig.7.

If at any time during a game a player's pieces are placed incorrectly play ceases and that game is abandoned.

Each player tries to move all his pieces into his inner table and then to bear them off the board passing through his 1-point. Fig.8 shows the notation used. There are no numbers on the actual boards. Play is towards each player's inner table.

Rules
1. At the beginning of a game each player throws one die and the player with the higher number has the choice of colour, the side of the board and the first throw of the game.
2. The opening player casts his dice and moves two pieces according to the two numbers scored. Each number can be used to move a separate piece, or one piece be moved by the two numbers in either order. A throw of 3 and 2 may move one piece by three *points* and two *points*, or by two *points* and three *points*, or else two pieces, one by three *points* and one by two *points*.
3. Each *point* played onto must be 'open', that is either empty or occupied by the player's own pieces or by a single enemy piece. It must not be 'closed' by two or more enemy pieces resting upon it.
4. If a player throws a *doublet* (the two dice showing the same number) he scores twice the number thrown. A throw of 4 and 4 scores as four plus four plus four plus four. The player may move one piece the whole distance (if each stage of four is open), or two pieces by four plus four, or three pieces by four, four and four plus four, or four pieces by four each. When two or more scores are used to advance a single piece, each separate move must be on to an open *point*.
6. A *point* occupied by two or more pieces is 'closed' to the opponent's pieces and they cannot land on it.
7. Pieces can jump over hostile 'closed' *points* but cannot land on them.
8. A *point* occupied by only one piece is vulnerable to attack and is 'open'. An enemy piece landing on the *point* sends

the *blot* (singleton) off the board to stay on the BAR and the opponent is said to have scored a *hit*.

9. A player with a piece on the bar cannot move any of his pieces until the piece on the bar has returned to the game by re-entering the opponent's 'inner-table'. If the *blot* cannot re-enter, the throw is lost, as are all subsequent throws until the blot is back in play.

10. If White had a piece on the bar and threw a 5 and a 2, he could enter it on B5 or B2 if either were open, but not on B1, B3, B4 or B6, even if they were open.

11. If there is an opposing *blot* on the point of entry, this is hit by the re-entering piece and is itself sent to the bar.

12. If the opponent's inner table is completely closed, the player with a piece on the bar does not throw the dice but waits until a point in the opponent's inner table becomes open.

13. On re-entry the player may use the throw of the other die to move the re-entered piece or any other of his pieces as he wishes.

14. Players must use both numbers of a throw, or all four of a doublet, if this is possible, even if it is to a player's disadvantage.

15. When all a player's pieces are in his inner table (but not before) he may bear off pieces (remove them from the board) using the score of the dice to do so. If Black threw a 4 and a 1, he could bear off a piece from B4 and another from B1, or he might use the numbers to move a piece inside the inner table towards B1. Such a move might be important in protecting a *blot* by turning an open *point* into a closed one.

16. If a higher number is thrown than the position of any of the pieces in the inner table, this throw is used to *bear off* the highest piece. A number thrown may not be used to *bear off* a piece lower than itself if it is possible to move a higher piece. For example, if a player threw a 5 and a 4, he would have to move a piece or pieces on the six point, or five point or four point before he could bear off a blot on the three point.

17. When a number is thrown which is higher than the highest *point* on which the player has pieces, he must bear off a piece from the outermost occupied *point*. He may, however, use the numbers in either order and this may enable him to avoid leaving a *blot*.

18. If a piece is 'hit' after the player has started *bearing off*, it is placed on the bar and until the piece is once more in the player's inner table *bearing off* ceases.

19. The game ends when one player has *borne off* all his pieces. There are degrees of losing.
    a) If the loser has *borne off* a piece he loses by a single game and his stake.
    b) If he has not *borne off* a piece, he loses by a 'Gammon' and has to pay double the stake.
    c) If he has not *borne off* any piece and has a piece on

the bar or in the opponent's inner table, he loses by a 'Backgammon' and has to pay a triple stake.

20. The size of the stake is agreed between the players before they throw their single die to decide the colour of the pieces and the side of the board taken by the opening player.

21. Before the game begins the players may decide to play a DOUBLING GAME. This adds to the excitement if the players are gambling. In the doubling game the stake may be doubled at any time by either player immediately before casting if he thinks that he has an advantage. The opponent has the option of accepting the double when the game continues with the stake doubled, or of refusing when the game finishes and the loser pays double the original stake. (He avoids, however, the risk of a gammon or backgammon). A double may be refused if the challenged player feels that he is too far behind to have a chance of winning, but if he feels that the immediate disadvantage may pass, he will accept and the game proceeds. He now has the right to re-double the stake, if he wishes, immediately before making a throw. The right to redouble alternates between the players until one of them refuses or the game finishes in the ordinary way with the raised stakes to be paid by the loser.

To keep track of the number of doublings in a game a special die is used with faces marked 2, 4, 8, 16, 32 and 64.

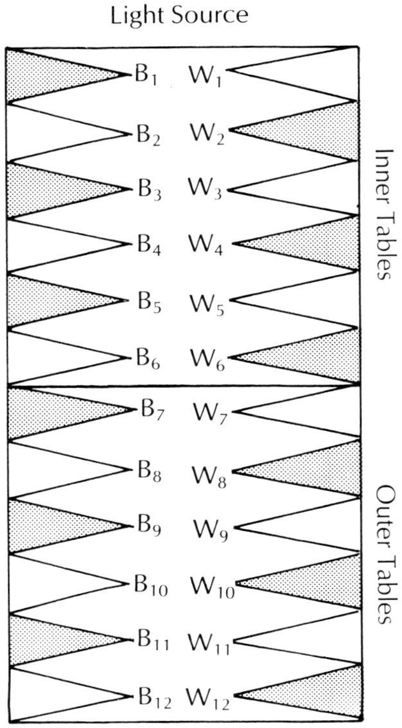

Light Source

Fig. 8.

25

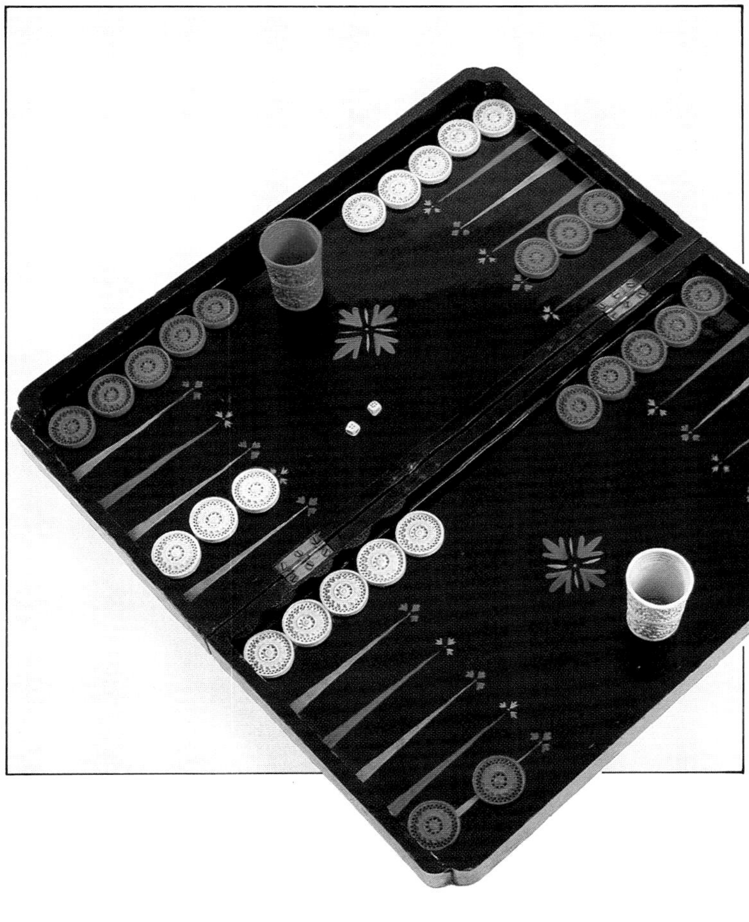

26

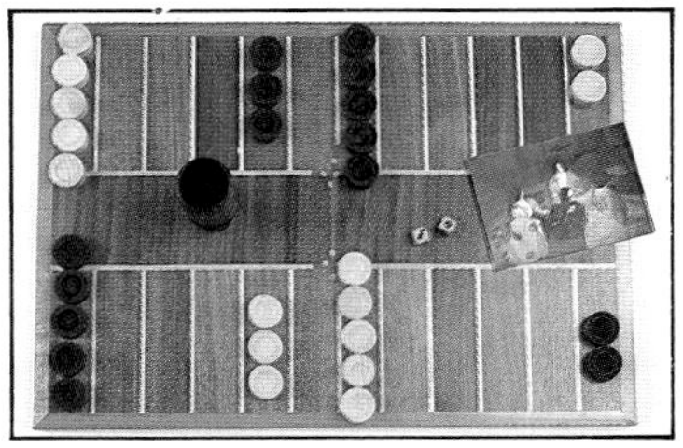

(**25**) A Chinese lacquered backgammon board, *c*.1870.

(**26**) Japanese *Sugoroku* (backgammon) board and pieces.

19

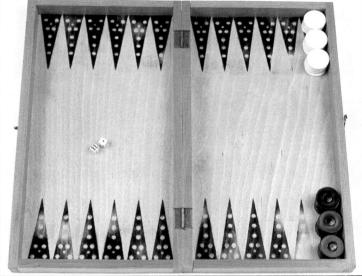

TAVLI (Cyprus)

An interesting variant of backgammon is *Tavli*, popular in the taverns and cafés of Cyprus.

Starting position: Each player starts with his fifteen pieces on his opponent's 1-point in five stacks of three. See *(28)*.

Opening play: Each player throws a die and the player with the higher score then throws both dice to start the game. If the first throws are equal, the players throw again.
Equipment: Only two dice are used, the players casting them in turn and the players can throw into either half of the board, directing the dice against the bar to make them rebound. This makes cheating more difficult.

Rules

1. Doubles count double; a throw of two 3's is played as 3 + 3 + 3 + 3.
2. A singleton *(blot)* on a *point* is vulnerable to attack but if a hostile piece lands on the same *point*, the *blot* is not sent to the bar as in backgammon, but is trapped and cannot move. See fig.9. The capturing piece is placed nearer the tip of the *point* and the *point* becomes the capturing player's *point*. He may move any number of his pieces on to it, while it is closed to his opponent.

(27) Scottish chess and backgammon board, *c.*1870.

(28) *Tavli* board set for the start of a game.

(29) *Saka* (Siamese backgammon) board at the start of a game with the pieces off the board. Dice, dicing cup and dice box.

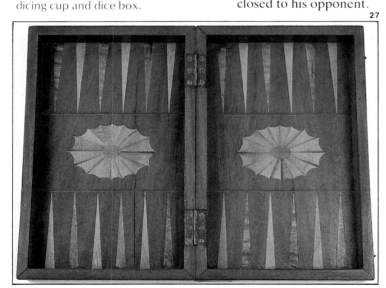

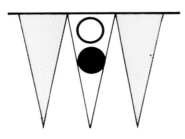

Fig. 9.

The White piece is trapped, and the point is closed to White pieces.

3. Alternate throws are made by the players, each player completing both his moves before the other player lifts the dice for his throw. The player throwing the dice has the choice of moving two pieces each by the cast of one die, or of moving one piece by the cast of both dice, but only if both *points* are open. If a player threw a 4 and a 1 and the *point* five away from a particular piece was open, the player could not move his piece unless either the point one away or four away was also open.
4. A *point* is held by two of a player's pieces on it or by one piece accompanied by a captured piece.
5. All a player's pieces must be within his inner table before he can begin to *bear off* and he must use the whole of a throw if possible. If a 5 is thrown, a piece on the *5-point*

must be *borne off*; it is not permitted to use the throw to *bear off* a piece on a *lower* point unless the *6-point* and the *5-point* are empty.

6. The first player to *bear off* all his pieces wins the game and scores one point for each of his opponent's pieces in the latter's inner table; two points for any piece in the latter's outer table; three points for any piece in the winner's outer table, and four points for any piece in the winner's inner table.

TACTICS

In *Tavli* the pinning of a *blot* by an opposing piece is often a more severe penalty than being sent to the bar in backgammon. The captured *Tavli blot* is immobilized until the opponent chooses to release it and the *point* is also held by a single piece. More care is needed to prevent leaving singletons than in backgammon and a piece trapped within the opponent's inner table usually results in the loss of the game and a four-penalty-point penalty for the piece.

In *Tavli* every piece has to pass over all the twenty-four points of the board before the player can win. A minimum of 15 x 24 = 360 *pips* is required from the dice to accomplish this, whereas in backgammon the minimum required is only 2 x 34 + 5 x 13 + 3 x 9 + 5 x 6 = 190 *pips*. The average game of *Tavli* therefore lasts approximately twice as long as a game of backgammon.

(30) Exterior of Turkish box backgammon board with book of instructions in Turkish, English, French and German.

(31) Syrian chess and backgammon board bought in Riyadh, Saudi Arabia in 1987. See also (52).

THE SNAIL GAME (England)

This nursery game *(32)* could be played by up to six children, the more the merrier. Each player threw the die; the highest scorer started the game, the player on his left being second and the rest following in clockwise direction around the table. The opening player threw the die again and placed his marble in the appropriate hole on the board. To quote from a contemporary Victorian description:

'Should a player throw a number which carried his marbles to an occupied hole, he says "You go back!" and takes his opponent's place, the latter beginning again at the start.'

Readers will realize that this Victorian game is very similar to the Snake game of the Ancient Egyptians, pages 11 and 104.

Historical events may, in the terms of the Old Testament, begat games and that described below is an example. The discovery of gold in payable quantities near Bathurst in Australia was followed shortly afterwards by the finding of much richer deposits at Ballarat and Bendigo. A few months later Port Phillip bay was full of ships bringing people and goods from all over the world. The alluvial deposits were soon exhausted and by 1857 deep shafts were needed, requiring considerable capital. The day of the speculative miner was over. To capitalize on the public's enthusiasm for these so called Gold Rushes old games were adapted by the games manufacturers *(33)*. One such, called Voyage to the Gold Diggings, traces the route of the thousands who left England to dig for gold in Australia and is reproduced on page 96 along with its rules.

(33) Up to the Klondyke, *c.*1898.

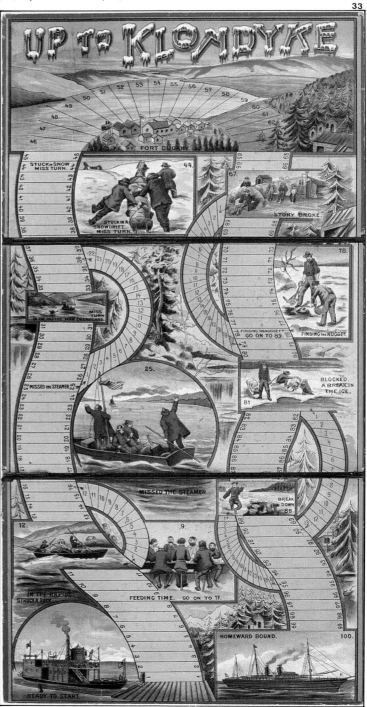

(32) Victorian nursery Snail Game, *c.*1880, with bone markers, marbles and die. The last two are modern replacements.

(34) Reproduction limestone *Ludus Latrunculorum* board and pieces. The latter are made of genuine fragments of Roman pottery. The Dux are pebbles.

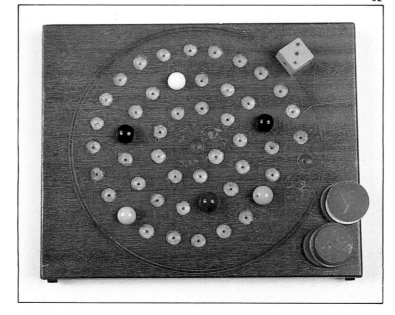

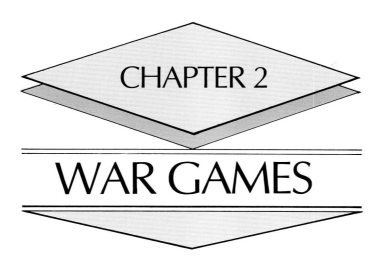

CHAPTER 2
WAR GAMES

LUDUS LATRUNCULORUM (Rome)

War games seem to have been invented long after the appearance of race games. One of the earliest was *Ludus Latrunculorum*, popular with the Roman soldiery *(34)* and a board has been reproduced to playable size, together with the suggested rules, on page 84.

Egypt was within the frontiers of the Roman Empire and Somaliland just outside. *Ludus Latrunculorum* may well have survived among the country people when it was forgotten elsewhere after the fall of the Roman Empire. Lane, in his *The Modern Egyptians* written in Egypt between 1833 and 1835 described a game played by the Egyptian *fellaheen* called *Seega (35)*. Marin, a hundred years, later found the same game being played by the Somali.

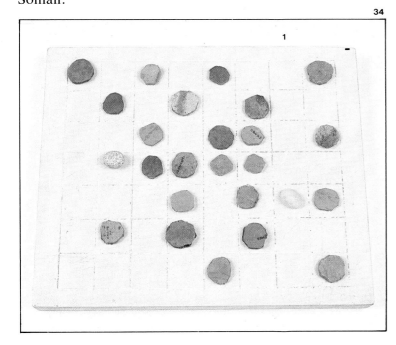

SEEGA (1) (Egypt)

A board of 5 x 5 squares is marked out on the ground. The two players each have twelve distinctive pebbles or pieces of broken pot.

First phase

1. The players place two stones at a time on any two vacant squares, except for the central square which is left empty in this first phase.
2. When all the twenty-four stones have been placed, the player placing the last couple in position begins the second phase.

Second phase

3. A stone can move at right angles to any adjacent vacant square, including the central one.
4. If a player can trap an enemy stone between two of his own (the custodian capture), he removes it from the board and continues to move the same stone as long as he makes captures with it.
5. A stone may make more than one capture in a single move. See fig.11.
   The white stone captures three black stones by moving on to the central square.
6. A player can move a stone between two enemy stones safely.
7. A stone on the central square cannot be captured, even though it is trapped between two enemy stones.
8. When a player cannot move, his opponent must make an opening for him by taking an extra turn.
9. The boards may be increased to 7 x 7 or 9 x 9 squares, each player then having twenty-four or forty pieces.

A weak feature of the game is the frequency of a draw. Each player may make a barrier behind which there are only his own pieces and these can be moved without fear of attack. The initial placing of the stones is important in planning such barriers or in preventing their construction. If a player captures all the enemy stones, he has a clear win; if a barrier position arises, the player with most stones on the board wins; if they have the same number, the game is drawn.

(35) Reproduction *Seega* board and pieces.

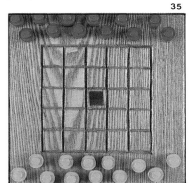

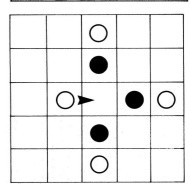

Fig. 11.

White moves to capture three Black stones

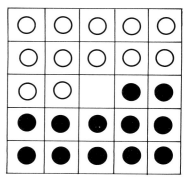

Fig. 12.

(36) Reproduction *Hnefatafl* board based on an illustration in an English manuscript written during the reign of King Athelstan (AD 925-40). The pieces are based on a *hunns* found at Woodperry, Oxfordshire.

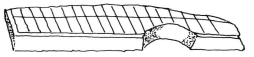

Fig. 13.

A. bone

Fig. 14.

B. Jet

24

HIGH JUMP (Somalia)

The Somalis play another game on the same board with the same pieces.

Rules

1. The initial positions of the players' stones are shown in fig.12.
2. The stones move as in *Seega*, but they capture an opponent's stone by jumping over it at right angles and several captures can be made in one turn of play, the capturing piece being allowed to change direction.
3. Capturing is not compulsory.

HNEFATAFL (Scandinavia)

A fragment of a gaming board was found in a Roman Iron-Age grave at Wimose in Fyn, the second largest of the Danish Islands. This period ended about AD 400. Fig 13. Eighteen squares are visible along one side, and if the board was symmetrical it contained at least 18 x 18 squares, each being about 1 x 1 inches (2.5 by 2.5cm) in area.

The Scandinavians took *Tafl* with them to Iceland and Britain. The later sagas mention the development of *Tafl* into *Hnefatafl* and an Anglo-Saxon manuscript written during the reign of King Athelstan (AD 925-40) contains a diagram of a Saxon form of *Hnefatafl* which corresponds with the Wimose fragment.

· A bone piece found at Woodperry in Oxfordshire gives the shape of the ordinary pieces *(hunns)* fig. 14a. The king or *Hnefi* was larger and more elaborate. In 1969 a jet playing-piece was found at Bawdsey in Suffolk and is now in the Ipswich Museum. It is 1.9 inches (4.7 cm.) high and of square cross-section, but with rounded edges. The flat top has been facetted to form a triangular field at each corner. This may have been a *Hnefi*. Fig. 14.b.

The reconstruction of the *Hnefatafl* board *(36)* is based on a translation of the Athelstan manuscript, the latter being a description of *Hnefatafl* used as an allegory of Christian life. The reproduction board has been made one square larger on rank and file to permit the pieces to be placed on the spaces instead of on the points as shown in the tenth-century manuscript. The board represents the open sea and the pieces, ships. The smaller fleet is under the direction of a Kingship *(Hnefi)*.

Suggested rules

1. The opening position of the opposing fleets is shown *(36)* the black kingship is on the central square surrounded by his twenty-four vessels.
2. The larger white fleet is stationed around the black fleet waiting engagement.

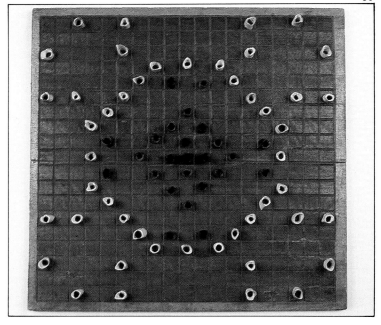

36

3. Black has first move and then the players move alternately.
4. Any piece can move along rank or file any number of vacant squares. (The rook's move in chess).
5. A capture is made by trapping an enemy piece between two of the player's pieces on rank or file (custodian capture) but not diagonally.
6. A piece may move on to the square between two enemy pieces without harm, but if one of these moves away and then back again at a later move, a capture is made.
7. The kingship can only be captured by being surrounded on all four sides by enemy ships.
8. Black wins if the kingship reaches any square on the periphery of the board (escapes from the encircling fleet) and loses if the kingship is captured.

The board illustrated *(37)* is a reproduction of a wooden board 9 inches (24cm) square with 7 x 7 holes for the insertion of pegged men. It was found when a lake-dwelling at Ballinderry, Co. West Meath, Eire was being excavated and is now in the National Museum of Ireland. The central hole is surrounded by a circle and the four corner holes by quadrants. The frame is decorated with various tenth-century patterns, suggesting manufacture in the Isle of Man. No pieces have survived, but the reconstruction is supported by a drawing on a golden drinking horn found at Gallehuus, South Jutland in the seventeenth century. The game seems to be a simpler form of *Hnefatafl* as does the game played on the board *(38)* on sale at the Jorvik centre in York and based on fragments of a board recovered from the site.

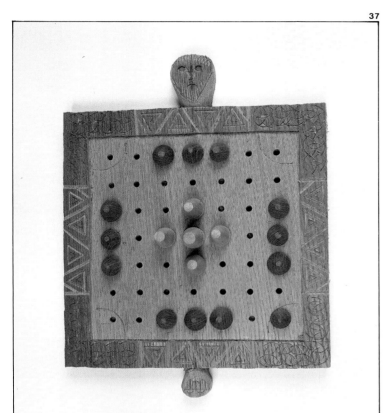

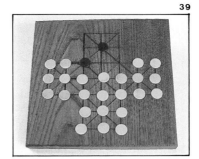

(37) Reconstruction of the Ballinderry board with pieces. (Arrangement based on *Tablut*.) There were no pieces found with the original board, *c*.AD 950, which was probably made in the Isle of Man.

(38) Commercially produced board on sale at the Jorvik Centre in York and based on fragments of a board recovered from the site.

(39) Bone disc Officers and Sepoys on oak Fox and Geese board.

(40) Reproduction *Tablut* board and pieces at the start of a game.

13 Geese

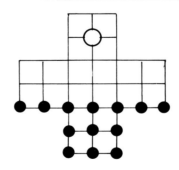

Fig 15a

17 Geese

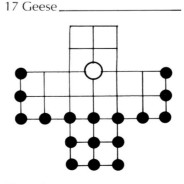

Fig 15b

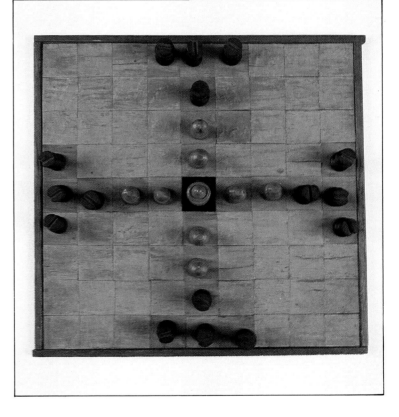

HALATAFL (Iceland)

Halatafl (The Fox Game) is mentioned in the Icelandic *Grettis Saga*, believed by the literary historian Dr. Finnur Jonsson to have been written after AD 1300 by a priest living in the northern part of the island.

Thirteen geese were arranged on the board as shown in fig. 15a and the fox was placed on any vacant point. The fox and the geese can move in any direction along a line to the next contiguous point. The fox can also jump over a goose if the point immediately beyond is vacant and the goose is eaten and removed from the board. Two or more geese can be eaten in the same move by a series of short jumps by the fox. The geese cannot jump over the fox, but try to crowd him into a corner and make it impossible for him to move. If the fox is trapped in this way he loses the game, but if he can destroy enough geese to prevent them being able to immobilize him, he wins.

If the geese are correctly played, the fox must lose. In later forms of the game the geese were increased to seventeen, but were deprived of the power of moving backwards. See figs. 15a & b.

ASALTO (England)

In this late form of Fox and Geese *(41)* twenty-four geese try to trap two foxes. The pieces can move along the marked lines at right angles or diagonally and the foxes can capture by diagonal short leaps as well as along rank or file.

During the Indian Mutiny in 1857 the game was renamed *Officers and Sepoys* and nine of the points were marked off as a fortress *(39)*.

On page 92 a beautiful board, a fine example of Bombay Inlaid Work, is reproduced to playable size with the rules of play.

25

SIXTEEN SOLDIERS (Shap luk kon tsu tseung kwan) (China)

Sixteen Soldiers (42) is a popular game with Chinese children, the board often being marked out on the ground. One player has sixteen rebel soldiers, and the other their loyal general. The pieces are arranged as in the illustration. All the pieces can move one point along any marked line, but only the general may move on to the three points within a triangular 'Sanctuary'. If he is confined there and unable to re-enter the main field of play, his player loses the game.

The methods of capture of the two sides are different. The general captures by occupying a point immediately between two rebels on the same marked line when he removes them both by *intervention*. The rebels capture by occupying the points immediately on both sides of the general, all three being on the same marked line, known as custodian capture. The rebels make the first move and then the players move their pieces alternately.

COWS AND LEOPARDS (South East Asia)

This is the best of a group of related games played widely throughout Southern Asia (43). A board from an antique games compendium from Mysore has been reproduced to playable size on page 90 with the rules.

TABLAN (Southern India)

This traditional Running-fight game (44) comes from Mysore in South-west India. The board is about a hundred years old.

Rules
1. The board consists of four rows of twelve squares.
2. Each player has twelve pieces of his own colour, placed at the beginning of the game on the squares of the player's back row.
3. The four throwing sticks are painted on one side and plain on the other. They are thrown up into the air, caught and thrown again two or three times before they are allowed to fall to the ground.

Scores
One plain surface up	2 and throw again.
Four plain surfaces up	8 and throw again.
Four painted surfaces up	12 and throw again.

No other throw scores and the sticks are passed to the opponent.

4. The first move of a piece can only be made on a throw of 2, though this can be split into two 1's if required and two pieces moved one square instead of one piece, two squares.
5. Throws of 8 and 12 can similarly be split in half into two 4's or two 6's.
6. The pieces move in the direction shown in fig. 16. Black's pieces move A to L, L to M, M to X, X to m, m to x, x to a. Yellow's pieces move in the opposite direction and finish in Black's back row.
7. The pieces can only capture pieces when they are on the two central rows or when displacing them on the opponent's back row. Captured pieces are removed from the board.
8. Once a piece lands on a square on the opponent's back row it is immobilized and does not move again. It cannot be captured.
9. The enemy row is occupied, square by square in order from a to l (A to L). This rule is optional.
10. More than one piece can be moved in any turn of play and more than one capture can be made, but the pieces must move in the direction shown and when they reach the last

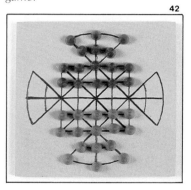

(41) Late Victorian mahogany Asalto board and original marbles. Note metallic flecking, c.1860.

(42) Reproduction Sixteen Soldiers board and pieces at the start of a game.

42

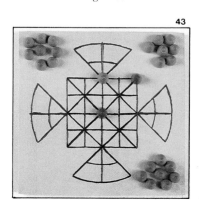

(43) Reproduction Cows and Leopards board and pieces at the third move of a game.

43

41

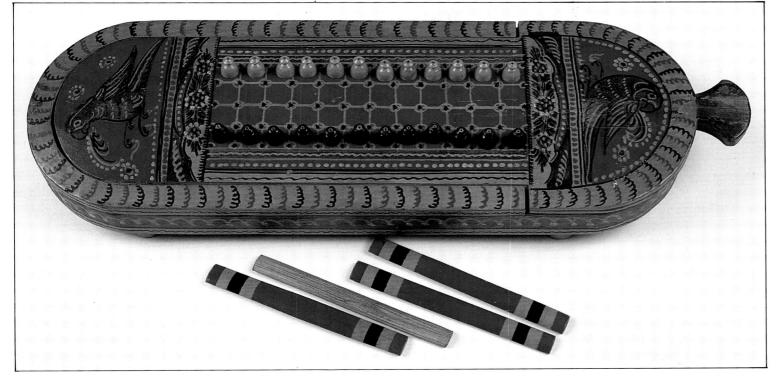

(44) Antique compendium of games from Mysore, with *Tablan* pieces and throwing sticks ready for play.

square of their middle rows they must turn off into the enemy home row and become immobilized. If they displace an enemy piece in doing so, it is captured and removed from the board.

11. A player has to use a throw, convenient or not, unless he has only one piece left near the end of the middle row next to the enemy home row and the throw does not allow him to occupy a square in the enemy camp. These squares must be occupied one after another in the order of a to l, (A to L). This rule is optional.
12. There is no DOUBLING UP of pieces on any square.
13. The player occupying most enemy home squares wins the game.

l	k	j	i	h	g	f	e	d	c	b	a
m	n	o	p	q	r	s	t	u	v	w	x
X	W	V	U	T	S	R	Q	P	O	N	M
A	B	C	D	E	F	G	H	I	J	K	L

Fig. 16.

THE CHESS GROUP

CHATURANGA (India)

In Ancient India a spiral racegame called *Ashtapada* was played on a board of sixty-four squares. Pieces on the marked squares were probably free from attack. Fig. 17. Each player's pieces started from their right-hand marked square and proceeded in an anticlockwise direction around the board in a decreasing spiral, ending in the left-hand marked central square.

In the fifth century, the *Ashtapada* board was used for playing a new wargame, *Chaturanga (47)*, which was a miniature battle between four armies each under the control of a Rajah and each containing representative pieces for the four corps of the ancient Indian army, Infantry, Cavalry, Elephant troops and Boatmen, the last being used in fighting across rivers and over flooded fields. In *Chaturanga* two players were loosely allied against the other two, Yellow and Green opposing Red and Black. The pawns in *Chaturanga* represented infantry, the ship boatmen, the horse cavalry, the elephant elephant-troops and a human figure the rajah. Each piece had a different power of movement. The RAJAH moved one square in any direction.

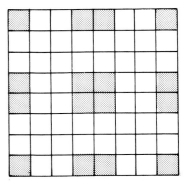

Fig. 17.

The ELEPHANT moved forwards, sideways or backwards any number of unoccupied squares along rank or file. The elephant could not jump over a piece.

The HORSE moved two squares along rank or file, followed by one square along file or rank. (The L shaped move of the knight in chess.) The horse could jump over intervening pieces.

The SHIP moved two squares diagonally in any direction and could jump over an intervening piece.

The PAWNS moved one square forwards along a file, unless they were making a capture when they moved one square diagonally forwards.

Ships and pawns were minor pieces and could capture each other, but were not allowed to capture the three major pieces. The moves of the pieces were controlled by the casting of a foursided long die marked 2, 3, 4, 5.

On throw of 2 the ship moved.
On throw of 3 the horse moved.
On throw of 4 the elephant moved.
On throw of 5 the rajah or a pawn moved.

Rules

1. If it was impossible to move a piece in accordance with a throw, the throw was lost, but if it were possible to move, this was compulsory even it were to the player's disadvantage.

2. If a piece moved on to a square occupied by an enemy piece, the latter was removed from the board. Minor pieces could not move on to squares occupied by the rajah, elephant or horse. The illustration *(47)* shows the arrangement of the board at the beginning of a game with the Black army at the northeast and the allied Red army in the south-west, while the enemy Yellow army was stationed in the north-west and the other enemy army, the Green, was in the south-east. Each army was drawn up in the same battle order with the boat on the corner square, then the horse, the elephant and the rajah on the back line, all protected in front by four pawns. The rajah's square was marked and known as the THRONE.

3. At the beginning of a game each player put an agreed stake in a pool, the prize of the victorious allies at the end of the game.

4. Each player threw the die in turn and the player with the highest score threw again and made his first move in accordance with this throw, unless it was a 4, when the elephant could not move and the die was passed to the player on the left.

5. An indicated piece was compelled to move if this were possible, though there might be a choice of pieces. For example, If a 5 was thrown the rajah or a pawn could obey the command, or if an ally's pieces had been taken over, one of his pawns or his rajah.

(45) An Indian painting on silk, c.1984, but the game is somewhat of a mystery.

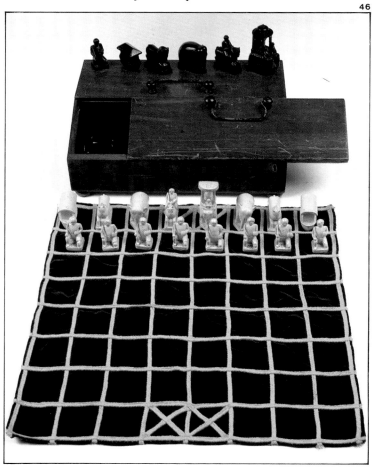

(46) Indian cloth chess board with four of the original *Chaturanga* marked squares surviving, with carved wooden pieces and original box. Late nineteenth or early twentieth century. Probably from Northern India.

(47) Reproduction *Chaturanga* board and pieces at the start of a game. The long die is marked 2,3,4,5.

6. SEIZING A THRONE When a rajah occupied the throne of an enemy he "Seized a Throne' and won a single stake from the despoiled opponent. If he captured either enemy rajahs at the same time, he won a double stake. If a rajah mounted the throne of his ally, he assumed command of the allied forces as well as his own and at his own or his partner's throw he could move either his own or his ally's pieces, a considerable advantage.

7. REGAINING THE THRONE If a player whose ally's rajah had been captured, captured a hostile rajah, he could propose an exchange of prisoner rajahs with the player owning the remaining rajah, but the latter had the option of accepting or refusing the exchange. A rescued rajah re-entered the board on his own throne square, or if this was occupied, on the nearest vacant square.

8. If a player whose own rajah was still on the board, but whose ally's rajah was a prisoner, captured both enemy rajahs he could claim the restoration of his ally's rajah without exchange or ransom. This also restored his ally's control of his own pieces.

9. BUILDING AN EMPIRE A player who succeeded in siezing his ally's throne and in capturing both enemy rajahs built an empire.
   (a) If the player's rajah made the capture on the hostile rajah's throne square, he won a quadruple stake from both opponents.
   b) If the player's rajah made the capture on some other square, he won a double stake from both opponents.
   c) If the capture of the second hostile rajah was made by any other piece, he won a single stake from both opponents.

10. CONCOURSE OF SHIPPING Each ship sailed on a different course and controlled different squares and they could never attack each other directly. However, if three ships were on adjacent squares and the fourth moved into position to occupy the fourth square, this player completed a 'concourse of shipping' and he captured the two enemy vessels and took control of the moves or his ally's ship. On throwing a 2 he could move his own ship or his ally's and also when his ally threw a 2 he had the same choice. There are only five positions on the board where a concourse of shipping can occur.

11. PROMOTION OF PAWNS If a pawn reached an unmarked square on the opposite side of the board, it was promoted to the piece of that square, either a horse or an elephant. Promotion only occurred if the player had already lost one or more pawns. He was not allowed to have a promoted piece and three pawns on the board and promotion was delayed until a pawn had been lost. A pawn reaching a marked square was not promoted and could take no further part in the game except to be captured, unless it became a privileged pawn. See rule 12.

12. PRIVILEGED PAWN If a player had only a ship and a pawn left, this pawn became privileged and, on reaching any square on the opposite side of the board, could be promoted to any piece at the choice of its owner.

13. DRAWN GAME If a player lost all his pieces except his rajah he was considered to have fought to an honourable peace and the game was drawn.

14. Each player paid any special debts accruing during the game to the player winning them: for example, a stake to the first enemy player seizing his throne; a double stake if his rajah is captured in the same move and a quadruple stake if one of his opponents built an empire.

15. The allies did not win from each other.

Chaturanga was used for gambling and when this became forbidden in Hindu culture, players evaded the law by discarding die, thus making the game one of skill. Other changes followed, one of the first being the concentration of the allied armies into single forces on opposite sides of the board and the game for four players became a game for two. Since there could only be one commander of an army, one of the rajahs was changed into a prime minister and the loss of rank was reflected in a loss of power, the piece only advancing or retiring one square diagonally.

About the same time the moves of the ship and elephant were transposed, the elephant moving diagonally two squares, while the ship, *roka* in sanskrit, assumed the powerful right angle moves of the ancient elephant. The game ceased to be *Chaturanga* and became *Shatranj* or medieval chess.

SHATRANJ (Persia)

Although *Shatranj (48)* and its development into modern international chess is of considerable interest to the chess historian, any lengthy description would seem to be out of place in the present work. Those requiring further information are referred to the author's account in *Board and Table Games from Many Civilizations Vol. 1,* where *Shatranj* and two variants are described; Circular Chess played on a round board and Courier Chess, popular in Germany in the thirteenth century, played on a checkered board of 8 x 12 squares, each player having twenty-four pieces, four extra pawns, two couriers, a jester and a sage.

MODERN INTERNATIONAL CHESS

Information and advice on the playing of chess is so readily available that only a description of the moves of the pieces and a bare outline of the rules will be given.

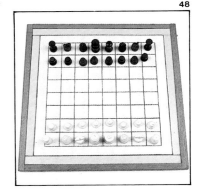

48

(48) Reproduction *Shatranj* board and pieces in ivory and ebony. Note that the white King's Knight has been placed accidentally on the Bishop's square.

The game is played on a chequered board of sixty-four squares with the black-squares double-corner on the player's right. Usually the pieces are white and red or cream and brown *(49)*. The players sit facing each other across the board and White makes the first move. Each player has sixteen pieces: eight pawns, two castles, two knights, two bishops, a queen and a king, with the queen resting on a square of her own colour, fig.18.

Power of movement

Pawns These move forwards one square at a turn of play. On their first move they may advance two squares, but if an enemy pawn could have captured them had they only advanced one square, the capture may still be made by 'capture in passing'. This can only be done on the opponent's next move. Pawns can only capture by advancing one square diagonally to replace the piece that is taken. Unlike every other piece, a pawn cannot move backwards and on reaching the eighth rank must be exchanged for another piece of the player's choosing, other than a king. The choice is usually a queen, although occasionally a knight with the power of jumping may be more valuable, fig.19.

Castle (Rooks) The Castles can move over any number of vacant squares along rank or file and capture by occupying the square of the captured piece, fig.20.

Knights The Knight moves three squares in a letter L. Either one square along a file and two along a rank, or one along a rank and two along a file. The Knight is permitted to jump over an intervening piece of either colour to reach the end square of the L, fig.21.

Bishops The Bishops move diagonally over any number of vacant squares, always remaining on a square of the same colour, fig.22.

Queens The Queen is the most powerful piece on the board and can move over any number of vacant squares along rank, file or diagonal (the combined moves of the Castle and the Bishop).

Kings The Kings can move one square in any direction, but not on to a square under threat from a hostile piece.

Castling This is a special move that can only be made once in a game and only then if the king and the castle concerned have not already moved. The King moves to either of the nearest squares of the same colour on its rank and the Castle towards which the King has moved goes to the square the King has just crossed. The King must not be in check or move across or to a square which is under attack by the opponent, fig.23.

(49) Modern wooden Russian chess board with notation letters and numbers, and painted wooden chessmen.

Arrangement of Black pieces to start a game.

P = Pawn
R = Rook
B = Bishop
K t = Knight
K = King
Q = Queen

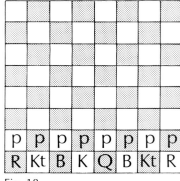

Fig. 18.

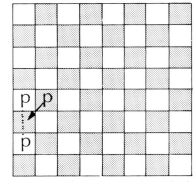

Fig. 19. White pawn takes Black

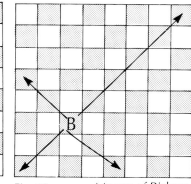

Fig. 22. Moves of Bishop.

Fig. 20. Moves of a Castle. Fig. 21. Moves of a knight.

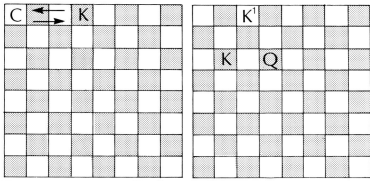

Fig. 23._____ Castling. Fig. 24._____

K¹ is not in check,
but cannot move. Stalemate.

Pieces capture by moving on to a square occupied by one of the opponent's pieces. The King cannot be captured, but instead if he is threatened by an enemy piece he is 'in check' and must move out of check or a piece be interposed to relieve the attack. If the King cannot escape from check, CHECKMATE has occured and the player has lost the game. The object of the game is to checkmate the opposing King.

DRAWN GAME This can arise in four ways:
A. The player who has the move is not in check, but cannot move without becoming so. This is known as STALEMATE. Fig 24.
B. Fifty moves have been made without capture, or the movement of a pawn.
C. The same position with the same player to move, repeated three times.
D. By agreement between the players.

FOUR-HANDED CHESS_____

This variant of the game was invented towards the end of the eighteenth century and was still being played by enthusiasts towards the end of the nineteenth century. The games-table *(50)* is a replica of a table made about 1820 in England. The original was recently sold to an American dealer for £1250/$2275. She usually bought porcelain, but liked its appearance and thought it would provide a good display stand for interesting ceramic pieces, besides being a useful conversation piece. It is somewhere in the USA.

The rules are taken from Chess Eccentricities by Major Hope Verney, published in 1885.

'Four-handed chess is not chess, though the same pieces are used, and the moves of the pieces are nearly the same. Bridge and Rummy both use a 52 cardpack, but there the similarity finishes.' Fourhanded chess is a light-hearted affair using a special board. fig. 25 and two sets of chessmen which are easily distinguished. The illustration *(50)* shows the opening position of the pieces.

Fig. 25.

50

(50) Reproduction four-handed chess table. Original *c.*1830.

Rules

1. The chequered board consists of 160 squares.
2. Each of the four players has 8 pawns and 8 pieces.
3. The players sitting opposite are partners and they try to checkmate the other two.
4. Note that all the queens are on a white square.
5. First move is decided by calling correctly the colour of a pawn held in a closed hand, but the winning partners have the option as to which makes the first move. In subsequent games each pair of partners starts alternately, but which partner is their decision.
6. The partners with the second move may change seats if they wish when the first move has been made.
7. Each player makes a move, in turn, in clockwise rotation around the table.
8. No consultation is permitted between the players. A feature of the game is appreciating the reason for each move made by the other players and silently assisting one's partner and foiling the plans of the opposition.
9. Partners' pieces have no antagonistic influences over each other and the partners' kings can move on to adjoining squares.
10. No player can move a piece which would expose his partner's king to a check any more than he can his own king.
11. One partner's king cannot move out of check if this exposes his partner's king. Unless a piece can be interposed, the game is lost.
12. Castling is not permitted.
13. Pawns only move one square at a time, and they are not allowed to move two squares on their first move, thus there is no capturing *en passant*. Pawns capture by moving one square diagonally.
14. For a pawn to queen it must reach an opponent's rear rank and this requires it to make at least three captures, a rare event.
15. If a pawn reaches the partner's rear rank it remains a pawn with no promotion, but it can move back again, one square at a time towards the player's own rear rank. Such a pawn is marked by sliding a paper collar over its head. Should this pawn eventually reach the player's rear rank, the collar is removed and it sets off once more in its original forward direction.
16. If two friendly pawns meet on the board either is permitted to jump over the other but remains on the same file. They only leave their file when making a capture.
17. The game is won when both opposing kings are checkmated. Should one be checkmated and the other stalemated, the game is drawn.
18. The game is also drawn if:
    a) both a partnership's kings are stalemated;
    b) one king is checkmated and it is impossible to mate the other;
    c) if a mate is impossible on either side;
    d) if each partnership has only one minor piece and two kings left;
    e) when only pawns are left on the board so that a double checkmate is impossible.
19. If a player is checkmated, his pieces remain on the board but do not move. His partner continues this struggle single-handed and the neutralized player misses his turn. While his pieces are immobilized they cannot be captured, but block the squares they occupy.
20. A partner may shelter his pieces behind the immobilized pieces of his checkmated partner.
21. If he is able to do so a partner may release his checkmated partner by capturing the checkmating pieces, or by forcing them to move. As soon as the checkmate is lifted the immobilized pieces regain their power of movement and their vulnerability to attack.
22. A player holding an opponent's king in checkmate can release it at any time should he wish, although he cannot capture any of the immobilized pieces in the same move. Immediately the checkmate is lifted all the immobilized pieces are vulnerable to attack even though the player so released has not had a turn in which to make a move.
23. Should a player point out in any way to his partner a desirable move, the opponents can object to the move being made until three moves have been made by all the players.
24. If a player touches a piece when it is his turn to move, he must move it, unless this discovers check to his own or his partner's king. Should he touch an enemy piece he must take it, if it is possible to do so.
25. If a player's king is checked by the player moving immediately after him, it gives the other adversary a clear move in which to attack or to take any piece of the player receiving check, since the latter at his next move must release his king from check, unless his partner has already given assistance.
26. The relative values of the pieces in four-handed chess are different from those in the standard game.

Pawn	1
Knight	5
Rook & Bishop	9
Queen	20

Reference: Verney, G.H. *Chess Eccentricities*, Longmans, Green & Co, 1885 pps. 6-70.

(51) From Szechwan in Western China this pottery piece portrays an old man about to teach a young one the finer points of *Siang K'i* (Chinese chess). No pieces are yet on the board, being still in the bowls by the players' left hands, c.1985.

51

(52) Beautiful inlaid chess board from Syria. See also (31).

(53) A Burmese chess set (*Sittuyin*) in Pinkadoo wood. The shapes are traditional and were carved in Rangoon in 1960.

(54) Magnetic Chinese chess set (*Siang K'i*) and board; and a larger folding wooden board and pieces.

OTHER FORMS OF CHESS

Many forms of chess are played throughout the world, but space limits their consideration to reproducing illustrations of some of their boards and pieces. Those requiring further information may turn to the author's *Board and Table Games from Many Civilizations*, Dover Publications Inc. New York, 1979; or H.J.R. Murray's monumental *History of Chess*, Clarendon Press, Oxford, 1913.

Those interested in *Siang k'i* (also translated as *Hsiang-chi*) *(54)* are recommended to read an article 'Bold Moves in Chinese Chess' by Chang-Ichu in *Free China Review*, Vol. 37, No. 7, July 1987, pp. 53-60. This is a well-illustrated and fascinating account of a recent design exhibition in Taipei's Fu-Hua Gallery of new shapes and styles of Chinese chess pieces. Replacing the simple, traditional, checker-like pieces were beautiful creations by some of Taiwan's best-known artists, architects and country craftsmen skilled in folk art. To quote:

'Originally imported from India the game developed Chinese roots in the Tang Dynasty (AD 618-907). By the time of the Sung Dynasty (AD 960-1279) the game had acquired Chinese literary, historical and poetic references

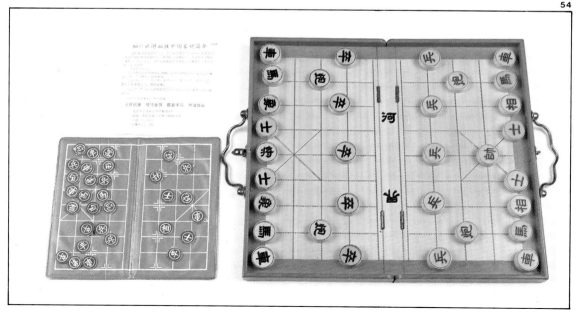

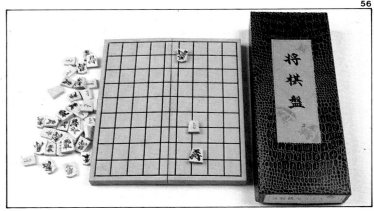

(55) Reproduction Korean chess board (*Tjyang keui*) and pieces.

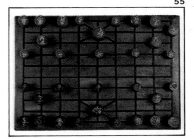

(56) Modern *Shogi* board and pieces (Japanese chess).

(57) Reproduction Abyssinian cloth chess board (*Santarij*) and painted wooden pieces.

(58) Siamese chess board (*Makruk*) and pieces at the start of a game. Note the large size of the Knights compared with the other pieces.

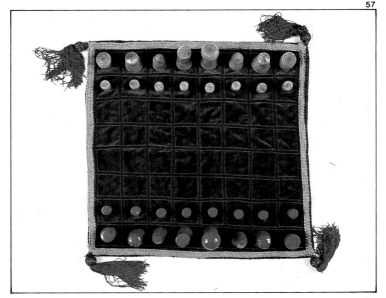

founded in *Yin* and *Yang* (male and female) philosophy coupled with a classical warfare etiquette.

'The two armies of sixteen units face each other across a river, the Chu, running across the middle of the board, dividing the warring states of Chu and Han, a reference to an historical situation prior to the establishment of the Han Dynasty in 206 BC.'

The new style of *Hsiang-chi* pieces blend traditional and modern shapes and materials, amongst the most attractive being cylindrical pieces of clear plastic containing sculptured figures embedded within them and with the ranks of the pieces engraved on their flat top-surfaces.

The author's collection also contains a chess set made in white and black resin, every piece having erotic connotations. Said to be a reproduction of a rare nineteenth-century ivory and ebony set, it may well be of recent conception produced for pornographic sale. (Not illustrated.)

THE MAHARAJAH AND THE SEPOYS

This light-hearted variant of International Chess is useful in stimulating quick and unorthodox thinking. One player has a full set of chess pieces arranged in standard fashion on his side of the board. The other player has a single knight which is called the Maharajah, and has the Knight's L-shaped move and power of jumping over pieces, in addition to the right angle and diagonal moves of the Queen. The Maharajah is placed on any free square.

The object of the game is for the first player to checkmate the Maharajah while the latter tries to checkmate the King. Games provide many interesting problems, although a careful player who supports his pieces properly will finally hem in the Maharajah. If he makes a mistake, however, the Maharajah's great mobility may allow the latter to win quickly by trapping the King behind his own pieces or later when the board is clear he can drive the King into a corner which is followed by an inevitable checkmate.

The board and pieces shown here *(61)* are Hungarian. A few years ago the author wrote an article on games for a Hungarian magazine and to avoid currency exchange complications, the editor sent a traditional Hungarian carved wooden set and board as a gift. It now has an honoured place in the collection.

Perhaps mention should be made of three dimensional chess *(60)*. This is a twentieth-century variant, but with little popular appeal and will probably join the serried ranks of chess curiosities invented and discarded over the centuries.

59

61

(59) A political chess set of resin compound. *c.*1970. From back to front, the characters are: Enoch Powell, white knight: Door of a bank, white rook: Door of a co-op, black rook: Barbara Castle, black queen: Sir Douglas Home, white bishop: Sir Harold Wilson, black king: Edward Heath, white king: Bernadette Devlin, black knight: George Brown, black bishop: Faceless city gent, white pawn: Margaret Thatcher, white queen: Faceless British worker, black pawn.

(60) Three dimensional chess set, *c.*1980.

60

ALQUERQUE (Ancient Egypt)

Cut into one of the roofing slabs of the Ancient Egyptian temples at Kurna is an unfinished *Alquerque* board, (*c.*1400 BC) probably abandoned through a mistake in cutting a diagonal line. Fig. 26.

More than two thousand years later a game called *Quirkat* is mentioned in an Arabic work, *Kitab-al Aghani*, whose author died in AD 976. When the Moors invaded Spain they took *El-quirkat* with them and it is described under its Spanish name, *Alquerque*, in the Alfonso X manuscript (1251-1282). An *Alquerque* board and pieces arranged for the beginning of a game is shown (*62*).

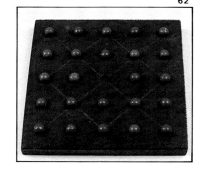

62

(61) Modern wooden Hungarian chess board and chessmen, *c.*1980.

(62) Reproduction *Alquerque* board and modern coloured clay marbles.

Rules

1. The pieces move from any point to any adjacent empty point along a line.
2. If the adjacent point is occupied by a hostile piece and the next point beyond it on the line is empty, the player's piece can make a short leap over the opponent's piece and remove it from the board.
3. If another piece is then at risk, it is taken in the same move by a second short leap, a change of direction being permitted.
4. If a piece can make a capture it must do so, otherwise it is HUFFED and is removed from the board.

These rules are from the Alfonso manuscript. One more rule seems to be needed.

5. If there is a choice of capture, a greater number must be taken in preference to a lesser, otherwise the capturing piece is huffed.

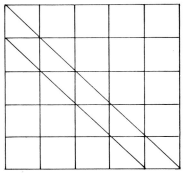

Fig. 26.

FANORONA (Madagascar)

This Madagascan game was used to foretell the future and the initial position of the pieces is illustrated *(63)*. During the attack by the French on the island's capital in 1895 the Queen and her advisers placed more faith for victory on the result of an official game between chosen professionals than in their army. *Fanorona* developed from *Alquerque* about 1680 by doubling the board, increasing the number of pieces from 24 to 44 and changing the method of capture.

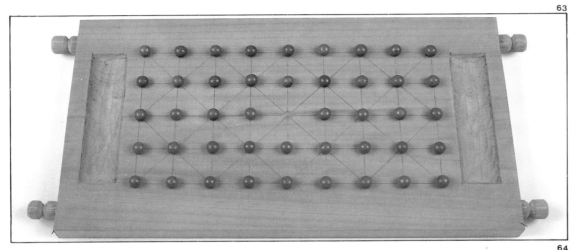

63

Rules

1. White starts and moves along any line to an adjacent empty point.
2. If a move ends on a point in contact with a point or points beyond in the *line of movement* occupied by enemy pieces in an unbroken sequence, these are captured and removed. This is capture by APPROACH.
3. Capture may also be by WITHDRAWAL. A player's piece moving away from a contiguous point with a point or points occupied by enemy pieces in the *line of movement*, these pieces are removed from the board.
4. Captures are compulsory, but on the first move by each player only one sequence can be taken.
5. On the second and later moves a player may make several captures, either by approach or withdrawal, but each move must be along a *different marked line*; i.e. the piece must change direction to make each capture.
6. If a move places enemy pieces in two directions at *risk*, the player can choose to remove the pieces in either direction but not in both. He is not compelled to capture the larger number, but must capture all possible pieces in the direction he has chosen.

The second or *vela* game is played differently. The losing player starts and the winner of the previous game sacrifices piece after piece until he has lost seventeen. During this *vela* play the previous winner refrains from making any captures, and his opponent may only take one piece each move.

Readers should play these games a few times to familiarize themselves with the very unusual method of capture by APPROACH AND WITHDRAWAL.

(63) Reproduction *Fanorona* board with pieces set for play.

(64) A board for quadruple *Alquerque*.

(65) Late nineteenth century travelling chess and draughts (chequers) set. The pieces have pegs to fit in holes in the board to prevent movement. With it is a 1970 magnetic draughts set.

(66) Public house draughts (chequers) board painted on glass, c.1890.

64

QUADRUPLE ALQUERQUE

The board is four times the size of the normal *Alquerque* board and each player starts with forty pieces of his own colour *(64)*. Such a board has been found cut into a roofing slab at Kurna, and similar boards are still in use in parts of India, Indonesia and the Sahara. The game described here is from the Punjab.

RATTI-CHITTI-BAKRI (India)

1. The players alternate in playing Black who always moves first in a game.
2. The players arrange their forty pieces on the points as in fig. 28, leaving the central point empty.
3. A piece on any point can move forwards or diagonally forwards along any marked line through that point to the next which must be empty.
4. If the adjacent point is occupied by an opposing piece and the point immediately beyond is empty, then the player's piece can jump over the enemy piece to the vacant point beyond and capture the piece by a *short leap*. If another enemy piece is then *en prise*, it can be taken by a second short leap and further captures may be made in the same turn of play, as long as an enemy piece is at risk after each capture. When making a capture a piece can move backwards.
5. Capturing a piece at risk is not compulsory and there is no huffing.
6. When a piece reaches the opposite side of the board it is promoted to a new power and can move over any number of vacant points along marked lines in any direction.
7. Promoted pieces can jump over a single enemy piece by a long leap, passing over any number of vacant points before and after the leap. If another piece is then *en prise*, it can make a second leap, either along the same line or with a change of direction. Promoted pieces are distinguished in some way.
8. Captured pieces are left on the board until the end of the turn and a previously captured piece forms an impassable barrier to further movement by its captor.
9. When a player has lost all his pieces he has lost the game.

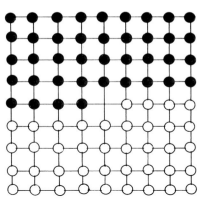

Fig. 28.

DRAUGHTS

About AD 1100 someone, probably in the south of France, invented a new game *Fierges*, using backgammon pieces on a chess board with the diagonal move and method of capture of *Alquerque*. Each player had twelve pieces of his own colour. *The Chronique* of Philip Mouskat (1243) refers to a KING of *Fierges*, indicating the existence of promotion at this early period. Later the game became known as *Dames*, and a single piece as *Dame*. In *Dames* there was no compulsion to take an enemy piece, but about 1535 a compulsion rule was introduced in France, and the old nonhuffing game became known as *Le Jeu Plaisant De Dames*, or '*Plaisant*' for short, in contrast to the huffing game called *Jeu Forcé*. Modern English draughts is the *Jeu Forcé* of the sixteenth century.

Man

King

Fig. 29.

68

67

69

70

(67) Official issue American Army chequers (draughts) board from the Second World War.

(68) Backgammon and draughts (chequers) board from Granada, Spain, 1970, set for a game of draughts with the six extra pieces for backgammon at the sides.

(69) Inlaid Indian draughts (chequers) board with Turkish bone draughtsmen in position to start a game. Board, c.1920, pieces, c.1910.

ENGLISH DRAUGHTS (England)

The object of the game is to capture or immobilize the twelve opposing pieces. The double black corner must be on the player's right (68). A capture is made by jumping diagonally over an enemy piece and landing on a vacant square immediately beyond. If the capturing piece can continue to leap over other enemy pieces (it can change direction to do so), they are also captured and removed from the board. When a piece finally comes to rest the move is finished.

Rules

1. The pieces move on the black squares and Black begins.
2. The players change colours at the end of the game.
3. The draughtsmen move diagonally forwards one square at a time. They cannot move backwards.
4. If a piece reaches the opponent's back row, the player's eighth rank, it becomes a KING and is crowned by having a captured draughtsman placed on top of it. Fig. 29. Crowning ends a move.
5. After crowning the turn ends and the new king cannot make further captures until the player's next turn. Kings can move diagonally backwards or forwards one square at a time and capture by a short leap over an enemy piece. There may be several kings of both colours on the board at the same time.
6. If a player has a choice of captures he may take a smaller rather than a larger number if he wishes, but whichever he chooses, he must then capture all the pieces at risk.
7. If he does not make a complete capture, he becomes liable to one of the following three penalties, which are also levied against a piece failing to make a single capture when this is possible.
   a) The opponent may insist that the piece moved is returned to its position and the proper capturing move is made.
   b) The opponent may remove the piece which should have made the capture and then continue with a move of his own. This is called HUFFING and is not a move in itself.
   c) The opponent may accept the move which was made, but the piece able to make the capture must do so at the player's next move or it again becomes liable to huffing.
8. A player need not point out to his opponent an opportunity to make a capture and that a piece is liable to be huffed.

There are two variants of the English game which make light-hearted changes from orthodox draughts.

LOSING DRAUGHTS

Each player has twelve draughtsman arranged in the conventional manner and the moves and method of capture are as in the standard game, except that only a) under rule 7 applies. Each player tries to force his opponent to capture his pieces and the first to lose them all wins the game.

DIAGONAL DRAUGHTS

The rules are the same as in the English game except that the pieces are arranged at the start of the game as in fig.30.

CONTINENTAL DRAUGHTS (France)

Jeu Forcé (English draughts) only lasted a few years in France and was replaced about 1650 by a variety known as *Le Grand Forcat*. This became obsolete within fifty years to be replaced by the game now known as Continental or Polish draughts and a board is reproduced to playable size on page 80 complete with the rules of play.

TAMS (Singapore)

This draughts variant, popular in Singapore, is played on a chequered board of 12 x 12 squares *(71)*.

Rules

1. Each player has thirty pieces which move diagonally and capture by a short diagonal leap. They can capture more than one piece in a turn of play.
2. Kings can move any number of vacant squares and can capture from any number of vacant squares before and land any number of vacant squares beyond the captured piece.
3. Multiple captures with change of direction are permitted in a single turn of play.
4. If a piece can be taken it is compulsory to do so under penalty of huffing.

Tams is frequently played in the open air outside cafés and in the streets using a painted wooden board and pieces from two Chinese chess sets, ignoring the ranks and using only the colours usually red for one side and blue for the other. Alternatively bottle tops may be pressed into service, one side being upside down and the other right way up.

(70) Double board for English and Continental draughts (chequers). The wooden pieces are stored in the troughs at the sides. For display a Scottish set of serpentine draughtsmen are placed ready for a game of draughts (chequers).

Le jeu de dames canadien, a form of draughts played in the French-speaking provinces of Canada, is very similar to *Tams*. The moves of men and kings and the rules of capture are those of Continental draughts. The board is chequered with 12 x 12 squares. Huffing was abolished in 1880, following a dispute during a match for the championship of Canada.

71

THE L'ATTAQUE FAMILY OF GAMES

L'ATTAQUE

The first of a new group of war games was advertised in *La Samaritaine*, Paris, in 1910. In chess, draughts fox and geese, and a host of other war games the players' pieces are in full view of the opponent. In the new game, *L'Attaque (72)*, each player (General) had the same pieces in his army, but they were made of cardboard held in tinware stands and the side of the piece facing the opponent was

Diagonal Draughts

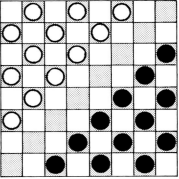

Fig. 30.

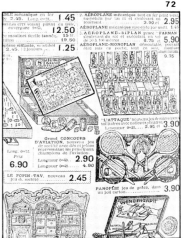

(71) *Tams* board in green and white paint, Singapore, 1979. The pieces are from two Chinese chess sets. The ranks are ignored and only the red and blue colours are significant.

(72) A page from *La Samaritaine* catalogue, Paris, 1910. Note the advertisement for *L'Attaque*.

either plain red belonging to the Red Army, or plain blue if belonging to the Blue Army. Each player was free to position his pieces ranging from a general to a private, with additional pieces guns, land mines, etc, as he saw fit. Every piece was vulnerable to some other piece in the enemy force and every piece could destroy specified hostile pieces. The initial placing of one's units to provide mutual support could be crucial later. Once an enemy piece had been challenged and its identity known, if it were not captured, the player tried to remember its identity through future moves until an opportunity occurred to attack with an appropriate piece. Equally, after a sucessful attack on an enemy piece, the player attempted to move his piece away and conceal it behind the rest of his force.

73

(73) *L'Attaque*, Tri-Tactics and Aviation sets.

DOVER PATROL

The next game of the series was Dover patrol. The board and pieces shown are post-World War II, and plastic stands replace the earlier tinware ones.
Equipment A folding board represents the North Sea with two opposing harbours, on each player's left, both protected by a harbour wall. Each player (Admiral) has forty pieces consisting of the following units in his fleet:

	Fire power
1 Flagship	10
2 Vice-flagship	9
1 Battle Squadron	8
2 Battleships	7
3 Battle Cruisers	6
4 Light Cruisers	5
4 Destroyers	4
4 Auxiliary Cruisers	3
5 Motor Torpedo Boats	2
5 Patrol Vessels	1

Auxiliaries and Mines
1 Mine Layer, 2 Mine Sweepers, 3 Submarines, 1 Flying Boat, 3 Mines.

The object of the game was to seize the flag of the opposing fleet and convey it back to one's own base, but a player could not place the enemy's flag on his base unless his own flag was in his possession on his own side of the board.

At the beginning of the game each admiral arranged his pieces as he wished, with their backs to the opponent and their identity concealed. The pieces occupied the spaces of the first five rows and one piece was placed anywhere on the sixth row. The base contained the flag, where it remained unless it was captured by an enemy unit arriving at the base.

Moves were made alternately, one space at a time forwards, sideways or backwards but never diagonally. There is no advantage in having first move.

The winner was the player who placed the enemy's flag on his own base, together with his own flag, or at least when his own flag was on one of his own ships in his own half of the board. A player also won the game if he hemmed in his opponent's pieces preventing them from being able to move when it was their turn to do so. His own flag, however, must be on his own base, otherwise the game was drawn.
DOVER PATROL. Copyright in all countries by H.P.Gibson & Sons Ltd.

AVIATION

The third game of the group, Aviation *(73)*, is probably the best of the four. The board represents air space over Europe and the players (rival Air Marshals) each have an airforce of 42 units representing aircraft, anti-aircraft guns, observation balloons, searchlights, etc. There is an aerodrome in each half of the board and its capture by troops in an enemy 'Troop Carrier' ends the game. Each Airmarshal sets out his pieces to his own plan and their distribution is concealed from the opponent. The pieces in the earlier sets have tinware bases, and the reconnaissance planes (1) are known as 'Scouts'. Otherwise the game has remained unchanged since it was played by the author at school in 1930. Modern packaging shows jet aircraft on the top of the box, but not on the pieces; indeed an airship flies bravely with a firepower of 5 and is the only piece which can attack the troop carriers (4½) in their hangers!

(74) Reproduction *Yoté* board and pieces.

TRI-TACTICS

The last of the games in this series combines elements of the other three in a tactical battle involving all three services, Navy, Army and Airforce. The game for two players uses a board with a headquarters, a land mass, a stretch of sea and a lake for each player who controls fifty-six pieces each, one force being coloured blue and the other red. The object of the game is to occupy either the opponent's Headquarters or his lake which lies up a river from the sea. A player can also win by blocking his opponent and immobilizing all his pieces.

The basic moves are similar to those in other games, though pieces can 'bluff' by moving out of their element, i.e. ships travelling over land, or an army piece moving on to the sea. If pieces are attacked out of their element, however, they are vulnerable to even the weakest of the units of the environment. To the purist this artificially detracts from the game.

HASAMI SHOGI (II) (Japan)

Unfortunately two games played in Japan on a quarter of the *Go* board and using *Go* stones have the same name, *Hasami shogi*. One is a war game, described here as *Hasami shogi* (II) and the other a game of position described on page 47 as *Hasami shogi* (I).

Rules
1. A piece may move any number of unoccupied squares on rank or file in any right hand direction. Diagonal moves are not allowed.
2. Each player has nine stones arranged on the squares of his back row.
3. A stone cannot land on a square occupied by another stone.
4. A stone can jump over an adjacent hostile stone to land on a vacant square beyond, but it cannot jump over a vacant square and an occupied square in the same turn of play.
5. When a player traps an opposing piece between two of his own rank or file (custodian capture), it is removed from the board. Any number of pieces can be trapped between two opposing stones as long as there are no gaps.
6. A stone may move safely between two enemy stones.
7. A stone on a corner square may be captured by blocking its movement with pieces on the two adjacent right angle squares. See fig. 31.
8. The object of the game is to capture all an opponent's pieces and remove them from the board.

YOTÉ (West Africa)

This West African game is popular throughout the area. The board may be made of wood (74) but is often scooped out of the sand. Five rows of six holes are required and the counters are pebbles or shells on one side and small pieces of stick or large seeds similar to acorns on the other.

Capture in a corner

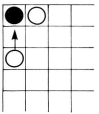

Fig. 31.

Rules
1. Each player starts with 12 counters.
2. The opening player places a pebble in any hole and the second player replies with a stick in another hole.
3. Only one piece may be played in each turn of play.
4. A player does not have to have all his pieces on the board before he starts to move those he has already put down; he has a choice of holding some in reserve for later in the game if he wishes.
5. Pieces may be moved one hole in a straight line along rank or file, but not diagonally and only to a vacant hole.
6. A player may capture one of his opponent's pieces by jumping over it and remove it from the board. He is then allowed a bonus capture with the choice of removing any one of the opposing pieces still on the board. He is not, however, permitted to make multiple short leaps.
7. Most *Yoté* games come to a quick and decisive conclusion, but a game can end in a draw when each player has three or fewer pieces left on the board.

Yoté can undergo rapid and surprising changes in fortune, making it an highly successful medium for gambling. In Senegal especially it is nearly always played for gain.

Reference: *Games of the World*, Holt, Rinehart & Winston, New York, 1975, pp. 90-1.

KONANE

Captain James Cook mentioned in his *Voyage in the Pacific* (1776-1780) that the Hawaiians played a game resembling draughts. Several stone boards for this game *Konane* have been found on prehistoric sites. The playing pieces were stored in a deep wooden bowl black stones of basalt, and white stones of coral. The boards varied in size. The reproduction board *(75)* is based on two in the Bernice P. Bishop Museum in Honolulu. One of these is made of wood with ten by thirteen depressions; the other is a flat piece of lava with ten by ten depressions cut into it to receive pebbles.

Equipment

Konane is played on a board of 10 x 10 depressions, with 50 black and 50 white pebbles. In this game for two, the players face each other across the board, each trying to capture or immobilize the opponent's pieces.

Rules

1. Each player arranges his 50 pieces on the board in alternate holes.
2. One player takes a piece of each colour and shuffles them behind his back and then offers them in his closed hands to his opponent who chooses one. This decides the colour of the players' pieces in the first game.
3. Two pieces are then returned to their holes on the board.
4. Black always starts and begins by lifting either one of the two central black pieces or one from a corner of the board. This piece is placed in front of his opponent as a capture.
5. White then lifts a white piece which must be adjacent to the vacancy left by Black's first turn. This piece is placed in front of Black as a capture.
6. The game continues by alternate turns of play, pieces jumping over an opposing piece into a vacant hole beyond by a *short leap*, forwards, sideways or backwards, but not diagonally.
7. Several jumps can be made during a turn as long as the movement of the capturing piece is in a straight line. A change of direction is not allowed.
8. When making multiple captures the pieces must be separated from each other by one empty hole.
9. A player has free choice of how many pieces to capture. He need not take all the pieces 'at risk'. There is no huffing.
10. As pieces are removed from the board, jumping becomes more difficult. If a player is unable to take a piece when it is his turn to play, he loses the game.
11. If a player loses all his pieces, the game is over and his opponent has won. Drawn games cannot occur.
12. At the end of every game the players exchange colours, their new pieces having accumulated in front of them during the preceding game.
13. A match consists of the best of an agreed number of games.

Cowrie shells, natural white and dyed red, blue or green make attractive pieces.

MING MANG (Tibet)

This game, popular with Tibetan monks before the Chinese invasion in 1959, is played on a board of variable size, but commonly uses a grid of 17 x 18 lines. A replica board made recently in England is illustrated using pieces from a *Go* set *(76)*.

Rules

1. Each player lines up his 34 counters on the points of two contiguous sides of the board.
2. The players move one piece in alternate turns of play at right angles to any vacant point along a line. There is no jumping.
3. All captured pieces are replaced by pieces of one's own colour.
4. A piece is captured if it is trapped between two hostile pieces along a straight line. This rule applies to any number of contiguous pieces in a straight line with a hostile piece at both ends. The trapped pieces are removed from the board and replaced by pieces of the captor's colour.
5. If a player has two pieces in a straight line with an empty point between them, his opponent may move a piece on to this point without it being taken but if the player moves one of the pieces away in any direction and at the next turn moves it back again, the opponent's piece is captured.
6. Pieces in the corners of the board cannot be captured because they cannot be in a straight line with opposing pieces. The corners are crucial points and if a player loses them he is likely to lose the game.
7. When one player can no longer move a piece on the board, either because they have all been captured or trapped in corners, the game is finished and lost.

GERMAN TACTICS (France)

Asalto has been described on page 25, but the version called *German Tactics (77)* is from the time of the Franco-Prussian War and contemporary with *The Siege of Paris*, page 43. The pottery board in the illustration came from the family home of an old lady and pre-dates 1900. The two ornamented pegs represent officers and the twenty-four plain pegs, private soldiers. The officers are placed on any two marks within the garrison and the soldiers on the twenty-four outside.

Rules

1. A soldier makes the first move along any single line to the next intersection.
2. The officers are able to advance or retire from intersection to intersection along both single and double lines (fig. 32)

Soldiers only along single lines.

Officers along single or double lines.

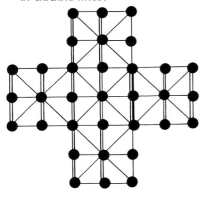

Fig. 32.

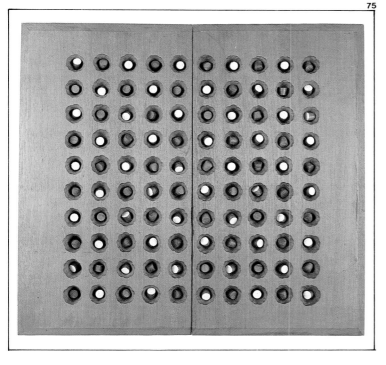

75

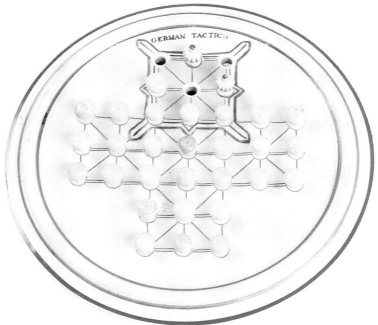

77

(75) Reproduction *Konane* board and pieces.

(76) Reproduction *Ming Mang* board, 1987. The pieces are from a *Go* set *c*.1850.

(77) Pottery German Tactics board and pieces, *c*.1870.

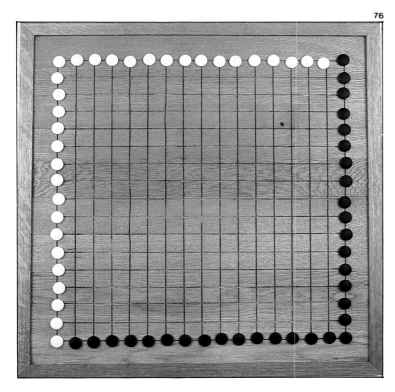

76

and to capture soldiers by jumping over them to a vacant point immediately beyond. They are permitted to make several short leaps in a single turn of play, thus making multiple captures.

3.	An officer need not make a capture, but if he does not, he is removed from the board.
4.	The soldiers cannot capture an officer, they can only advance and along single lines.
5.	The officers win by reducing the soldiers to eight, or if the soldiers manoeuvre themselves into such a position that they cannot move, or if they have blockaded the officers in the garrison so that the latter cannot move.
6.	The soldiers win by occupying the nine points in the garrison. The other side of this board is marked out for French solitaire, with thirty-seven holes instead of thirty-three as in the English board. There are six pegs missing, otherwise the board and pieces are undamaged.

SIEGE OF PARIS (France)

This game is usually played by two players, but three can take part, one player controlling the force within the garrison and each of the other two being in charge of an attacking force.

The game commemorates the encirclement of France's capital city by the German Army under General Moltke from 18th September 1870 for 132 days. On 1st March,

1871 the Germans held a triumphal march down the Champs Élysées.

The game only enjoyed a brief popularity and then disappeared, though boards and pieces are occasionally seen in antique shops. The board illustrated here *(78)* is made of two hinged pieces of mahogany-covered plywood. The dark squares of the board are of rosewood and the light of a fruitwood, probably pear. The fortress is of the same light wood. The black pieces are of ebony, the white of pear, and the brown probably of laburnum heartwood. When closed one surface forms a board for the Snail game, see page 22, and the other is for Asalto, see page 92.

The central 6 x 6 squares of the Siege of Paris board are replaced by a square marked with eight circles and linked with lines, representing the fortress. The restriction of certain pieces to squares of one colour is derived from chess; but the unequal forces engaged in a battle for different objectives is borrowed from the Norse *Tafl* group of games, Fox and Geese springing to mind.

A board is reproduced to playable size on page 88 together with the rules of play.

● Cavalry
○ Indians

Fig. 35.

allude to the Custer affair of 1876 when the Sioux chief Sitting Bull led his tribesmen against the U.S. Cavalry General and wiped out the entire force at the Battle of Wounded Knee?

Rules

1. The starting position of the pieces are shown in fig. 35 with the Indians placed on the perimeter ring and the cavalry on the inner ring and at the angles of the cross.
2. Pieces move one point at a time along any marked line.
3. A capture is made by jumping over an adjacent enemy piece on to a vacant point beyond.
4. Any number of pieces can be captured in a turn of play by a series of short leaps, a change of direction between one leap and the next being permitted.
5. The Indians always make the first move.
6. The object of the game is for either player to gain control of the board (Territory) by eliminating or blocking the pieces of his opponent.

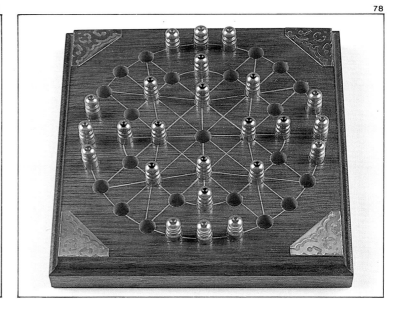

79

78

(78) Siege of Paris board and pieces set out for the start of a game, *c.*1870.

(79) Stockade board and pieces at the start of a game.

STOCKADE

This modern modification of Fox and Geese *(79)* produced by Slater and Futton, designers of executive games, is given a Wild West setting in mid-nineteenth century North America. The traditional English Fox and Geese board has the addition of two concentric circles. See fig. 35. Twelve Indians try to trap or destroy twelve members of the United States Cavalry who emerge from a fort represented by the empty central hole. Does the game

In this modern variant of *Freyerstafl* both players have the same number of pieces and the same power of movement. The game is thus closer to draughts than to its classical ancestor; only the different, though balanced, initial positions of the pieces retains an element of the old Norse war game.

CHAPTER 3

GAMES OF POSITION

TIC-TAC-TOE (Ancient Egypt)

The board contains nine points (fig. 36a) and each player has five counters of distinctive colour or shape. The players place one counter alternately on a point and if one player can place three in a straight line he wins the game.

Noughts and Crosses is the same game but using a different board. See (80).

Cut into the roofing slabs of the Ancient Egyptian temple at Kurna is a more elaborate board, fig. 36b. Each player had three men of his own colour and entered them in turn on any vacant point on the board. Then the game continued with alternate moves of a piece to a contiguous vacant point until one player succeeded in placing his three men in a straight line. As the opening player can always force a win by correct play, dice may have been used to decide the advantage of first entry.

Two boards of this type have been found in Roman Britain, one cut into a stone at the Roman supply base at Cortopitum and now in the museum there, and the other on a stone quarried from Hadrian's wall is in the wall of the vicarage garden at Lanercost Priory. They date from the second or third century.

The game was widely played in England in the fourteenth century, and boards can be seen in several cathedrals carved by monks who perhaps found the long hours of devotion tedious.

ACHI (Ghana)

Achi is played by the schoolchildren in Ghana, the board being marked out on the ground, fig. 37. Each player has four little sticks, one side with the bark left on and the other peeled. In the first phase the sticks are entered on to any empty points on the board in alternate turns of play. When all eight sticks are positioned, the second phase begins. Each player moves one stick along a line at each turn of play, trying to obtain three markers in a row, thereby winning the game.

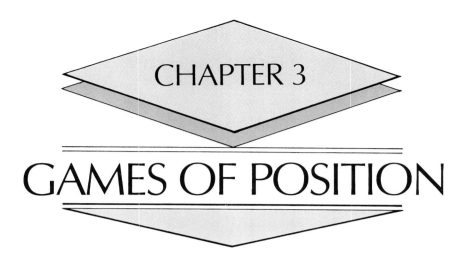

80

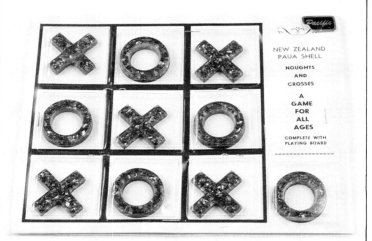

(80) *Pau* shell Noughts and Crosses board and pieces from New Zealand.

NINE MEN'S MORRIS (Ancient Egypt)

Nine Men's Morris reached its height of popularity in the sixteenth century and superb illustrations of the game are preserved in the codices of the North Italian Academies' manuscripts intended for use at court. Boards made in the shape of a shallow box with a hinged lid were popular from this time onwards. When closed, one surface was marked out for chess and the other for Nine Men's Morris; when open the interior was inlaid with the twenty-four points of a backgammon board and the hinged half sides of the box formed the bar. Some were superb *objets d'arts* worked in mother-of-pearl, ivory and precious metals.

This game for two is reproduced to playable size on page 76 together with some of the game's history and the rules of play.

Fig. 36a

Fig. 36b

Achi board and pieces

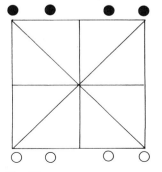

Fig. 37.

45

DARA (Nigeria)

Dara (82) played by the *Dakarkari* people of Nigeria is eminently suitable for a holiday game on a beach. The board consists of thirty small hollows made in the sand in five rows of six each.

First Phase Each player has twelve distinctive pieces — these may be stones, shells, pieces of pottery or small sticks. They are placed one at a time in any empty hole in alternate turns of play. When all the pieces have been positioned the second phase begins.

Second Phase In alternate turns, each player moves a piece along rank or file to the next empty hole, his objective being to form a line of three pieces in consecutive holes, at right angles but not diagonally. When a THREE is formed, the player removes one of his opponent's pieces from the board. The game ends when one player is reduced to two pieces or has pieces trapped and is unable to form a line. Lines of four or more do not count. Success in the second phase depends on skilful placing of pieces in the first.

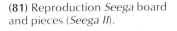

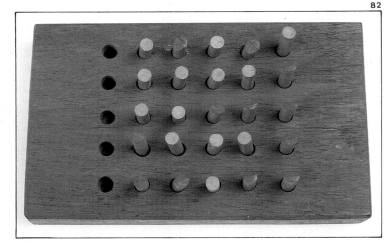

(81) Reproduction *Seega* board and pieces (*Seega II*).

(82) Reproduction *Dara* board and pieces.

(83) *Go* board and pieces, *c.*1950, at the start of a game of *Go-moku*.

(84) A *Go* board set out for *Hasami Shogi I*.

GO-MOKU (Japan)

Go-moku (83) also known as *Renju*, is played on a *Go* board of 19 x 19 points.

Rules

1. The board is empty at the beginning of the game, and the players have 180 stones each.
2. In alternate turns of play, the players place a piece on any empty point.
3. Players are not permitted to construct open-ended forks with branches of three stones each. Forks of three and four or four and four are allowed.
4. The first player to form a continuous line of five pieces on rank, file or diagonal wins the game.

Go-moku was introduced into Europe about 1885. In England it was marketed as 'Spoil Five' and was played on the squares instead of on the points.

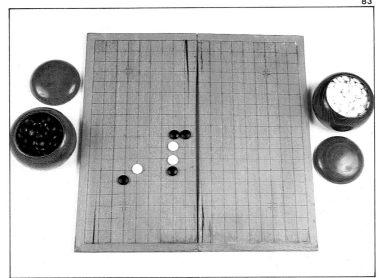

HASAMI SHOGI (I) (Japan)

This game is also played on a *Go* board (83) but only one quarter of the board of 9 x 9 squares is used, and the pieces are placed on the squares and not on the points, fig. 38.

Rules

1. Each player has eighteen *Go* stones of his own colour and they are placed on the squares of the back two rows.
2. A stone may be moved any number of unoccupied squares on rank or file in any direction.
3. No diagonal moves are permitted.
4. The players try to form five stones in a line excluding the home two rows. The first to do so wins the game.

The reader is referred to *Hasami Shogi* (II) in Chapter two, page 41. Unfortunately these very different games, both played on one quarter of a *Go* board have the same name.

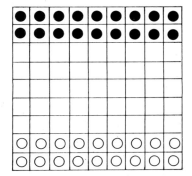

Fig. 38.

FOUR BALLS (Provenance unknown)

Each player in the game starts with 21 wooden balls of his own colour and in alternate turns of play tries to arrange 4 of his balls in a straight lines, vertically, horizontally or diagonally. There are seven columns, each capable of holding six balls. Unlike *Go-moku* and *Hasami Shogi* (I) the order of placing the balls is dependent upon gravity. The game is more difficult than it appears.

The upper surface of the fine box board has a thin green skiver covering, with gold blocking and a small centaur about to throw a spear at the top and at the bottom in gold lettering is RÉMY MARTIN COGNAC. The date of the board is uncertain, but probably it is Edwardian, *c*.1901-10. The wooden balls are made of beech, the yellow being clear varnished and the brown stained and varnished.

This may have been a pub game, standing on the bar ready for customers' use and advertising cognac at the same time.

(85) Four Balls. The upper surface of the mahogany box is covered with green skiver blocked in gold RÉMY MARTIN COGNAC, *c*.1901-10.

(86) Three-dimensional three-in-a-row game.

THREE DIMENSIONAL THREE-IN-A-ROW (Provenance unknown)

The board *(86)* consists of a central peg and three pairs of pegs set at 120 degrees to each other. There are eleven white wooden rings and ten black wooden rings which the players place by alternate turns of play over the ends of the pegs, each trying to make a row of three of his own rings vertically or horizontally. White starts and the players change colours after each game. The winner of a match is the first to win an agreed number of games.

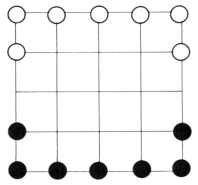

Fig. 39.

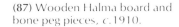

Starting position of pieces in Five Field Kono.

(87) Wooden Halma board and bone peg pieces, c.1910.

(88) Display of Halma boxes.

87

88

FIVE FIELD KONO (O-pat-ko-no) (Korea)

This Korean game is played on a grid of 5 x 5 lines, either scratched on the ground, drawn on a piece of paper or cut into a wooden board. Each player has seven distinctive pieces placed as in fig. 39. The players move their pieces by alternate turns of play of one piece diagonally across a square to the next point, either forwards or backwards. No jumping over pieces is allowed.

The object of the game is to manoeuvre one's pieces across the board onto the points originally occupied by the opponent at the beginning of the game; the first to do so being the winner.

HALMA (USA) — (once known in Britain as Hoppity)

Halma (87) was invented about 1880, the name being based on the Greek for jump. When played by two players, each has nineteen pieces of his own colour arranged in a CAMP on his own side of the board, the walls of which are marked by a thicker line. A board is reproduced to playable size on page 112 together with the rules for both two and four players.

CHINESE CHECKERS (USA)

About the same time as Halma was invented, Chinese Checkers was put on the market in the US. The board illustrated here (89) is an early one manufactured by Parker Bros. at about the turn of the century and was bought in 1977 in a second-hand shop in Kaslo, a small town in central British Columbia. The previous owner had been a lady of 95 who had owned it since childhood.

Rules
1. If there are two players each has fifteen pieces of his own colour and places them on fifteen spaces of his home base, one of the points of the star. When two play they use opposite points of the star.
2. If there are three players each takes ten pieces of his own colour and places them on the ten nearest spaces of the star, leaving alternate star-points empty, each player's pieces facing an empty corner.
3. With four or more players they may choose which points to use as their base.
4. The object of the game is for a player to be first in transferring all his pieces to the star-point opposite his home base.
5. The order of play is in clockwise rotation.

6. Each player in his turn may move a piece on to an adjoining empty point along any line, or he may jump over a single piece of any colour on to an empty space immediately beyond. If he can make further jumps in any direction he may do so, but jumping is not compulsory.

7. Only one piece can be moved in any turn of play.
Strategy Players place some of their pieces to form a ladder along which other pieces can jump towards their goal. Such a ladder may be equally useful to the opponent who is moving his pieces in the opposite direction and either player may decide to 'block' a ladder rather than use it.

(89) Chinese checkers board manufactured by Parker Bros. USA, c.1900.

(90) Three early Reversi sets (none complete) with the original paper board from one of them, c.1910.

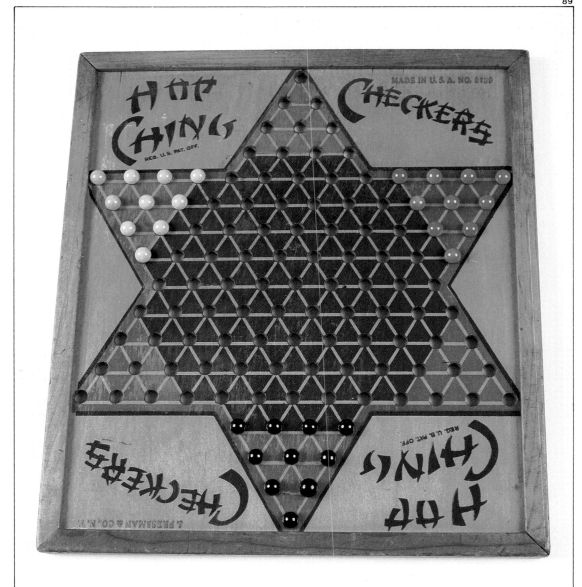

89

REVERSI (England)

Reversi was invented by Mr Waterman in 1888 and was published by Messrs Jacques & Son. The game is played on a draughts board of sixty-four squares with sixty-four pieces which are different colours on their two sides (90). Each player begins with thirty-two pieces.

Blue begins by placing a piece, blue side up, on one of the four central squares on the empty board. Yellow replies by placing his first piece, yellow side up, on another central square. These four squares must be covered first and then the players play alternately, each piece being placed on a square adjacent to one occupied by an enemy piece. Any enemy pieces directly intervening between this piece, either on rank or file, and another piece of the player's colour are captured and turned over to show the player's colour uppermost. A piece may change colour and ownership several times during a game. When all the squares on the board are covered with pieces, the player with most pieces of his colour showing wins the game.

90

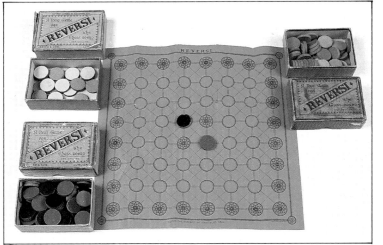

91

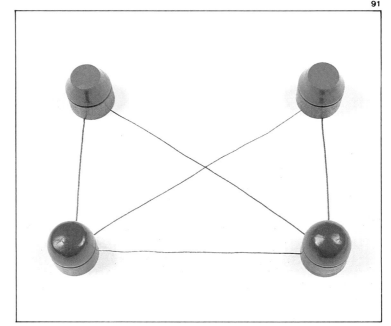

(91) Reproduction *Pong Hau K'i* board approximately 6 inches (15cms) square.

(92) Reproduction *Mu Torere* board and pieces (New Zealand Maori game).

92

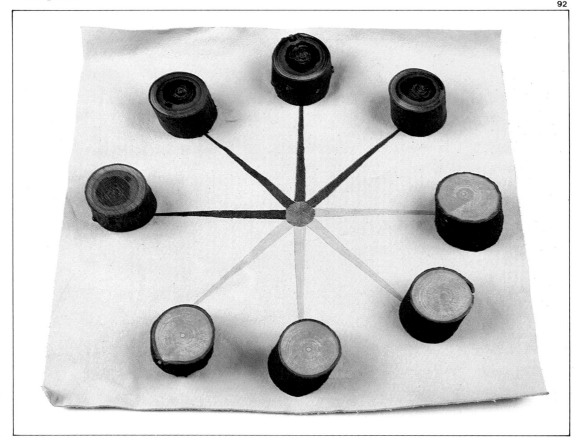

PONG HAU K'I (China)

Pong hau k'i is played in Canton, the board usually being drawn on a piece of paper or on the ground. Each player has two distinctive markers; their initial positions being shown in the illustration *(91)*.

The players move one marker at a time along a line onto an empty point, the object being to block the opponent's markers. Some players do not start from a set position, but place the markers on any empty point in alternate turns of play, and then continue as described above.

MU TORERE (New Zealand Maori)

The board consists of an eight pointed star with a circular area at the centre *(92)*. Each player begins with four pieces of a distinctive colour arranged on four adjacent peripheral points of the star. Each player tries to block the opponent's pieces and prevent their being able to move.

Rules

1. Black begins and the players move a piece alternately. Only one piece is allowed on each point. Jumping is not permitted.
2. There are three types of move:
   a) a piece may be moved from one of the arms to an adjacent arm;
   b) from an arm to the centre, providing that one or both of the adjacent arms are occupied by a hostile piece;
   c) from the centre to an arm.

Variant The restriction on the movement of a piece from the arms to the centre is sometimes observed only for the first two moves of each player.

GO (China and Japan)

Go, also known more correctly as *I-go*, or in China as *Wei-ch'i*, is possibly the premier intellectual game. Originating in China, Wei-ch'i (pronounced Way Chee), was first mentioned in writings from Honan c.625 BC. The first books on the subject were written much later during the Tang Dynasty, AD 618-906. *Wei-ch'i* was introduced into court circles in Japan about AD 500, probably during the reign of Empress Suiko. In the museum at Nara is a *Go* board — said to have been used by Emperor Shomu, AD 724-48. By 1066 when the Normans invaded England, *Go* was beginning to be played by the common people in Japan, and in the thirteenth century it was popular with the Samurai, boards and stones being regarded as essential pieces of military equipment and taken on active service.

As soon as fighting ceased, *Go* contests began.

In the sixteenth century a State Academy was founded for the teaching and advancement of the game, and several master players were engaged as professors with substantial salaries. The director, Honinbo Sansha received 1,400 square yards of land and an annual income of 1,000 bushels of rice. The Academy awarded professional players degrees, the first or lowest carrying the title 'Shodan' and the ninth or highest, 'Kudan'. The highest degree has very rarely been granted. A system of handicapping was also devised, the weaker player being allowed first move, or being granted one, two, three or four stones, the last being the highest handicap permitted among players holding degrees. The highest recognized handicap for a novice is seventeen stones.

With the fall of the *Shogunate* in 1868, state regulation of the game ceased and the *Go* Academy closed, but about 1880 there was a revival in interest in the game, and today there are about some eight million *Go* players in Japan and nearly a hundred professional players. *Wei-ch'i* is played widely in China and *Pa-tok*, the same game, is popular in Korea, though the standard of play in both mainland countries is well below that of Japan.

Traditional Japanese boards *(94)* are made of a solid block of wood about 18 inches (45.5cm) long, 16 inches (40cm) wide, and 5 inches ((12.5cm) thick, fitted with four detachable feet about 3 inches (7.5cm) high. The board and feet are stained yellow. A square depression is cut into the underside of the board to lighten it and also to increase the resonance; the pieces make a pleasant click when placed upon it.

The upper surface of the board is marked out with thin black lines of lacquer into a grid of 19 x 19 forming intersections or points. Nine of these are marked to assist in rapid orientation and in handicapping.

A board of playable size has been reproduced on page 98 with the rules and tactics.

The wood carving *(93)* was exported from Japan in 1898 and was probably made in the same year. It depicts a desperate encounter on a *Go* board between a gambler on the right and a demon on the left. Watching them is the god of gambling. Both spirits have blue eyes. The intense anxiety of the human as he struggles to preserve his soul is strikingly portrayed.

References: Iwamoto, K. *Go for Beginners*, Penguin Books Ltd, 1976. Smith, A. *The Game of Go*, Charles E Tuttle, Rutland, Vermont, 1958. Takagawa, K. *How to Play Go*, Japanese Go Association, 1956. Takagawa, K. *The Vital Points of Go*, Japanese Go Association, 1958.

93

(93) Japanese carving in wood of a gambler playing *Go* with a demon. The God of Gambling watches from behind waiting for the human's soul. Note the blue eyes of the devil and god. The heads are hollow. Height 13 inches (32cm). Brought to England in 1898.

(94) *Go* board and stones, *c.*1880. The pieces demonstrate a *seki* position.

94

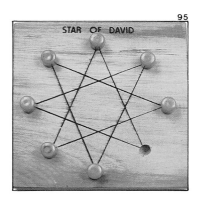

Fig.49 _____

(95) Star of David board and pieces. New Zealand, 1983.

Solution:

3→6, 4→1, 7→4, 2→7, 8→3, 6→8, 6→2.

(96) Reproduction *Pasang* board, central bowl, and cups for each player with cowrie shells and acorns as pieces at the start of a game.

Notation for English Solitaire.

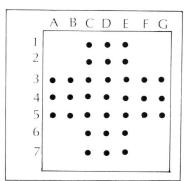

Fig.50 _____

PASANG (Brunei)_____

This traditional game is played by the women in Brunei (96). Two, three or four players can take part. A common size board is 11 x 11 holes with the central holes omitted and the space occupied by a store bowl leaving 112 holes in play.

Equipment With 112 holes, 56 white stones worth two points each, and 56 black stones worth 1 point each are used as pieces, and each player has a store bowl. Cowrie shells (white), and acorns (black), are used as pieces.

Rules _____

1. One player arranges the stones in any way she fancies, but often attractive geometric forms are created, some having special names, such as 'Flowers in a vase', 'Ascent to a palace', 'Day and night', and 'Chicken leg'.
2. When all the holes are filled, the player on the left of the sower begins by lifting a piece from any of the four corner-holes and places it in her store bowl.
3. The turn of play then passes to the next player on the left who lifts one of the three possible pieces to jump over a piece into the vacant hole.
4. A piece can only jump along rank or file or along one of the marked diagonals. Pieces passed over are lifted and placed in the player's bowl.
5. Play proceeds in a clockwise direction around the board.
6. Pieces can only move by making a short leap and one, three, five, seven or more odd number of pieces can be captured in the same move, but not an even number.
7. If four pieces are at risk, only one or three can be captured.
8. A player is not compelled to make all the captures possible in a move and there is no huffing.
9. When no more captures can be made the game is finished, and any stones left on the board are ignored.
10. The player making the highest score, with white stones counting 2 points and black 1 point, is the winner.
11. Each of the losers pays the winner her total score and then she arranges the stones in a pattern of her choice for the next game.
12. When the board is reset the player on the sower's left begins the new game by lifting one of the corner stones and play continues as before.

POSITIONAL GAMES FOR ONE PLAYER (Patience)_____
STAR OF DAVID_____

The board and pieces illustrated (95) were bought in Hamilton, New Zealand in 1982. Made by I.Q.Products, Lake Taupo, N.Z. In this solitaire game, the player starts with the board empty and places a peg in any hole on the point of the star, moving it along one of the lines to occupy the opposite point. This same manoeuvre is repeated at every turn of play. To win the player must introduce seven pegs onto the board. Solution, see fig.49.

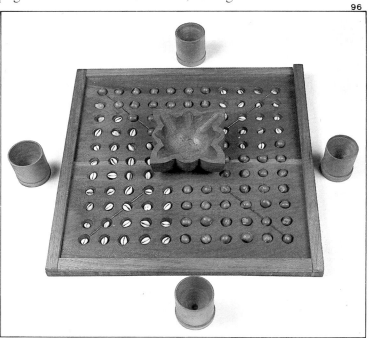

SOLITAIRE (France)_____

Solitaire is said to have been invented during the eighteenth century by an imprisoned French count. The new game for one player used a Fox and Geese board and pieces and provided a series of interesting problems. Fig. 50 shows notation used for recording them.

The basic puzzle is to remove the marble in D4 and then, at each turn of play one marble must jump along rank or file over an adjacent marble into a vacant hole immediately beyond. The marble passed over is removed from the board. The object of the game is to remove all the marbles from the board except one and this should be left in the central hole. D4, fig 50.

FRENCH SOLITAIRE (France)

In England, solitaire continued to be played on the original Fox and Geese board of thirty-three spaces, but in France four more spaces were added. This change was followed by the invention of several neat and attractive problems.

Examples Starting with a full board:

'the professor and his students' — lift the piece on 19, and end as fig. 51a;

'St Andrew's Cross' — lift the piece at 19 and end as fig. 51b.

'the Cross Moline' — lift the piece at 19 and end as fig. 51c.

The lovely solitaire board of ivory (98) was made about 1780, probably at Dieppe in France, and may have been brought to England by a refugee from the French Revolution. In the 1950s it belonged to a very old lady who had an antique shop in Penrith. During her lifetime she refused many offers for it, but after her death her daughter sold it to the author. Unfortunately the board's history has been lost.

97

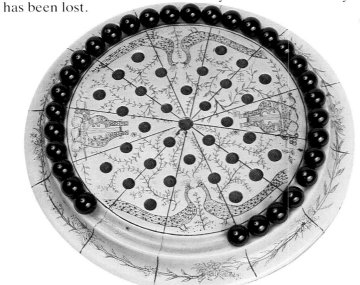

LAM TURKI (India)

A variant of *Pentalpha* known as *Lam Turki* is played in Northern India. The first part of the game is the same as the *Pentalpha* still played in Crete, and the same board is used, fig. 52. In this game for one player, there are nine pieces which he attempts to introduce onto the board of ten points. The board, which forms part of a compendium, is reproduced to playable size on page 90 together with the rules of play.

Notation for French board.

	1	2	3		
4	5	6	7	8	
9	10	11	12	13	14	15
16	17	18	19	20	21	22
23	24	25	26	27	28	29
	30	31	32	33	34	
		35	36	37		

Fig.51

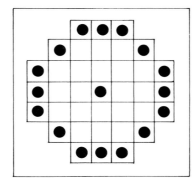

Fig.51a

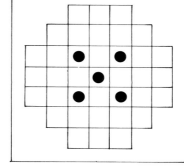

Fig.51b

Fig.51c

98

(97) Italian replica in resin compound *c.*1987 of a scrimshaw solitaire board, original in an Italian museum.

(98) French ivory Fox and Geese board with pieces, also used for solitaire problems, *c.*1780.

Pentalpha Board

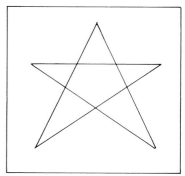

Fig.52

53

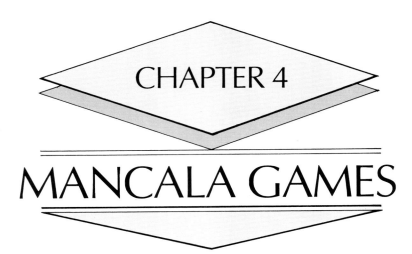

CHAPTER 4

MANCALA GAMES

Mancala is the generic name for a large family of games played widely throughout Africa, the Near East, India, Indonesia and the Islands of the Caribbean, but virtually unknown in Europe, North America and Australasia in spite of many attempts to popularize various members of the group *(100)* and *(101)*. Sir William Finders Petrie described and illustrated a stone *Mancala* board in his *Objects of Daily Use*, Aris & Phillips Ltd, 1974, first published in 1929, p.55 and Plate XLVII, under the title 'The Game of Forty-two and Pool' *(99)*.

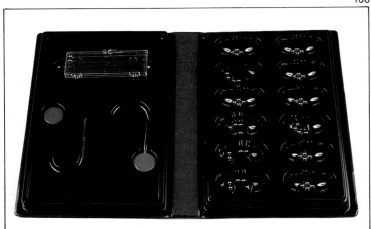

(99) A plate from Prof. Flinders Petrie's *Objects of Daily Use* showing an early limestone *Mancala* board from Memphis. No date given.

(100) This thin plastic *Asanti* board was produced as a promotion item by Puffed Wheat breakfast cereal (Quaker Products) for 2 tokens and £4.35/$8.

Petrie wrote: 'One instance of a board of 3 x 14 holes with a pool was found on a rough block of limestone at Memphis. The lines are not regular, but it seems probable that it was played like *Senat*, but with a longer range between players. The pool suggests that pieces were taken in this game. The holes are so small that the pieces were probably beans or little chips of pottery.

He does not give any clue to the age of the board, but it is certainly Ancient Egyptian, probably dating from 1500 BC or earlier. A much later *Mancala* board was discovered cut into the flat roof of a small Ptolemaic temple at Deir-el-Medina *(102)*. This probably dates from the occupation of Thebes by Roman troops in 89-85 BC. The troops occupied

the whole temple complex and the soldiers probably occupied this vantage point for guard duties and cut the boards to relieve the monotony of day after day on duty.

There are three classes of *Mancala* games: those with two rows of holes, those with three rows of holes and those with four rows of holes. The last are confined to the south and east of Africa and the three row form to Ethiopia and neighbouring Somaliland. By far the commonest is two rank *Mancala*, played over the rest of Africa and the Orient.

Two Rank Mancala

SUNKA (Indonesia)

This board *(103)* was manufactured commercially in Indonesia and bought from Lib's Art and Craft shop in Singapore in 1978. The game is also played in Malaysia. Note the carrying handle, also useful for suspension from a wall hook, and is the only board among the twenty in the author's collection of *Mancala* boards with this feature. With the board was a cotton bag holding 98 cowrie shells.

To enable the game to be played in this book it has has been re-drawn as a flat board and it can be found on page 110 along with the rules.

Definitions As the *Mancala* games will be new to many readers the following terms will be defined.

LIFT Lifting all the shells from a hole ready to begin sowing.

SOWING Placing one shell in each consecutive hole in the direction of movement. In some games this is clockwise, in others anticlockwise, and in a few in either direction.

LAP This may involve several lifts and sowings and ends when the last shell of a lift falls into an empty hole.

ROUND This lasts from the setting out of the shells in the holes until no more play is possible. A game may consist of

a single round, although more commonly of several, until one player is no longer able to fill even one hole with pieces.

GAME When a decision has been reached and one player emerges as the winner.

These terms will be used in describing all the *Mancala* games in this chapter. Incidentally there are probably as many *Mancala* games as there are card games and they are equally varied.

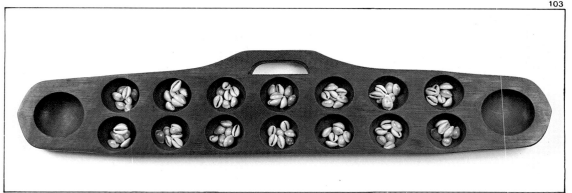

PALLANGULI (India and Sri-Lanka)

Four boards are illustrated under this section and three varieties of the game described. The first board *(105)*, made of white metal and chromium plated with little brass wheels, was brought to England in 1954 from Ernakulam in Travancore-chochin. *Pallanguli* is usually played by women.

Rules For Two Players

1. Two three or four can play and the players start with six seeds in each of their seven holes.
2. The opening player lifts the seeds from any hole on her side of the board leaving it empty and sows anticlockwise one seed into each hole. If she reaches the end of her side of the board she continues sowing into the opponent's holes.
3. When the last seed of a lift falls into a hole, either on her own side of the board, or her opponent's, she lifts all the seeds in the next hole and continues sowing as before.
4. If the last seed of a lift falls into a hole with an empty hole beyond, any seeds in the hole immediately beyond the empty hole are captured and put in the player's store; she then continues playing from the next hole beyond, but if the last seed of a lift falls into a hole with two empty holes beyond, she wins nothing and the lap ends.

(101) *Tsolo*. This very cheap production of the Bantu game published by HPG Series about 1955 is made of cardboard with the rules on the underside of the lid. These are the same as given for *Baré* on page 60. A provisional patent was taken out on 25th May, 1954. This particular one obviously did not sell well and was finally bought for one shilling; less than the value of the cowries.

(102) A *Mancala* board found at Deir-el-Medina. *R. C. Bell.*

(103) *Sunka* board from Indonesia with seven cowrie shells in each hole.

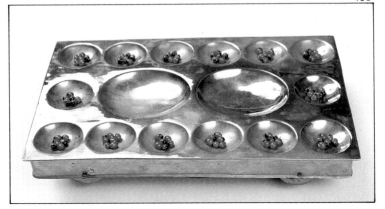

5. Her opponent then plays by lifting the seeds or seed from any hole on her side of the board and sows in an anticlockwise direction. Her turn also ceases when the last seed of a lift falls into a hole with two empty holes beyond.

6. The game continues by alternate moves.

7. Four seeds in a hole are called a COW and, irrespective of the sower, become the property of the owner of the hole and are lifted at once and put in her store while play continues.

8. At the end of the first round players empty their store hole and put six seeds into as many holes on their side of the board as they can, any remainder are returned to store.

9. The loser of the first round will be unable to fill all her holes and these are marked with a little stick and are known as RUBBISH HOLES. The winner of the round fills all seven of her holes and returns any surplus to her store.

10. The player having first move in the first round, has second move in the second and first move in the third round, etc. Each round is played in the same way as the first, except that rubbish holes are not used.

11. The game ends when one player is unable to fill even one hole with six seeds.

12. During any round the losing player may win enough seeds to re-open one or more rubbish holes in the next and eventually defeat her opponent. A game between well-matched players can last a very long time.

The antique board (104) is part of a compendium of six games which belonged to a family in Mysore and was bought to England thirty years ago. It had been in the family for at least fifty years and probably longer. The instructions for playing the game are the same as the above.

(104) *Pallanguli* board from the antique compendium of games shown on page 27 in picture no. 44.

(105) *Pallanguli* board in white metal from Ernakulum, Travancore-cochin. Six seeds per hold. Note the little brass wheels, 1954.

TAMILNADI (India)

The third board (106) of brass made in two halves and hinged in the middle, came from Madurai and was bought to England in 1979, with its instructions for play, together with the bald statement that the game was played by the Pallawa kings in about AD 900. Two, three or four players can take part. See figs. 53a, 53b, and 53c.

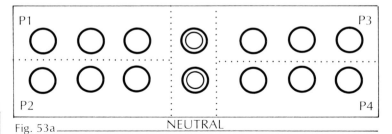

Fig. 53a — NEUTRAL

Fig. 53b — NEUTRAL

Fig. 53c — NEUTRAL

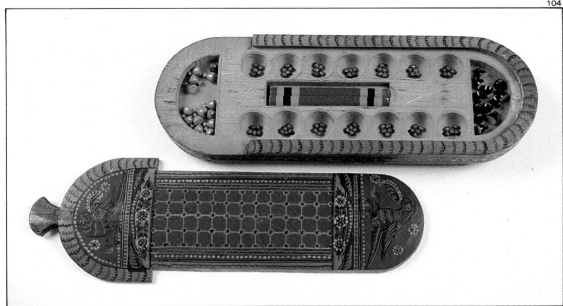

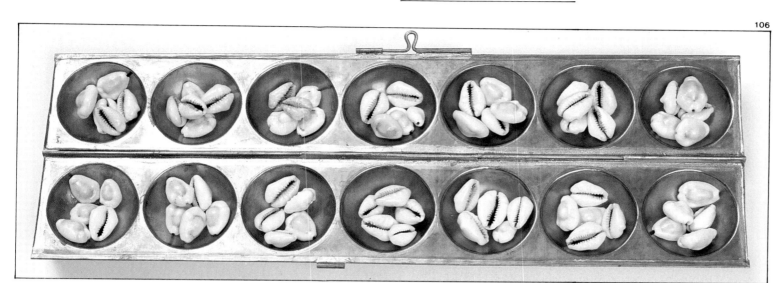

Rules

For four players

1. If four play each player owns three holes, see fig.53a and there are five shells in each hole. The Tamil name for cowrie is *chovi*.
2. The opening player lifts from one of her holes and sows in an anticlockwise direction, lifting from the hole immediately beyond the hole where the last shell of a lift was placed.
3. If the hole beyond where a sowing ends is empty, the player wins the contents of the next hole and puts them in her store.
4. If the hole beyond the empty hole is a neutral hole, the sower does not win the contents of the hole and the lap ends.
5. When there are four shells in a hole, these are taken by the owner of the hole and placed in her store, regardless of who is sowing.
6. As the players' holes become empty and they are unable to start a lift, they drop out of the game. The last player to be left in play wins.

For three players

7. Each player has four holes, see fig. 53b. Otherwise the play is the same as in the four-handed game.

For two players

8. Each player has six holes, see fig. 53c, otherwise the play is the same as in the four-handed game.

OLINDA KELIYA (Sri Lanka)

In Sri Lanka *Pallanguli* is known as *Olinda Keliya* (The Olinda game).

This board *(107)* from Sri Lanka is made of a heavy wood painted dark brown. There are two store holes, with a central hole for holding sticks to mark rubbish holes. The game is played almost exclusively by women and usually at the New Year Season.

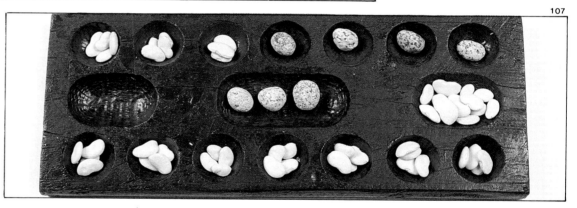

Rules

First Round

1. Four beans are placed in each hole.
2. There are several laps to the move.
3. There are several rounds to the game.
4. All moves are made in the same direction, all clockwise, or all anticlockwise, and in passing a bean is sown into the players's store, but not into her opponent's.
5. The opening player usually lifts the beans from the second hole either end of her row and sows the first bean in the adjoining end hole, thereby fixing the direction of play for the round. Subsequent moves may start from any of the player's holes.
6. Singletons cannot be lifted if the player has a more heavily loaded hole and a singleton in her leading end-hole cannot be moved if she has other singletons.
7. When sowing beans, none can be sown in a hole which already contains three beans, except the last bean of a lift, and then the four resulting beans are taken by the player and put into her store and the contents of the next hole in

(106) Brass folding *Tamilnadi* board from Madurai. Brought to England in 1979. Five cowries per hole.

(107) *Olinda Keliya* board with four seeds per hole. (White beans substituted for olinda seeds.) Four 'dead' holes are filled with pebbles, and three more pebbles ready for use are in the central hole.

(108) *Conglak* board from Indonesia and five cowrie shells in each hole at the start of a game. Advertised in Oxfam catalogue, 1986. Similar to Sunka.

front are lifted for a new lap, or if it is empty, the move ends.

8. Otherwise, if the last bean falls in a loaded hole, its contents are lifted for a new lap and if in an empty hole, the move ends.

9. The round ends when all one player's holes are empty and any beans left in the opponent's holes are put into the opponent's store.

Second Round

10. The winner of the first round puts four beans in each of her holes, leaving any surplus in her store.

11. The loser then starting from one end of her row, puts four beans in as many of her holes as she can and leaves any beans over in her store. The holes she cannot fill become *Kana* 'blind' — a term used for the player herself and are out of play for the round. A stick is placed to indicate that it is out of use.

12. The blind player begins the round, moving towards her blind holes. The round is played in the same way as the first round.

Third and later rounds

13. The winner of the previous round puts four beans in each of her holes.

14. Starting from one end, the loser puts four beans in as many holes, as she can and the odd beans over in the next hole.
If this is one bean, it is called *puta*, 'son'.
If this is two beans, it is called *naga*, 'younger sister'.
If this is three beans, it is called *wala*, 'slave'.
The holes with no beans in are blind and are out of play for the round.

15. If the loser has a *puta* hole, the opponent removes one bean from her opposite hole.
If the loser has a *naga* hole, the opponent removes two beans from the opposite hole
If the loser has a *wala* hole, the opponent removes three

beans from her opposite hole, making one of her holes *wala*, *naga*, or *puta* respectively, with the contents of the two opposing holes adding up to four. The beans removed from the leading player's holes are placed back in her store. The *puta* and *naga* holes are marked by putting a piece of paper or a straw in them.

16. The blind player then begins, playing in the direction of her blind holes. This fixes the direction of play for the round.

17. Beans are sown in all the holes except the blind ones, but beans in *puta* or *naga* holes cannot be lifted for sowing, or taken; they accumulate for the player in whose row they lie. If the last bean of a lift falls in a *puta* or *naga* hole, the move ends. The round is played in the same way as the first round.

18. When a player has less than twelve beans at the beginning of a round she may arrange them differently if she wishes. See rule 19.

19. She may put one or two beans in one end-hole and not more than four in the other and one or two beans in some of the intermediate holes leaving the rest blind. Thus with eight beans she could arrange them as 2, 2, 1, 0, 0, 1, 2. Her opponent puts four beans in each of her holes. There are no *puta*, *naga*, or *wala* holes in the round and the players play in different ways.

20. The player with full holes plays as in the previous rounds, but the blind player only takes when her last bean in a lift falls in a hole on either row, making its contents three beans if she had put two beans in her first end-hole, or making its contents two beans if she had put one bean in her first end-hole.

21. Otherwise the blind player, except when sowing the last bean in hand, omits all holes containing one or two beans, but not those which contain three beans as in the first round. In this way the blind player may regain her lost beans and the game be prolonged considerably.

THREE RANK MANCALA

ABALALA'E (Ethiopia)

According to Richard Pankhurst, several games using three rank *Mancala* boards are still played in Ethiopia. One of the most interesting is *Abalala'e* or 'Eating', from the highlands of Eritrea, popular during the period of marriages, which usually takes place after the harvest season, between November and January. The board *(109)* consists of three rows of six holes each. Half the holes (A to I) belong to one player (P) and the other half (a to i) to the other player (p). See fig. 54.

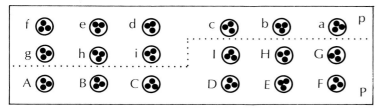

Fig. 54

(109) Reproduction three-rank *Mancala* board with two stores and three nuts per hole.

First phase

1. At the beginning of the game three pebbles are placed in each hole, and the players start simultaneously by lifting the entire contents of the left-hand hole in their back rows (player P from hole A, player p from hole a) and sowing one pebble into the adjacent holes in an anticlockwise direction. On sowing the last pebble of a lift into any hole the player lifts the entire contents of the hole, including the pebble just placed in it, and the sowing continues anticlockwise into the adjacent holes. Player P thus lifts from hole A and sows along his back row from left to right and along his half of the middle row from right to left and then passes to the opponent's back row from right to left (hole a to hole f) then along his opponent's half of the middle row (hole g to hole i). He then passes to his own back row at A and continues as before, until one of the players sows the last pebble of a lift into an empty hole.

   Up to this point the game is a race. Any pebbles held by the slower player in his hand are sown, but no 'pick up' is made if the last pebble falls into a loaded hole.

Second phase

2. The first player to halt in phase one starts the alternate moves of play in the second phase.
3. Each player always starts from one of his own holes by lifting its entire contents and sowing them one at a time into the consecutive holes in an anticlockwise direction.
4. If the last pebble of a lift falls into a loaded hole, the entire contents are lifted and the sowing continues until the last pebble of a lift falls into an empty hole.
5. If a lift ends in an empty hole on his own half of the board, the player captures any pebbles in the opponent's holes or hole along the same file.
6. He then lifts the pebble which made the capture and sows it in the next hole, when there are four possibilities:
   a) the capture of further pebbles from the opponent if the pebble falls into an empty hole on the player's side of the board facing an occupied hole or holes in enemy territory;
   b) the continued lifting and sowing if the pebbles falls into an occupied hole;
   c) the end of the turn if the pebble lands in an empty hole faced by empty hostile holes;
   d) the end of the turn if the pebble falls into an empty hole on the opponent's side of the board.
7. Play continues until one player's side of the board is empty. His opponent then wins all the remaining pebbles and adds them to his previous gains.
8. The two players then re-load their holes, three pebbles in each, in an anticlockwise direction, starting with their left-hand corner hole in their back row. (A & a)
9. If the players have won different numbers of pebbles, the weaker player fills as many holes as he can, being allowed to fill the last hole with two, or even one pebble.
10. The stronger player fills the corresponding holes on his side of the board with the same number of pebbles and places the remainder aside as his winnings.

110

(110) A small wooden carving, 3 inches (7.5cm) high, in four different woods of two men playing a two-rank *Mancala* game, probably *Wari*, West African, c.1975.

(111) Venerable *Baré* board from Zaire with two beans per hole at the start of a game.

(112) *Bao* board bought in Cape Town in 1983. Probably from Zanzibar or Swahili territory.

111

112

11. The holes in the empty part of the board belong to their original owners and are played over in the same way as in the opening round.
12. Eventually one player will capture all the pebbles and his opponent concedes defeat, although some games may last a very long time.

Reference: Pankhurst, R. Gabata and related board-games of Ethiopia and the Horn of Africa, *Ethiopia Observer*, Vol. XIV, 1971. Townshend, P. Les Jeux de Mankala au Zaire, au Rwanda et au Burundi, *Les cahiers du cedaf, No. 3*, 1977.

FOUR RANK MANCALA
BARÉ

Four rank *Mancala* games tend to be complex and difficult to understand from written descriptions. One of the simplest is *Baré (111)* played by the Anuk people of Ethiopia's far west. At the start of the game, there are two pebbles in each hole. The players own the two nearest to them and their pebbles circulate anticlockwise along these two rows. They do not venture into the opponent's half of the board.

Rules

First phase
1. The players start simultaneously from any hole in either of their rows by lifting the two pebbles up and sowing them in the contiguous holes in an anticlockwise direction, picking up the entire contents of the hole in which the last pebble fell and continuing in this way until the last pebble of a lift falls into an empty hole. This ends the first phase of the game.

Second phase
2. The player who first reaches an empty hole begins the next stage of the game by lifting all the pebbles from any hole in his front or rear row, provided that it contains two or more pebbles, and he sows them one by one into the following holes, picking up the contents of the hole in which the last pebble of a lift falls, and continues the sowing until the last pebble falls into an empty hole.
3. Captures are made by a player sowing the last pebble in his hand into a hole in his front row which contains one or more pebbles, while the two opposite enemy holes are both occupied. The player then lifts the pebbles from these enemy holes and sows them one at a time into his own holes starting immediately beyond the one from which he made his capture.
4. On the completion of this sowing, the player continues his turn of play by picking up and sowing pebbles from any of his holes.
5. If a player fails to lift enemy pebbles he could have captured his opponent may amalgamate these pebbles into one of the

two holes concerned, thus protecting them from further attack for the rest of the turn.

6. If a player forgets to amalgamate pebbles into one hole under rule 5 and subsequently his opponent attacks them, they are captured in the usual way.

7. The players have alternate turns of play.

8. The game ends when one player has only singletons left in his holes when he can no longer make a lift.

9. The player with the most pebbles at the end of the game is the winner.

Tactics Each player tries to keep his pebbles on his right and to capture those opposite him on his left. This form of four-rank *Mancala* is unusual in that a game finishes with a single round and setting of the board.

Made of a heavy black wood similar to ebony this board *(112)* is thought to have come from Zanzibar or Swahili territory and is for the Arab game of *Bao*. The square holes are reversing holes; if the last bean of a lift falls into them the direction of the sowing of the next lift is reversed. Note that there is only one store hole. As *Bao* is one of the most complicated of all the *Mancala* games, a lengthy description here seems out of place, but the fine board

deserves illustrating.

The other four-rank board from Zaire *(111)* was probably used for playing *Mangola*. The board's chief interest is in the extensive repairs that have been carried out. It is an old and very well-worn board. Although the pieces used were soft beans, the wood at the bottom of the holes has been worn away in many places through long use and has been repaired by nailing pieces of plywood over the erosions. In the eyes of native players, new boards lack 'character' and are spiritless and neutral but old boards have acquired great merit through the skill of the players taking part in contests upon them. This one has great merit!

WARI

The *Wari* board from Ghana *(113)* was made by P.O. Hpau of Old Asuoyo in 1954. It was the first he had carved for several years and he was delighted to receive the order. The basic shape is the same as the throne stool of the Old Ashanti kings.

(113) A *Wari* board from Ghana. Four seeds per hold and two empty store holes.

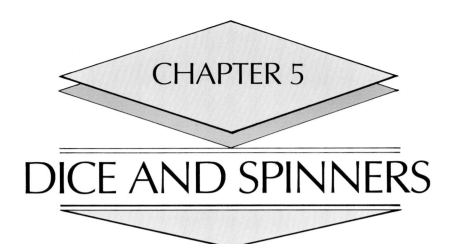

CHAPTER 5

DICE AND SPINNERS

Dice were used in prehistoric times and the pyramidal dice of Sumer and four-sided dice from Ancient Egyptian tombs, have already been described in Chapter 1. Six-sided cubic Etruscan dice made about 900 BC were found near Rome and are similar to the cubic dice of today but with the opposite faces being 1-6, 2-3, 4-5 instead of the modern 1-6, 2-5, 3-4, the sum of the opposite faces always being seven.

During the twelfth and thirteenth centuries, dicing spread throughout England. The favourite game in taverns was Hazard. Chaucer wrote in his 'Pardoner's Tale', in *The Canterbury Tales* 1-3:-

In Flaundres whylom was a compayne
Of yonge folk that haunteden foyleh
As ryot, hazard, *stewes and taverns.*

Hazard, for any number of players, became an obsession amongst gamblers in the seventeenth and eighteenth centuries and it survives in a modified form as Craps *(115)* so widely played by American and Canadian troops in the Second World War.

GAMES USING ONE CUBIC DIE

THIRTY-SIX

1. Any number can take part and each puts a stake into a pool and then throws the die for order of play, the lowest scorer starting and the highest having the advantage of playing last.
2. Each player in turn throws the die, adding each number thrown to his previous score, the object being to reach thirty-six, or to approach it as closely as possible without overshooting, known as GOING OVER THE TOP and out of the game.
3. The player with thirty-six, or nearest to it, wins, and if there is a tie, the pool is divided between the winners.
4. New throws of the die determine the order of play in the next game, lowest first and highest last.

USING TWO DICE

ACES IN THE POT

Two dice and a pot are used in this game for any number of players each of whom starts with two counters.

Rules

1. In rotation the players make a single throw with the dice, if two 1's are thrown, both the caster's counters are put in the pot.
2. On a throw of 6, a counter and the dice are passed to the player on the left.
3. On a throw of two 6's, the dice and both counters are passed to the left. If the player only has one counter this suffices.
4. The dice pass clockwise around the players until there is only one counter left outside the pot.
5. A player without a counter cannot throw the dice but passes them on.

(114) Korean porcelain figurine of a clown with two dice.

6. The player with the last counter makes three consecutive throws, and if he does not throw a 6, he wins the game. If a 6 is thrown, the counter and the dice pass to the player on the left, who in turn throws three times.

7. The first player to throw three times without a 6 wins the game and the contents of the pot.

This game is remarkable because every player has a chance of winning up to the very last moment.

ROTATION

Two dice are used in this game for any number of players. The order of throwing is immaterial.

1. In the first round each player throws once and tries to score 2. If successful he scores two points, and if not, nothing.

2. In the second round the target is 3, successful players scoring three points, and unsuccessful nothing.

3. In all there are eleven rounds in which totals from 2 to 12 are required.

4. At the end of the eleventh round the player with the highest score wins.

As the maximum possible score is 77 points, and scores of 40 are fairly common, each player will find a piece of paper and a pencil a help.

THE GAME OF THE PEDLAR

This very simple board *(116)* is attractive in its simplicity. It came from an antique dealer in Worcester and is undated, but was entered at Stationers' Hall, suggesting it was invented at the end of the nineteenth century. The rules are given at the bottom of the board in a copper plate hand:

(115) Miniature Craps table, bought in Reno, 1978.

(116) Board, dice and bone counters for The Game of the Pedlar, *c.*1890.

(117) Dicing tray with a variety of items: A Whiskey glass with three small dice in a false bottom. Alongside three minute dice in a brass and glass box, £1 coin as a size control. B Roman bronze astragal — 3rd Century AD from Lincolnshire, site unknown. C Six bronze astragals from Indonesia, *c.*1975. D Commercially reproduced astraguli on sale at Vincolanda museum, 1980. E Set of Jacks and rubber ball. F Cowrie shells. G Three shop dice, one coloured, with rounded corners. H Bone counters, late nineteenth century.

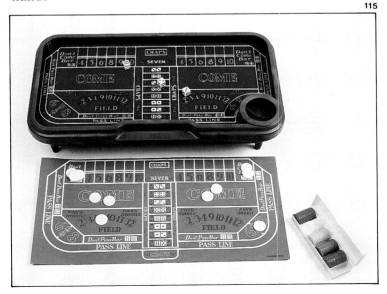

(118) Two white glass bottles made in the form of three poker dice. The designs were taken from Dondorff's famous 'Duchess' card pattern, c.1895). Bought for its games interest, on breaking the seal, the larger one was found to contain a high quality brandy. An unexpected smile from Dame Fortune.

118

'Directions

'This game is played either with a pair of dice or a teetotum marked with 12 sides, and any number of persons can play. In order to decide who shall begin the game, each person throws, and the highest number plays first; and the number thrown he must cover with a counter the corresponding one on the board, each in their turn doing the same (providing it is uncovered). If it is already covered he claims the counter on that particular number. Exception is taken to No. 7; anyone throwing that number pays to 'The Pedlar' which remains until one of the party throws 12 and he clears the board, including the Pedlar, and the game recommences.'

'The Game of the Pedlar was probably played in Victorian nurseries and it appears that the pair of dice, or the teetotum is not provided with the board. Possibly the players also supplied the counters from some other game or made their own from pieces of cardboard.

Twelve-sided teetotums are rarely seen; the usual are six or eight sided. The wooden dice and counters illustrated have been supplied from elsewhere.

GAMES USING THREE DICE

MARTINETTI

This game for any number of players requires three dice and a martinetti board, fig. 55. The board may be drawn on a piece of card. Each player has his own coloured counter and the board is marked from 1 to 12.

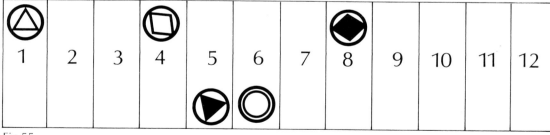

Fig.55

Showing 5 counters on the board.

Rules

1. Each player throws the dice from a cup, the highest scorer starting the game while the lowest plays last. Ties are thrown again. There is a slight advantage in playing first and players cast again at the beginning of each game for the order of play.
2. If the opening player throws a 1, he places his marker on space 1 on the board. If he throws 1, 2, on the same throw he would put his marker on the second space, while a throw of 1, 2, 3, would advance the marker to the third compartment.

3. Numbers may also be added together to make required number. A throw of 2, 3, 6 could be used to make 5 or 8 or 9 or 11.
4. Each player's turn lasts as long as he is using numbers thrown. If he fails to use any part of any throw the dice are passed to the player on the left.
5. If a player misses a number that he could have used, any player can make use of it by calling out as soon as the player passes the dice on and before they are rolled again. If two players call the number together, the one who is nearest the player's left takes precedence.
6. The first player to travel from 1 to 12 and back again wins the game.

GAMES WITH FIVE DICE

INDIAN DICE

1. Each player puts a stake in the pool.
2. The players throw a single die to decide on the order of play, high man playing first, the next highest second, etc. Sixes are high, deuces low, while aces are wild and can count as any number.
3. The opening player has a choice of making one, two or three throws, the other players being allowed only the same number as he has chosen.
4. After his first throw the opening player may put aside any of the five dice and place the others in the cup for a second throw, or he may throw all five. After his second throw, he may throw any or all of the five dice in a third throw, including any that were previously put aside.

Scoring combinations in descending order:
Five of a kind (Five 6's being above five 5's, etc)
Four of a kind
Three of a kind and a pair (known as a FULL HOUSE)
Three of a kind
Two pairs
One pair.

A hand without a pair scores nothing. Whatever the dice show after the third throw is the final value of the hand.
Example The first player throws 6, 6, 5, 4, 2. He may throw all five again, hoping to get better than a pair or he may put the 6, 6, aside and throw the remaining three dice. If he stood on his pair and did not throw again, the other players would also only have one throw.

If he decided to throw the three dice again and on this second throw the dice showed 5, 3, 1, he would add the Ace (Wild) to the 6, 6, making three of a kind. He might stand on this score, or attempt a third roll hoping to get another 6, or a pair which would give him a Full House.

Each round is called a *leg*. If there are only two players the winner of two out of three *legs* wins the game. When there are more players they all enter the first two *legs*, and

the high man of the first *leg* plays a two-handed deciding game with the winner of the second *leg*, the ultimate winner taking the pool.

Alternatively the two low men play off with the loser paying a forfeit, which is shared by the other two players and there is no pool.

GAMES WITH SIX DICE
SEQUENCES

Any number can play and each player throws six dice once and then passes them on clockwise around the table. A throw of 1, 1, 1, cancels a player's whole score and he has to start again. The first player to reach a hundred wins.

Scoring		Points
	1,2	5
	1,2,3	10
	1,2,3,4	15
	1,2,3,4,5	20
	1,2,3,4,5,6	25 (Some players allow 50 points for this throw)
	1,1,1,	Cancels the player's whole score and he must start again.

GAMES FOR FIFTEEN OR MORE DICE
ACES

This is one of the best of the dice games. Any number can play, but each player must have five dice and a dicing cup. Each player puts an agreed stake into a pool and then throws his five dice and the player with the highest hand takes any seat and is the first SHOOTER. The player throwing the second highest sits on his left and shoots second, etc. Tying players throw again. Aces count as seven.

1. The first shooter begins by throwing his five dice. Each 1 is placed in the centre of the table, all 2's are passed to the player on his left and all 5's to the player on his right. The player continues to throw until he fails to throw a 1, 2, or 5, or until he has no dice left.
2. The player on his left then begins his throw.
3. Players with no dice are still in the game as they may receive dice from their neighbours on either side.
4. When all the dice but one have been placed in the centre of the table, the player throwing the last 1 with the last die is the winner and takes the pool.

SHUT THE BOX (France)

For more than two hundred years *Shut the Box*, fig. 56, has been a favourite game amongst the sailors of Normandy and some of the other French coastal areas. It is not confined to seafarers, however, and versions are played by such inland communities as the Barotzi, a tribal people of Zambia in Central Africa *(119)*.

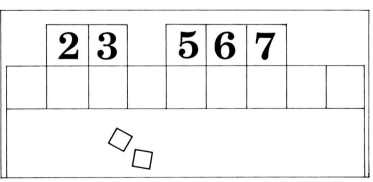

Fig. 56

(119) Board for African 'Shut the Box' type of game. Barotzi tribe, c.1900.

Boxes 1, 4, 8 and 9 have been shut.

'Shut the Box' is played by two or more players in competition, often for stakes.

Rules

1. At the beginning of a player's turn the hinged lids of the numbered compartments are all lifted.
2. The player rolls the two dice on to the felt area of the board. The two individual numbers thrown or the sum of the numbers permit the player to shut the box or boxes similarly numbered. For example, if a 5 and a 4 were thrown, the player could close boxes marked 5 and 4, or the box marked 9.
3. A turn finishes when the player cannot shut a box on a throw of the dice.
4. When the sum of the numbers of the boxes still open is six or less, the player throws only one die until he has shut all the boxes or throws an unusable number.
5. At the end of each player's turn, the total of the boxes remaining open is added to the player's score.
6. A player is out of the game when he has a score of 45 points or more.
7. The last player left in the game is the winner.

'Shut the box' can be played as a patience game with the player trying to close all the boxes in less than a chosen number of turns.

(120) Oil cloth Crown and Anchor board, c.1950, with special dice and pre-1971 halfpennies.

GAMES WITH SPECIAL DICE

120

K & C LONDON   MADE IN ENGLAND

CROWN AND ANCHOR

Crown and Anchor (120) is popular in the British Merchant Navy and Fishing Fleet. Three special dice are used with the faces marked with a Spade, Heart, Diamond, Club, Crown and Anchor. The players sit around a board or cloth marked with the same symbols.

The players place their bets on the devices of their choice and the dealer throws the three dice from a cup. He pays even money on singles, two to one on pairs, and three to one on three of a kind.

The banker's advantage is such that eventually he will always be well up on a series of games and therefore the bank should pass to each player in turn. (The bank's advantage is 7.87%).

POKER DICE

Five Poker dice (121) are used with their faces marked A,K,Q,J,10 and 9. Any number of players can take part, each player throwing a single die to determine the order of play, highest man going first, next highest second etc. The object of the game is to throw the highest poker hand in one, two or three rolls of the dice as chosen by the starter. After the first throw, the opening player may stand or pick up any number of dice he wishes from the table and roll again hoping to improve his score. A maximum of three rolls is permitted and the other players are entitled to the same number of throws as the starter.

Order of scoring.

Five of a kind (Aces count high, above Kings)
A Royal Flush (The five dice in sequence, Ace high)
A Low Flush, (The five dice in sequence, King high)
Four of a kind
Three of a kind
Two pairs
One pair

The extra die or dice not included in one of the above hands do not have any value. For example if two players threw the same four-of-a-kind, the fifth die does not help to decide the winner. Tying players throw off again.

The player with the highest combination wins the pool and rolls first in the next game. Some players play the Ace wild, allowing it to represent any wanted denomination.

In a two-handed game, the best three hands out of five win.

LIAR DICE

This game can be played with five standard dice but is more fun using Poker dice.

1. The opening player casts the dice on to a tray (121) from a cup and hides them behind his left hand from the other

players. He declares a score which may or may not be true and can be accepted or challenged by the player on his left.

2. If the declaration is accepted, the dice are passed still hidden to the next player who may retain or throw any number of dice. The number re-thrown must be announced, e.g. 'Throwing two'. He then makes a declaration which must be higher than the one he accepted and the player on the left in turn may accept the new call or challenge it.

3. If a call is challenged, the dice must be exposed immediately. If the throw is at least as high or higher than the call, the challenger loses a life. If it is below the declaration, the caster loses a life.

4. The order of scoring combinations is as in poker dice, see page 66.

5. Except for High and Low Flushes, sequences do not count. A hand without a scoring combination is called a PRYLE.

6. If a declaration of five Aces is made, the next player may challenge it accept it. If he accepts he is allowed five throws of the dice to equalize. If he succeeds, the caller loses a life, if not, the acceptor.

7. Each player has three lives and when these are lost he is out of the game.

8. The first player to lose three lives, however, is granted an extra fourth life, a favour known as being ON THE PARISH.

9. The last player left in the game is the winner.

The dicing tray and the dice in its edge (122) present a problem.

Bought in Amsterdam some ten years ago, they are of continental origin with the Queen carrying the indices D for *Dame*. At first glance the set seems to be for Liar Dice. But what of the sixth die, with the faces marked as in the exploded drawing, fig.57?

SPINNERS

PUT AND TAKE (England)

Once popular in mining communities, a spinner with six faces is used for Put and Take *(124)* marked:

TAKE 1
ALL PUT
TAKE ALL
PUT 2
TAKE 2
PUT 1

Each player starts with an equal number of counters and puts an agreed number into a pool. The opening player then spins the teetotum and obeys the instructions on the uppermost face before passing the spinner clockwise to the next player. When a player has lost all his counters he retires from the game. In some schools, players are allowed to resign or join at any time.

(121) Leather dicing cup and tray for Poker Dice, Mexico, 1975.

(122) A selection of Chinese dice on a continental dicing tray.

Exploded Sixth die.

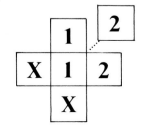

Fig.57

(124) Spinner tray with a variety of spinners: A 'Howzat' cricket game roller, *c*.1950. B Vegetable ivory teetotum, *c*.1900. C Lead teetotum. D Four 'Put-and-Take' spinners, one of plastic. E Plastic *Dreidel* (Jewish) *c*.1975.

(125) A selection of gaming counters, *c*.1970 and a brass counter holder. The latter probably late nineteenth century.

(126) A black bakelite Roulette wheel and layout with coloured bone counters, *c*.1935.

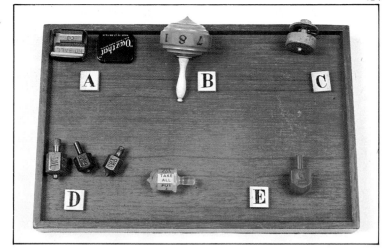

(123) *Hoca* board, top and wooden balls. Bought in the Austrian Alps, 1971.

DREIDEL (Israel)

This Jewish children's game is played during the eight days of Hannukkah, The Feast of Dedication. The four-sided spinner originated in medieval Germany where it was used for gambling. The original German characters on the four sides have been changed to the initials of the Hebrew message, *nes gadol hayah sham*, 'A great miracle happened there'.

According to the *Talmud* the miracle occurred when the Maccabees recaptured the Temple in Jerusalem from the Syrians in 165 BC. There was only a tiny supply of oil but, miraculously, the lamps continued burning for eight days until new supplies arrived.

Traditionally *the Dreidel* is made of wood or lead, but during the nineteenth century fine chased silver examples were created, mainly in the continent of Europe. The modern example (124E) is of red plastic.

WHIRLING BALLS ROULETTE (France)

Roulette (126) originated in France in the seventeenth century as a refinement of *Hoca*, which was very popular in southern and central Europe at that time. In *Hoca* a wheel was used to throw a ball into one of several pockets and stakes were wagered on the outcome. The autocratic Cardinal Mazarin opened *Hoca* gambling houses all over France; the immense profits derived from them were only discovered after his death in 1661 and the government promptly made the running of a *Hoca* house a capital offence.

Essentially *Roulette* involves spinning a ball around in a wheel containing pockets numbered 1 to 36 (but out of numerical order) and coloured alternately red and black, except for one pocket coloured green and numbered 0. On the early French wheels and still in America there is a second green pocket numbered 00.

Players bet against the house: 35 to 1 odds on any individual number, even money on red or black, odd or even numbers, high or low numbers. The green pockets give the house an eventual winning percentage. If the ball enters 0, bets are frozen, the ball spun again and bets are either forfeited to the house or returned to the player. The extra green pocket on American wheels doubles the house's winnings *(127)*.

Roulette made Monte Carlo the world's most famous and wealthiest resort. A banker, François Blanc, bought the gambling concessions of Monaco and opened a casino in 1863. By using only one green pocket instead of two, he attracted big-time gamblers and this innovation provided a financial bonanza. The lack of attraction of *Roulette* in the American casinos could well be through the retention of the 00 pocket.

HOCA (Alps)

Hoca (123) is still a winter evening's pastime of the villagers in the Dolomites. Any number can take part. The bowl, pockets, top and balls are made of a hardwood, usually beech. The pockets are glued to the side of the bowl after a hole has been drilled through the wall. The top has a six-sided base. The sides are unequal, thereby increasing the element of luck.

Rules

1. Before the start of the game the players agree a winning total, usually 301.

126

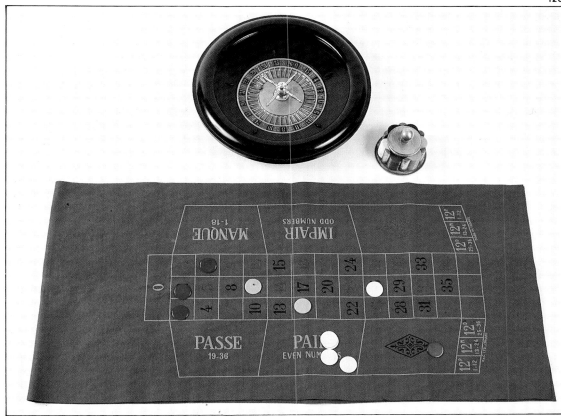

127

(127) Tinware Roulette wheel with plastic counters. Note 00 compartment. On the underside is a flying horse with the words 'TURF VIRGINIA CIGARETTES'.

(128) A walnut Roly Poly board with marble, (not original), *c.*1850 or earlier.

2. Before each player's turn, the five balls, four plain and one coloured red, are placed in the centre of the bowl. The player then spins the top using a sliding movement of the palms of the hands with the shaft of the top between them.

3. The balls are struck by the flat sides of the bottom of the top and knocked into the numbered pits or the pockets. When the top stops spinning the player's score is totalled, any score by the red ball being tripled.

4. If a ball jumps out of the bowl it may be returned as long as the top is still spinning and there is a chance that it may make score.

Although the way the balls strike the top is pure luck, skill in spinning the top will produce higher scores during a lengthy spell of play.

ROLY-POLY (England)

The small Roly-Poly table *(128)* is 8¾ inches (22cm) long, 4¼ inches (11cm) wide and 1¾ inches (4.5cm) high. Made of walnut it probably dates from the middle of the nineteenth century or earlier. The second row of figures, 1-9, 1-9, 1-6, is a later addition and may have been an adaptation for the French game of *Boule*. It appears to be

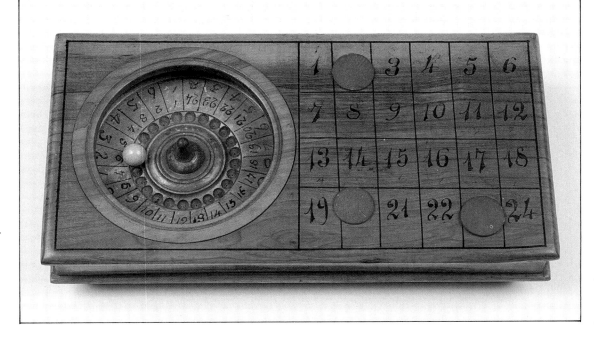

128

either a travelling board, or a toy miniature of a full-sized table. According to the third edition of Joseph Strutt's *The Sports and Passtimes of the People of England*, p. 333, 1845, Roly-Poly was prohibited by Act 18, Geo II '... and whereas a certain pernicious game called Roulet or Roly-poly in daily practiced...', the act then directs, '... that no place shall be kept for playing at the said game of Roulet, or Roly-poly, or any other game with cards or dice...', etc.

The border-line between games and toys may be ill-defined; two examples are described.

JEU DE COURSES (France)

This elaborate French tinware toy/game *(129)* was advertised in *Grands Magasine de la Samaritaine*, Paris, 1909; 'Jeu de Courses perfectionné garniture nickete piste drapée, Prix 9.75'. It simulates the carousel of the amusement park with the addition of the betting on a race course. In the advertising illustration, a tin flag flies from the finishing post. Only the base of the post remains in the example illustrated here *(130)*.

(129) A page from a catalogue *La Samaritaine*, Paris, 1910.

(130) Jeu de Courses, *c.*1910.

(131) Electric Derby game.

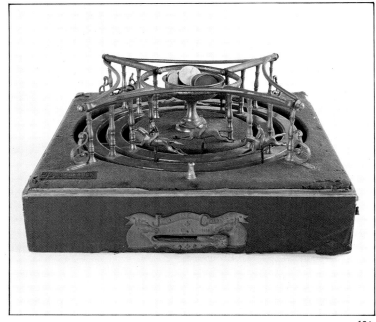

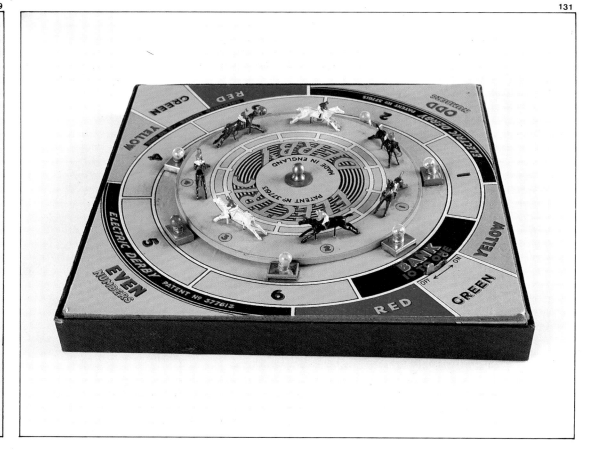

ELECTRIC DERBY (England)

The electrical components of the game *(131)* are powered by a three-volt flash lamp battery.

Rules

1. One player acts as the banker. The others place their bets on the board as they fancy. The banker switches on the light and spins the wheel.
2. When the wheel ceases to revolve, the lamp remaining on indicates the winner. The banker collects the losing bets and then pays the winners according to the following odds:
   Those who have backed 'odd' or 'even' receive evens.
   Those backing a colour — yellow, red or green receive two to one.
   Those backing a single number receive five to one.
   Those backing the bank — the white light — receive ten to one. When the white light appears the banker takes all stakes except those placed on 'BANK'.

FOUR NUMBERS (China)

Four Numbers *(132)* is a Chinese gambling game using a four-sided top and a *Fan Tan* board. The faces of the top are marked 1, 2, 3, 4 and it is spun in a saucer which is covered with a bowl while it is still spinning. When all the stakes have been placed on the board the bowl is lifted, exposing the winning number uppermost which is called out by the banker. Winning players retain their stakes and are paid dividends by the banker, while the losers' stakes are gathered up and passed to him.

The top is then spun again in the saucer, covered with the bowl and the punters place their bets for the next round. The method of placing the bets requires description. The First House is taken as the example, although the six methods apply equally to stakes laid in any of the other three houses.

1. *Koo Fan* The stake is placed in the centre of the First House. If 'ONE' is called as winner, the player is paid three times his stake. The stake is lost if TWO, THREE or FOUR is called.
2. *Kok* The stake is placed on the dividing line between the First and Second Houses. If ONE or TWO is called as winner, the player is paid a dividend equal to his stake. The stake is lost if THREE or FOUR is called.
3. *Lim* The stake is placed in the First House adjacent to the Second House. If ONE is called as winner, the player receives twice his stake, if TWO is called his stake is returned to him, and it is lost with a call of THREE or FOUR.
4. *Chuen* The stake is placed in the First House on the line separating it from the empty central square. If

ONE or THREE is called, a dividend equal to the stake is paid to the player. The stake is lost with a call of TWO or FOUR.

5. *Tong* The stake is placed in the First House adjacent to the vacant central square. If ONE is called, the player receives twice his stake, the stake is returned to him if THREE is called and is lost if the call is TWO or FOUR.
6. *Cheng Tau* The stake is placed outside the First House near the base line. If ONE is called, a dividend equal to the stake is paid to the player; if TWO or FOUR is called his stake is returned to him, and if THREE is called the stake is lost.

These six methods of laying stakes in the First House apply to stakes laid in any of the other houses. The odds are fair and to pay for overheads and make a profit the management deducts ten per cent from every winning dividend.

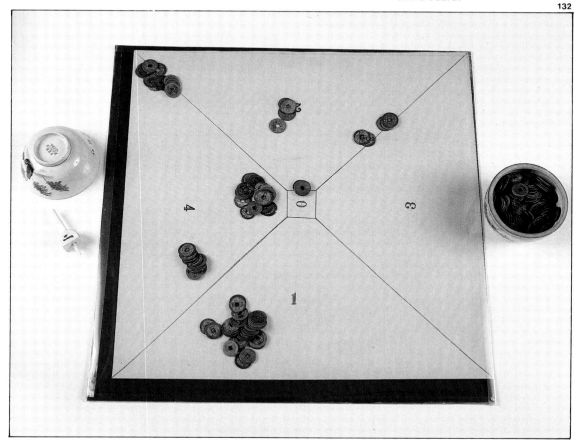

(132) Thin cardboard 'Four Numbers' board confiscated by the Malayan Police in 1955. Chinese cash is used as stakes on the board. Reproduction '4-numbers' top of ivory to the left of the board.

132

133

134

(133) Paper *Hoo Hey How* board and three special dice. Vancouver, Chinatown, 1970. Cash coins used as stakes.

(134) Tourists' souvenir from Winthrop, Washington State, USA. 'Last Chance Saloon'. 1984.

HOO, HEY, HOW (China)____

This Hokkien game 'Fish, Prawn, King Crab' *(133)* is a dice game requiring no skill. Three six-sided dice are usually used in this game. The facets of the dice are engraved with one of the following: a fish, a prawn, a king crab, a cockerel, a gourd and two coins. The staking board has six squares marked to correspond with the facets of the dice.

Players place their stakes on the board. The operator shakes the dice under a cover and then exposes them or he may throw them into a bowl. Players whose stakes on the board correspond with the uppermost facets of the dice receive from the banker:

a)   an equivalent of the stake for one die the same.
b)   twice the stake for two dice the same.
c)   three times the stake for three dice the same.

The actual stake is always returned to the winning punters. If operated by professionals 10 per cent is deducted from the winnings for the house.

Reference: Dobree, C.T. *Gambling Games of Malaya*, Caxton Press, Kuala Lumpur, 1955. p.123.

CHAPTER 6

GAMES TO PLAY

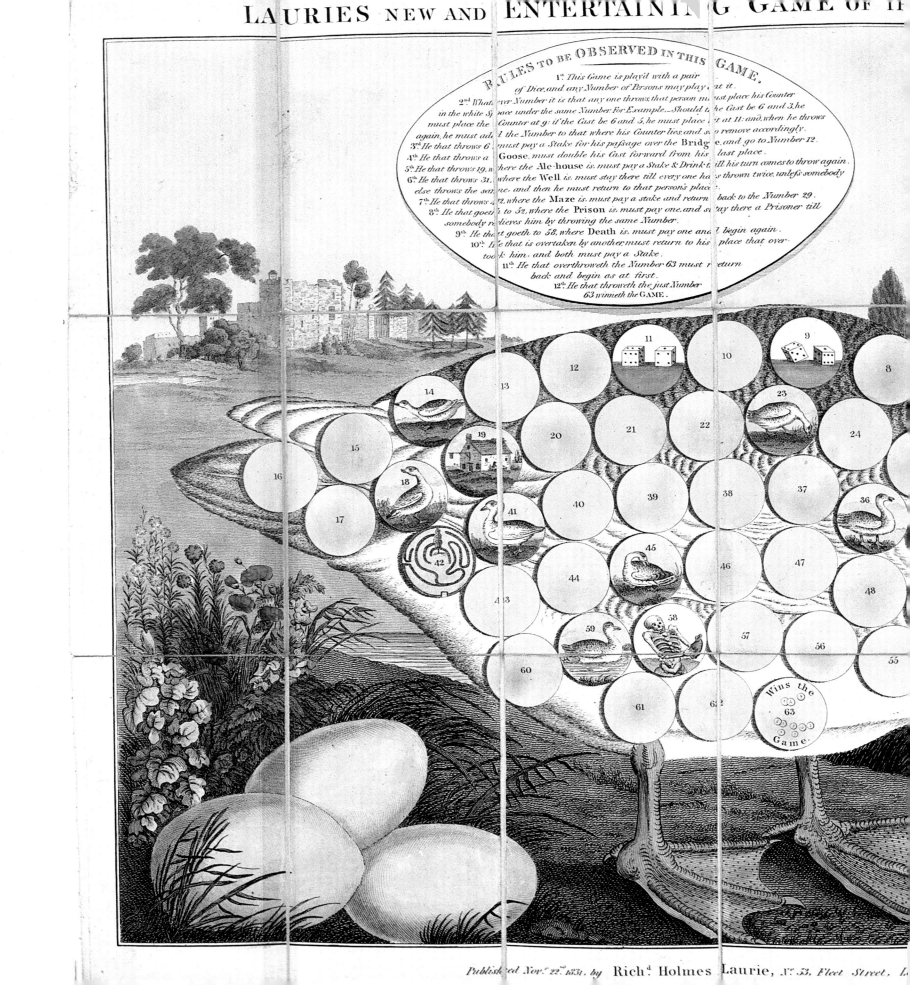

RULES TO BE OBSERVED IN THIS GAME.

1st. This Game is play'd with a pair of Dice, and any Number of Persons may play at it.

2nd. Whatever Number it is that any one throws that person must place his Counter in the white Space under the same Number For Example... Should the Cast be 6 and 3, he must place the Counter at 9: if the Cast be 6 and 5, he must place it at 11: and, when he throws again, he must add the Number to that where his Counter lies, and so remove accordingly.

3rd. He that throws 6 must pay a Stake for his passage over the Bridge, and go to Number 12.

4th. He that throws a Goose, must double his Cast forward from his last place.

5th. He that throws 19, where the Ale-house is, must pay a Stake & Drink till his turn comes to throw again.

6th. He that throws 31, where the Well is, must stay there till every one has thrown twice, unless somebody else throws the same, and then he must return to that person's place.

7th. He that throws 42, where the Maze is, must pay a stake and return back to the Number 29.

8th. He that goeth to 52, where the Prison is, must pay one, and stay there a Prisoner till somebody relieves him by throwing the same Number.

9th. He that goeth to 58, where Death is, must pay one and begin again.

10th. He that is overtaken by another, must return to his place that overtook him, and both must pay a Stake.

11th. He that overthroweth the Number 63 must return back and begin as at first.

12th. He that throweth the just Number 63 winneth the GAME.

Published Novr. 22d. 1831. by Richd. Holmes Laurie, No. 53, Fleet Street, Lo

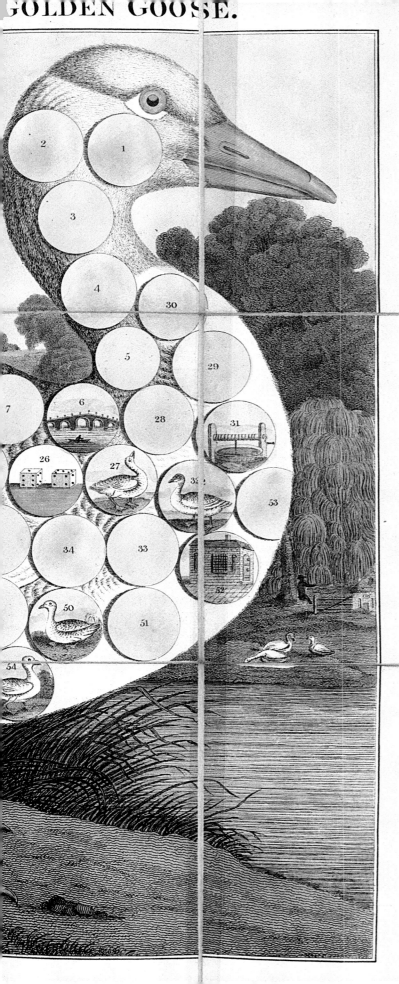

Royal Game of Goose (Italy)____

Spiral games first became popular in the eighteenth century. The Royal Game of Goose was one of the first and became the prototype for many that followed and some of its history can be found on page 11. The game illustrated on these pages was published by Richard Holmes Laurie on 22nd November 1831 and is for any number of players.

For any number of players

Equipment
2 dice
1 token and 12 counters for each player.

Rules_____

1. Each player starts with twelve counters and pays his debts into a pool which becomes the winners prize.
2. Each player throws the two dice in turn and advances his marker by the total of the cast, eg. if the player throws 6 and 3 he places his counter on the ninth space.
3. A player throwing to land on space 6 must pay a stake to pass over the bridge and go to number 12.
4. If a counter lands on a goose, it moves forward by the same amount as the throw which brought it there.
5. A player landing on 19 where the ALE HOUSE is must pay a stake before he can move on.
6. On reaching 31 where the WELL is, the marker must remain there until every player has thrown twice, unless someone else lands on 31 when they exchange places.
7. On landing on 42 where the MAZE is, the player must pay a stake and return to number twenty nine.
8. On reaching 52 where the PRISON is, the player must pay one and stay there a prisoner until another player relieves him by throwing the same number.
9. On landing on 58 where DEATH is, the player pays a stake and starts again at the beginning.
10. A player being overtaken by another player must return to the space vacated by the overtaker, and both must pay a stake.
11. A player overthrowing the number 63 must start again at the beginning.
12. .The first player to reach exactly 63 wins the game.

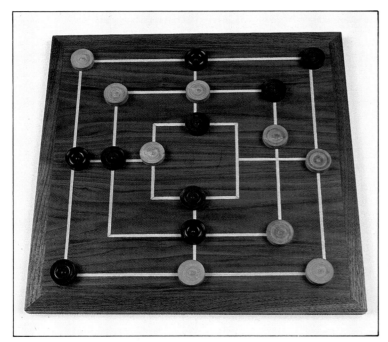

Equipment
9 pieces of his or her own colour.

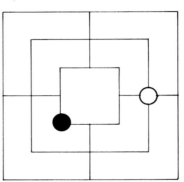

Fig. a.

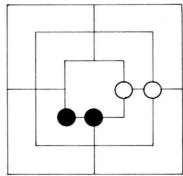

Fig. b.

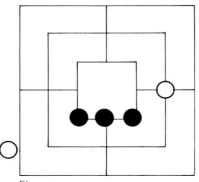

Fig. c.

NINE MEN'S MORRIS

A design 15½ inches (38cm) square for this game is cut into the roofing slabs at Kurna temple, *c*.1400 BC. Two similar designs have been found cut into the great flight of steps which ascend the lower part of the hill at Mihintale in Sri Lanka, carved by masons working during the reign of Mahadathika Mah-Naga, AD 921.

On the Gokstad farms near Sandefjord in Norway a large grave-mound was opened in 1880, exposing a Viking ship and on the deck was the burial chamber of a king. Among his many possessions was a portion of a wooden games board, carved on one side for Nine Men's Morris and on the other for a game that appears to have been a variety of *Hnefatafl*. In fact boards for this exciting strategy game have been found all over the world. In France, it was known as *merelles* and today is called *jeu de moulin* (Game of Mill) while in Germany it has always been known as Mill.

First Phase Each player has nine pieces of his own colour and enters them alternately one at a time onto any vacant point. Fig. a. If a player forms a row of three pieces, known as a MILL, he removes one of his opponent's pieces from the board, but not one which is itself in a mill. Figs. b and c. When all the pieces have been entered on the board the second phase begins.

Second Phase The players continue in alternate turns of play by moving a piece to an adjacent vacant point along a line. Each time a mill is made an enemy piece is captured and removed. A player reducing the opponent's pieces to two or blocking all the opposing men and preventing their being able to move, wins the game.

A mill can be made and broken any number of times, an enemy piece being removed from the board each time a mill is formed. Players try to form a double mill when a piece moves from one mill into the other and then back again, capturing a piece on every move.

If a player has three pieces left on the board and they are in a mill, if it is his turn to move he must do so even when this makes his pieces vulnerable to attack and means losing a piece and the game at the opponent's next move.

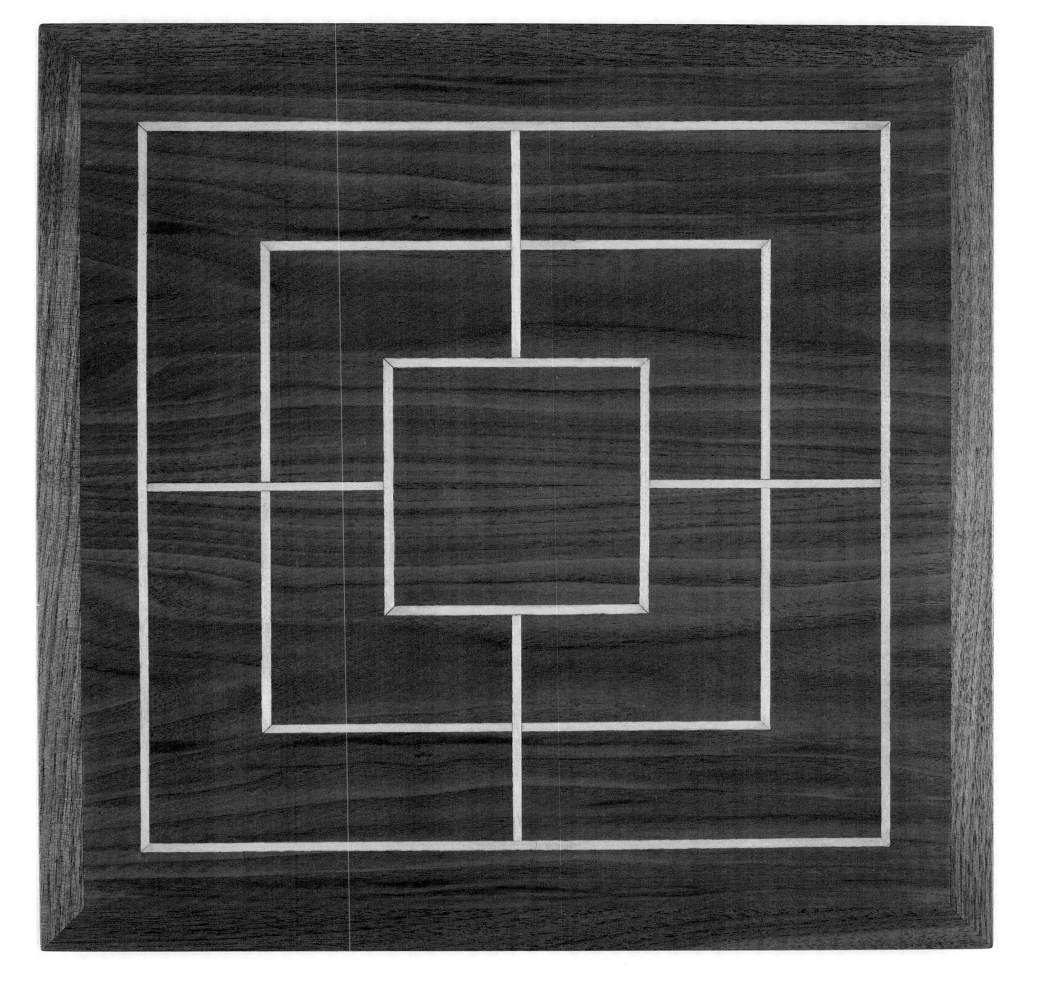

APHELION (England)

The Race to the Sun

Published by F. H. Ayers and entered at Stationers' Hall, it probably dates from about 1870. The earliest date of an Ayres product known to the author is a ball of 1864; and the latest, The New Game of Spoof (1889). To quote from the pamphlet accompanying Aphelion:

'This merry and instructive game will acquaint both young and old with the mysterious worlds and wonders which shine on the Celestial vault, and engrave in memory an everlasting idea of the Solar and Planetry system.'

'The large circle or orbit represents the sphere of the fixed stars. The two next circles comprise the twelve signs of Zodiac. The inner circle round the Sun is the Planetry orbit, and contains Mercury, Venus, Jupiter, etc. To give more amusement and sport to the game, the Earth and Moon have been placed in Zodiac circles.'

For 2 to 6 players

Equipment
1 die
1 token of his or her own colour
15 counters for each player.

Rules

This game can be played by two to six persons and each pays into the pool ten counters. The order of play being decided on, each player takes one of the markers (which are of various colours, *viz*: red, green, yellow, pink, blue and brown) and the first player commences the game by throwing with one dice *(sic)* (numbered from 1 to 6) and whatever number is thrown, he places his marker on that number on the board. The other players follow in order.

On the second and subsequent throws the number exhibited by the dice *(sic)* is added to the previous score, and the marker advanced accordingly, subject to the following regulations:

1. Should you throw No. 1 on the dice *(sic)* being the lowest number, you have to pay one to the pool and put your marker on the number. In passing No. 12 you have to pay one to the pool to enter the 2nd circle.
13. The 1st Quarter of the Moon — to receive three counters from the pool.
14. The Ram — to return to No. 12 and pay a fine of two counters to the pool.
16. The Bull — to pay a fine for butchering, pay two counters to the pool.
18. The Twins — stop here and throw the dice *(sic)* till you get six, then put your marker on No. 19 (the Earth), you are then to receive five from the pool.
20. The Crab — go back to No. 1 and pay a fine of five counters to the pool.
22. The Lion — to receive four from the pool and one from each gentleman playing, should a lady throw this number.
25. The Balance — to stop here until another throws the same number, or pay a fine of three to the pool.
26. The Cluster of Stars — to receive five from the pool.
27. The Scorpion — go back to No. 21 and pay a fine of three to the pool.
29. The Archer — you pay for the right to shoot, two to the pool.
30. The Full Moon — that being fine weather, to receive six from the pool.
31. The Goat — go back to No. 15 and pay a fine of three to the pool.
32. The Seven Stars — to receive seven from the pool.
33. The Water Bearer — pay for rain, four to the pool.
34. The Great Comet — to return to No. 18 and pay a fine of three counters to the pool, and go through the same ordeal as before on No. 18.
35. The Fishes — to receive three from the pool to get them cooked.
36. Venus — here you have to pay two to the pool to pass into the Planetry circle.
43. A Planet — go back to No. 37.
48. A Planet — go back to No. 45.
49. The Sun — this wins the contents of the pool.

There is no guidance as to what happens if a player throws a higher number than that required to reach 49 and therefore one must assume that the player wins the game.

The reader will also realise that this is really a spiral game, the dotted lines joining the concentric circles making the fact as inconspicuous as possible.

The markers are of painted wood, the counters are cowrie shells, the dicing cup of cardboard, and the die surprisingly of ivory. Scribbled on the bottom of the box in pencil is 1/-, the original price of the game.

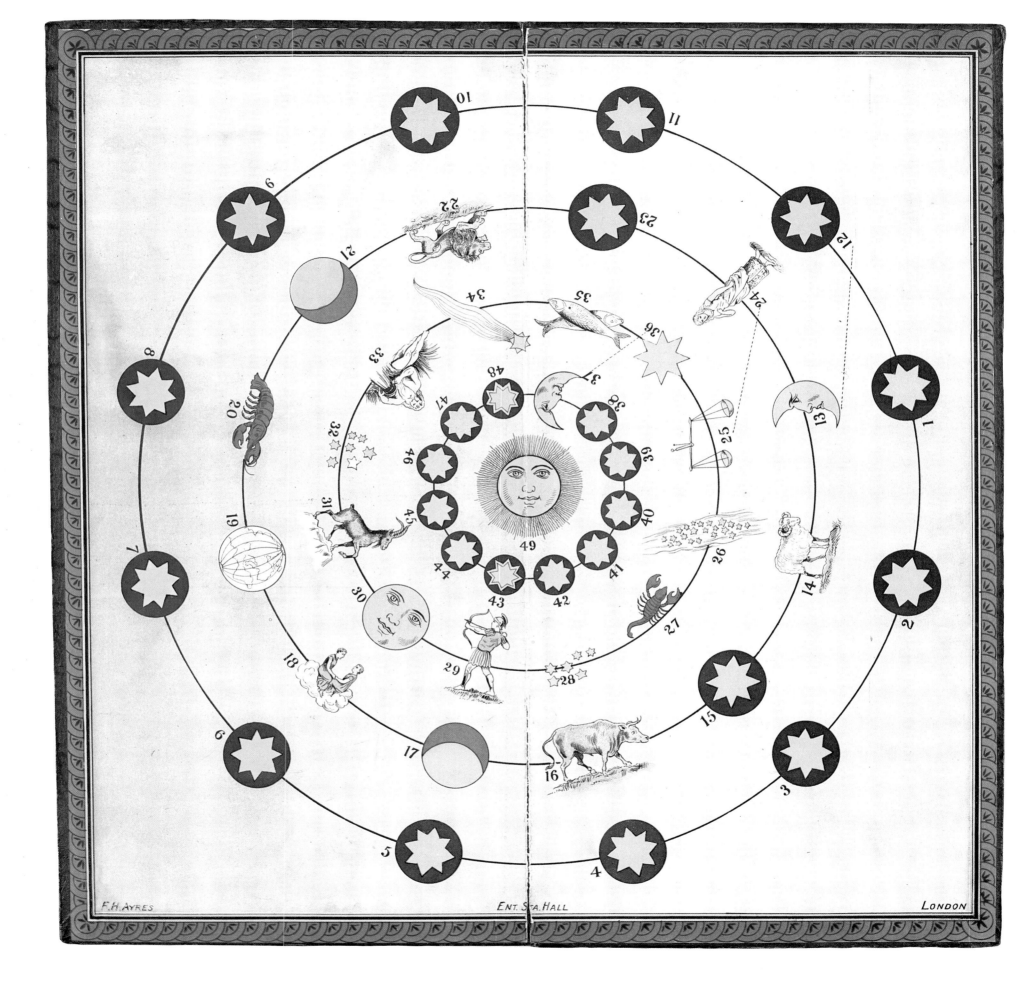

F.H. AYRES   ENT. STA. HALL   LONDON

For two players

Equipment
20 pieces of his or her own colour.

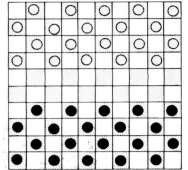

Fig. a

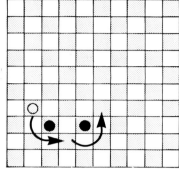

Fig. b

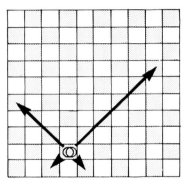

Fig. c

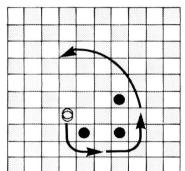

Fig. d

Continental Draughts (France)

Jeu Forcé (English draughts) only lasted a few years in France and was replaced about 1650 A.D. by a variety known as *Le Grand Forçat*. This became obsolete within fifty years to be replaced by the game now known as Continental or Polish draughts, first played in the cafés of Paris in 1727. The first book on the game published the same year by Quercetane, a pseudonym, was probably written about five years earlier. A 10 x 10 squares board was used.

Rules
1. Men move one square diagonally forwards.
2. Men capture by a short leap, either diagonally forwards or backwards. Capturing is compulsory. Fig. b.
3. A king can move diagonally forwards or backwards over any number of vacant squares. Fig. c.
4. A king can land any number of vacant squares beyond a captured piece. Rules 3 and 4 may occur together, a move known as a *'long leap'*. Fig. d.
5. If a player has a choice of captures he must take the greatest possible number of pieces, or if equal numbers are at risk, the player has the choice of which pieces he captures. He is not obliged to capture a king in preference to a man.
6. Captured pieces are only removed from the board at the end of a move and a dead piece forms an impassable barrier.
7. A man is only promoted to becoming a king when he remains on the opponent's back row. If on reaching the crownhead more captures are possible, they must be made and the move completed, the man remaining unpromoted until he again reaches the opponent's back row and remains there at the end of the move.

For any number of players

Equipment
2 dice
1 token of his or her own colour.

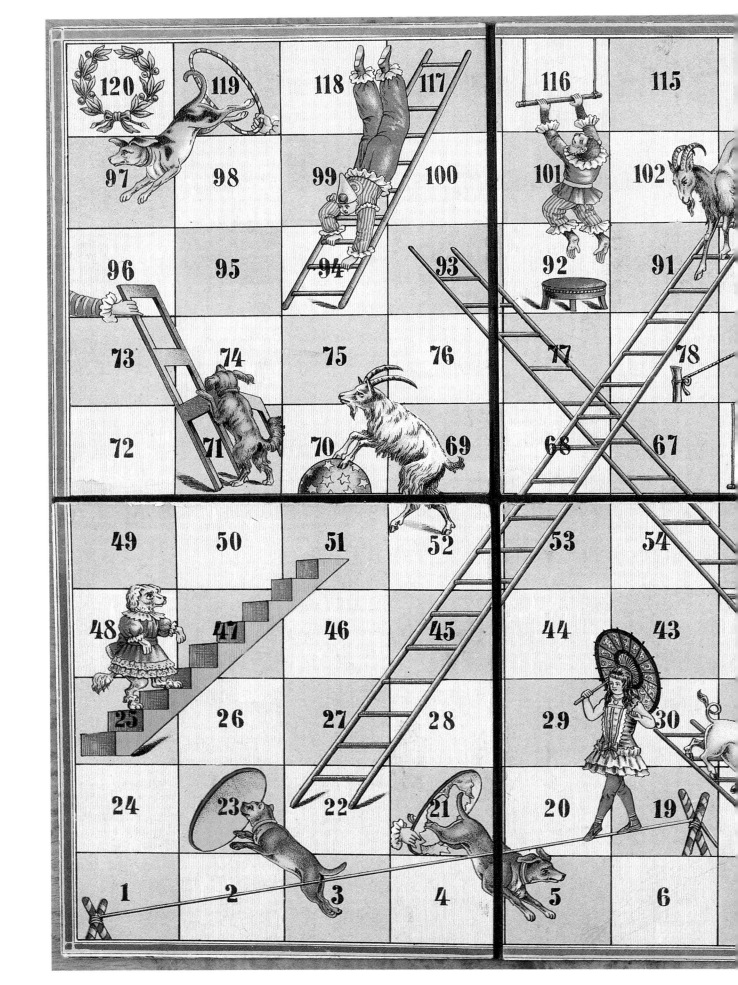

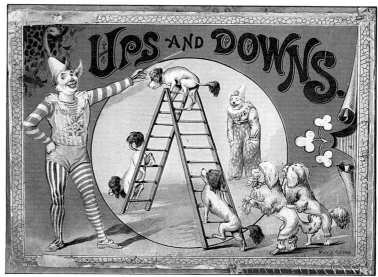

Ups & Downs

Snakes & Ladders is based on a very old Hindu game called *Moksha Patamu*. It was used for religious instruction with the snakes representing evil, the ladders, virtue and was regarded as a symbolic journey through life to Heaven. During the last century it was adapted into a simple race game and has been popular with children ever since. Ups & Downs is a variant of Snakes & Ladders and was produced around the beginning of this century. The following instructions are taken from the box-lid.

'The game represents a circus. Each player's object is to reach the highest number 120.

'Having selected one of the coloured men the player moves as indicated by a throw of the dice.

'Up to No.108 two dice may be used, above that only one — so that, if the player drops below 108 he may resume both again.

'Whenever the player reaches a number which is joined to another by a performer (whether man or beast) climbing upward, he is entitled to mount in one move to the highest number lying in this performer's course.

'In the same way, should the player reach a place with a performer climbing downward he is compelled to go down as far as this performer's course reaches.

'Each player's success varying very considerably during the game, much interest and amusement is evoked. The most successful already nearing a hundred may quickly lose his place whilst on the other hand, the lowest in the race may in a moment reach the winning post.

'The first player reaching or going beyond 120 wins the game.'

LUDUS LATRUNCULORUM
(Rome)

The first reference to this game was made by Varo (116-27 BC) but it was probably much older. He implied that it was played on a board marked with lines enclosing spaces.

Ovid tells us that the pieces were of different coloured glass or even precious stones. He also states that a piece was captured by being surrounded by two enemy pieces on rank or file and that backward moves were permitted. Our chief source of this information about the game comes from an ancient account in an obscure poem by Saleius Bassus known as *Laus Pisonis* written in the middle of the first century.

Many stone boards and fragments of boards have been found on Roman sites in Britain. They are usually marked with 7 x 8, 8 x 8, or 9 x 10 squares, the larger the board the longer the games lasted. The commonest are 8 x 8 boards and the rules are described here. The last reference to *Ludus Latrunculorum* being played in the interior of the Empire was about AD 400 when Macrobius rebuked those who played at *Tabula* and *Latrunculi*.

Becq de Fouquere and others have suggested that some of the pieces may have had increased powers, perhaps there was a leader who could move more than one square at a time by jumping over an enemy piece and trapping another of the opponent's pieces. This would permit a player to break up an otherwise stalemate position with the game finishing while many pieces were still on the board.

At Pompeii a wall-painting shows a board with yellow, black and white pieces on it; and in 1924, twenty-one white, five black and two blue counters were found in a room of one of the barrack buildings in a late first-century deposit at Chester. No trace was found of a board, though this could have been of wood and rotted away, or the board may have been marked out on the ground. The two blue counters (DUX) could have been leaders.

Suggested rules

1. Using an 8 x 8 grid each player has sixteen pieces of his own colour. They are placed on spaces anywhere on the board two at a time in alternate turns of play. During this first phase the pieces do not move and no captures are made.
2. When all the pieces are on the board each player adds his blue dux anywhere on the board.

Second phase

3. The players move one piece one square at right angles in any one direction in alternate turns of play.
4. A capture is made by trapping an enemy piece between two of one's own pieces on rank or file.
5. When a piece makes a capture it has another turn and can continue to make two or more captures in a single turn of play, fig. a.

For two players

Equipment
Each player has sixteen pieces of his or her own colour and one blue piece (dux) each.

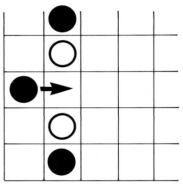

Black to move and capture two White pieces

Fig. a

6. It follows from rule 5 that an isolated piece may endanger itself and several of its fellows by starting a sequence of captures.
7. A piece may move between two enemy pieces without harm.
8. The dux moves in the ordinary way, but in addition it may make a short jump at right angles over an enemy piece, landing on an empty square immediately beyond. No capture is made by the leap unless by this manoeuvre an enemy piece is trapped between the dux and another of the player's pieces. If this happens the dux has another move.
9. The power of jumping permits the penetration of a defensive position which may start a series of captures from within.
10. The dux is captured in the same way as any other piece.
11. The game continues until one player has lost all his pieces, or a blockade has arisen which neither player can break. The player with most pieces left on the board is then declared the winner.
12. If no captures have been made in twenty moves a blockade has been established and the game is over.
13. There is no evidence whether huffing was involved. Players can decide for themselves at the beginning of the game.

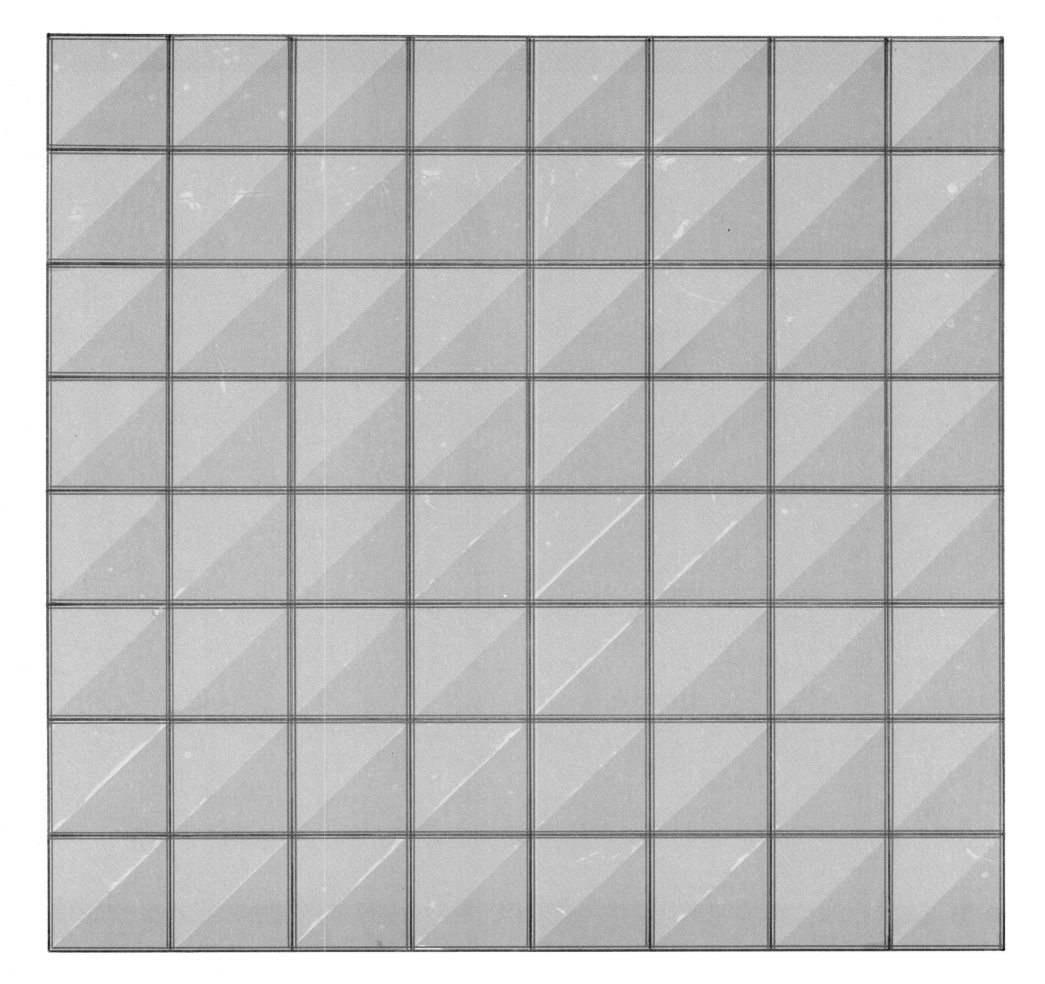

Equipment
A fifty-two card pack of
playing cards
1 token for each player
A number of counters for
paying fines.

THE ROYAL HURDLE RACE GAME (England)

This is a variant on The Game of the Race, illustrated in Chapter 1, page 14, using a pack of cards instead of dice or a teetotum. There are also rules in the centre of the board for the simpler game of Steeplechase.

Method of play

1. Each player chooses his horse and places it on the course at the starting post No. 1 in the same order as the players are sitting at the table.
2. The cards count as follows: King 16; Queen 14, Knave 12, Ace 1 or 11 and the other cards according to their *pip* value.
3. Cut for deal, the highest becoming the dealer who deals and the last card dealt represents TRUMPS, which belongs to the dealer.
4. To win a player must land exactly on No. 100.
5. Each player, except the dealer who pays double, contributes the value of the trump card to the pool. The cards are valued in three groups, the highest price for a court card, next price for Ace, 10, 9, 8, and the remaining cards the lowest price. These values should be agreed before starting the game.
6. The dealer leads by playing, say a king, and his horses's forefeet (or token) are placed on line No. 16. The others follow suit in turn and place their horses feet according to their card's value. The player with the highest card takes the trick and has the next lead.
7. Tricks do not count except to regulate the lead in the next trick.
8. In following suit, if the card you play does not clear your horse over the hurdle jump, but throws you on a blank, you do not move, but pay the value of the card to the pool.
9. If you cannot follow suit, play a trump and, if the number is suitable you move, if it is not, you do not move, but you do not pay a forfeit on trumps.
10. If you cannot follow suit, nor trump, a card is discarded and its value is paid into the pool and your horse does not move.
11. The highest card of the suit led takes the trick, unless a trump or trumps have been played when the highest trump takes the trick and this player has the lead in the next trick.
12. The lines marked with 10 or a multiple of 10 are regarded as hurdles, and if a horses's forefeet land on one of these lines they are assumed to have refused the hurdle, and rule 8 applies.
13. If the players wish, extra obstacles may be placed on the track, water jumps, walls, hedges, etc. When any horse lands on these, rule 8 applies.

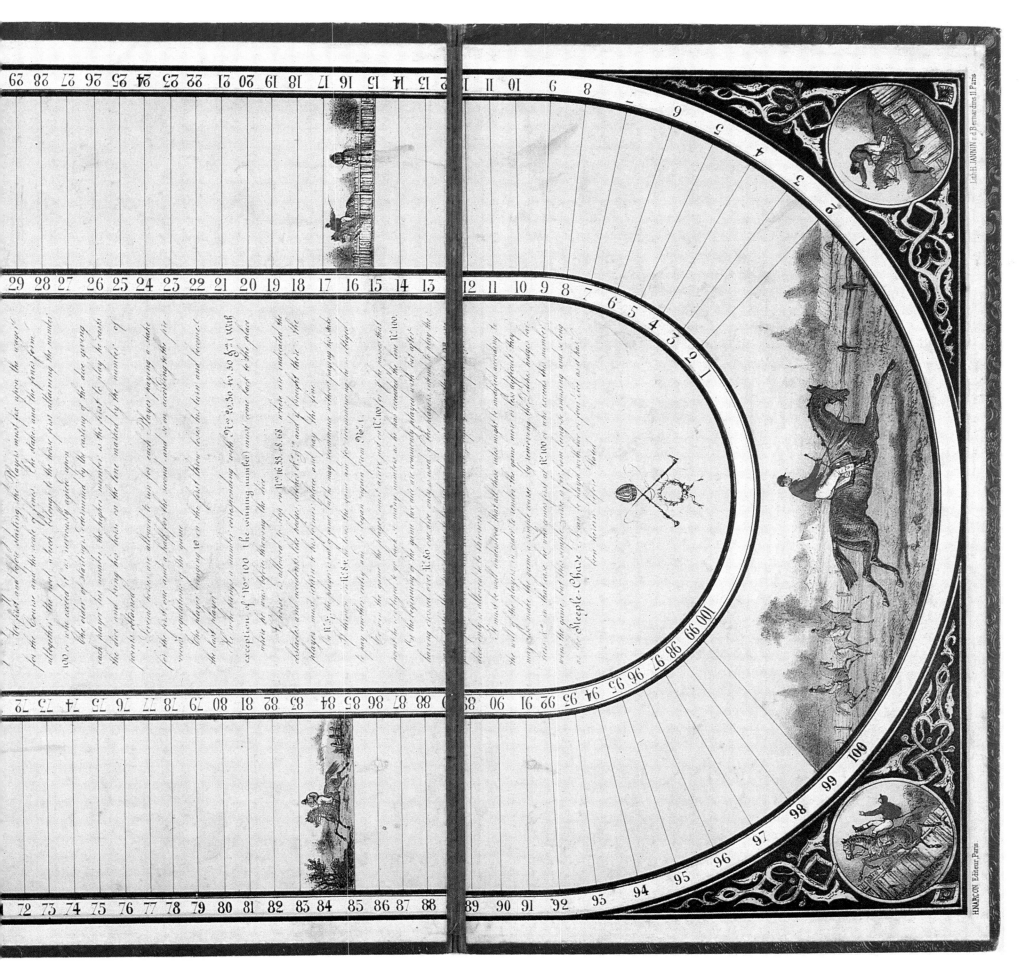

SIEGE OF PARIS (France)

For two or three players

Equipment
Two attacking forces
(one white and one black)
One defending force
(usually brown).

Each attacking force has eighteen pieces and consists of a General, a Colonel, two Captains, two Lieutenants and twelve soldiers.

The defending force consists of eight pieces and comprises a General, a Colonel and six soldiers.

The pieces can be simple pieces of card marked as in fig. b, for instance, SG — garrison soldier, LW — white lieutenant etc.

The game is a curious hybrid invented in 1871 in France, using an enlarged chequered chess board but with a central fortress. Most unusual however, is the different powers of the same pieces on the different sides. Note that the besieged General can only move one square in any direction at a turn, but can make a capture, whereas the two attacking Generals can move one, two or three squares forwards, sideways or diagonally forwards, but not backwards, and cannot capture.

Equipment. The chequered board is of 16 x 12 squares with the central 6 x 6 squares replaced by a fortress. The central garrison is defended by eight pieces, a General, a Colonel and six soldiers and there are thirty-six attackers divided into two equal forces of eighteen, coloured white and black respectively. Each of these forces has a General, a Colonel, two Captains, two Lieutenants and twelve Soldiers. The opening position of the pieces is shown in fig. a.

Rules

1. At the beginning of the game all attacking pieces are placed on squares of their own colour; the General at the extreme right of the back line, the Colonel at the extreme left, next to three senior officers are the two Captains, and occupying the two central squares of the back line are the Lieutenants. The twelve Soldiers occupy the two rows in front of their officers.

2. The fortress contains eight circles and the garrison forces can be arranged in any order. Movement in the fortress is along the marked lines, and there are two exits out of the fortress with a choice of the piece moving onto a black or white square.

3. The objectives of the two sides in winning are different. The besiegers try to immobilize the garrison force inside the fortress and prevent them coming out, or to place one officer and two men inside the garrison. Any attacking piece once inside the fortress is safe from attack. The defenders win by capturing twenty-four of the attacking soldiers and six officers of either colour.

4. The besieging soldiers always remain on squares of their own colour, but the officers can move onto squares of either colour.

5. **Moves of the attacking pieces:**
   (a) Generals move on white or black squares by one, two or three squares at a time, forwards, sideways or diagonally forwards. They may not change direction during a turn of play.
   (b) The Colonels move on white or black squares one or two squares at a time, forwards or sideways.
   (c) The Captains move on white or black squares — one square at a time forwards or sideways.
   (d) The Lieutenants move one or two squares diagonally, and always remain on squares of their own colour.
   (e) The attacking soldiers move one square diagonally, and cannot be captured once they are within the fortress, though they are vulnerable outside.

6. **Moves of the defending pieces:**
   (a) The General can move one square in any direction, forwards, backwards, sideways, or diagonally. He may capture by displacement either on a black or a white square.
   (b) The Colonel moves on black or white squares backwards, forwards, or sideways, one square in any direction and captures by displacement. (Note that he cannot move diagonally.)
   (c) The Soldiers move diagonally backwards or forwards one square at a time, and capture in the same way. Not more than three of the garrison soldiers may be on squares of the same colour (three on black and three on white) and they do not change the colour of their square on moving or capturing unless they return to the fortress and then emerge again.

7. The garrison pieces are of a different colour from either of the besieging forces.

8. The soldiers and officers of the garrison cannot be captured, but they can be hemmed in by the besiegers and if all are unable to move the game is lost.

9. The garrison player is compelled to capture an unsupported piece when requested to do so by the besieging player.

10. If an attacking soldier gains entrance to the fortress the game is drawn.

11. The garrison player has the first move.

12. Then the White player moves one of his pieces.

13. The garrison player replies with another move.

14. If there are three players Black then moves a piece, or if there are only two players the besieging player moves one of his black pieces, thus a white piece and a black piece are moved alternately separated by a move of one of the defender's pieces.

15. Only garrison pieces can capture, and this is by a piece moving onto a square occupied by a besieging piece which is unsupported by another besieging piece (c.f. the King in chess who can only capture a piece that is not supported).

    In fig. b the garrison soldier Sg could not capture the black soldier Sb since it is supported by the white Lieutenant, Lw.

    In fig. c the garrison general Gg could take either of the besieging soldiers Sb or Sw as they are not supporting each other, nor are they supported by any other piece.

16. Inside the garrison the pieces can move along marked lines from one circle to the next.

17. It is possible for the officers of the garrison to remain within the fortress guarding the entrances, but if their soldiers on the board outside are trapped one of them must venture outside to maintain movement on the board.

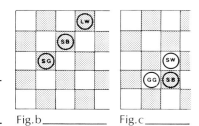

Fig.a

Fig.b   Fig.c

The board illustrated on these pages is the underside of the lid of an antique games compendium from Mysore and is marked out for Lau kati kata (right), Cows and Leopards (centre), and Lam Turki (left).

Lam Turki (India)

Played in northern India, this game is similar to *Pentalpha* which is still played in Crete and is a positional game for one player.

For one player

Equipment
Nine counters, pebbles or buttons.

1. A piece is placed on any unoccupied point while the player calls ONE. Then it is moved in a straight line through another point TWO onto a third point THREE.
2. This ONE-TWO-THREE sequence is followed for each of the pieces. The first and third points must be empty, but the second point can be occupied. When nine out of the ten points of the board are covered the player has solved the *Pentalpha* problem, but *Lam Turki* carries on with a second stage.
3. A piece is lifted over another onto an empty point beyond, the jumped-over piece being removed from the board.
4. In a series of such short leaps all the pieces but one are removed from the board.

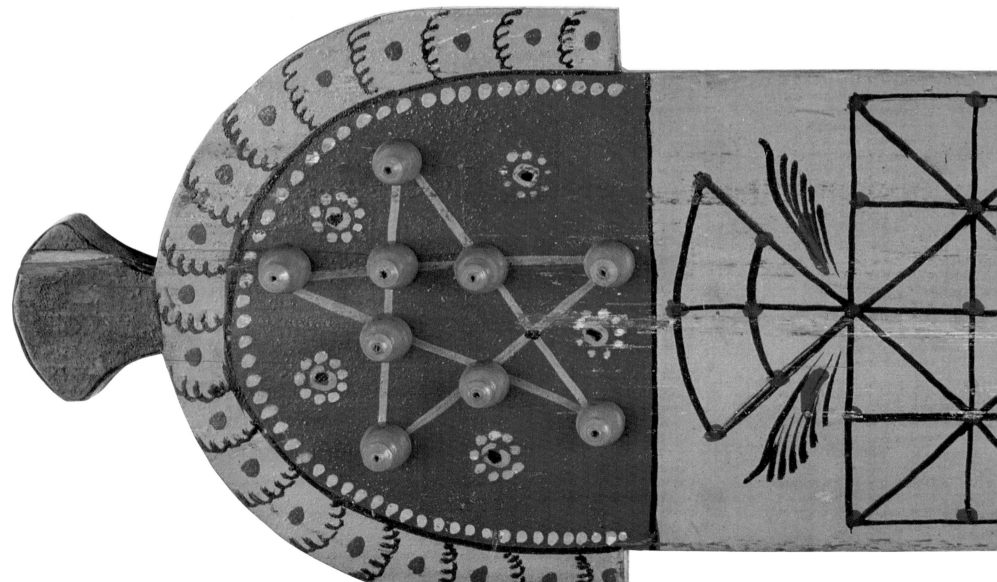

Lau Kati Kata (India)

The board on the right of this compendium is a variant of *Alquerque*, the rules for which will be found on page 35. The only difference is that the player has six pieces of his own colour which are placed on the intersections and the central *point* is left vacant at the start of play.

Cows and Leopards (South East Asia)

Played throughout southern Asia, it is a game for two players. The sides are of unequal strength but the players' objectives are different. One player has two leopards and the other twenty-four cows which try to hem in the leopards. The latter can kill a cow by jumping over her onto a vacant point immediately beyond. Cows and leopards move from one point to the next, along rank, file, or diagonally. (Sixteen Soldiers may be played on the same board and the instructions for that game are given on page 26).

Rules

1. The leopard player begins by placing a leopard on any point, usually the central one.
2. A cow is next put down on any vacant point.
3. The second leopard is placed on any chosen empty point and another cow follows.
4. After each move of a leopard another cow is added to the board until all twenty-four have been placed. Only then can any cow on the board be moved.
5. A cow 'at risk' must be taken.
6. While the cows are being introduced some will be *killed*, and removed from the board. If the leopards manage to kill eight cows they should win, but with careful play the cows will always succeed in trapping the leopards.

Lau Kati Kata
For two players

Equipment
Each player has six pieces of his or her own colour.

Cows and Leopards
For two players

Equipment
Two pieces of one colour and twenty-four of another.

Equipment
One player controls two pieces, the Officers, in the garrison while the other controls the moves of twenty-four pieces, the Sepoys, in the neighbouring countryside.

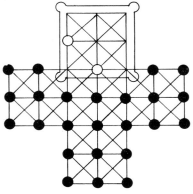

Fig. a

OFFICERS AND SEPOYS
(England)

This is a form of *Asalto* which in turn was adapted from the game of Fox & Geese, originating in Iceland hundreds of years ago and is a contest between two unequal opponents who try to outwit each other. During the Indian Mutiny in 1857 the game was renamed Officers and Sepoys and nine of the points were marked off as a fortress.

One player places his two officers on any two points within the walls of the fortress. His opponent controls the moves of twenty-four rebellious sepoys who occupy all the points in the neighbouring countryside. All the pieces move one point along any marked line, but the sepoys always move towards the fort.

The officers capture by a short leap, but are subject to *huffing* and if a capture is possible it must be made or the officer is removed from the board.

The sepoys win if they occupy every point in the fortress or if they trap the officers and remove their power of movement, but if they are so depleted that they cannot achieve either of these objectives, the officers win.

The opening position of the pieces is shown in fig. a.

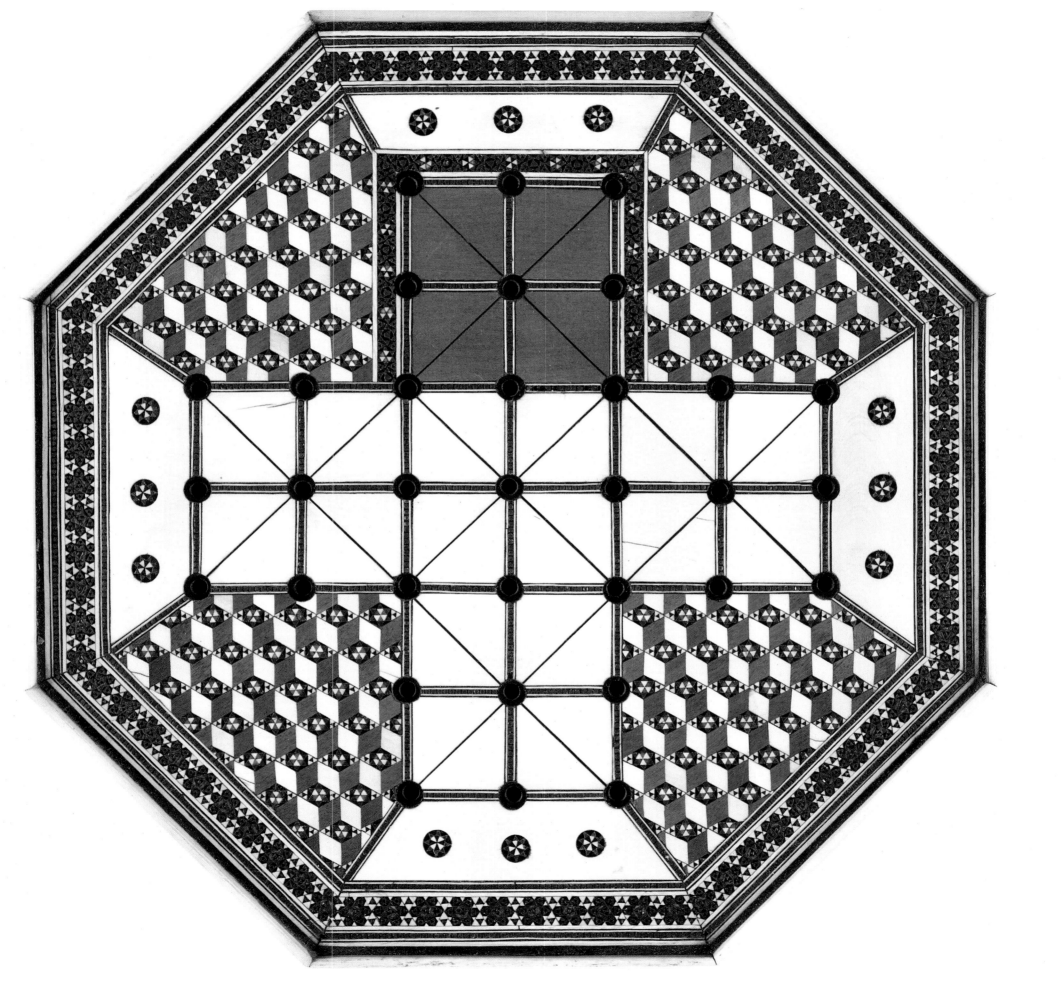

THE SUMERIAN GAME
(Iraq)

Sir Leonard Woolley's book *The First Phases* contains a plate showing two of the other boards, found during his excavation, in 1929, of several tombs in the Royal cemetary of Ur *c.*3000 BC. One is very simple, the spaces being little sheets of shell with red or blue centres set in bitumen which covers the wood base and forms a surround for the playing area. The other more elaborate board is completely covered with shell plaques inlaid with *lapis lazuli* and red limestone and separated by *lapis lazuli* strips. The boards were hollow and inside were seven black and seven white markers and six pyramidal dice with two of their four points dotted with inlay. Three white ivory and three blue *lapis lazuli* dice made a set. No account of how the game was played has survived, but there appear to have been lucky and unlucky squares.

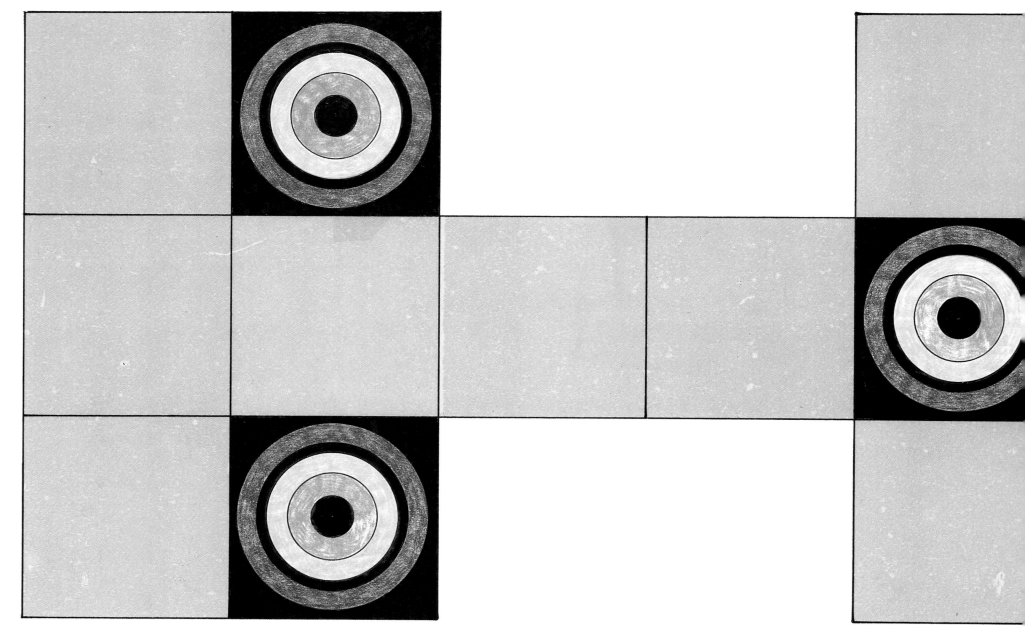

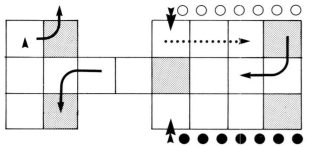

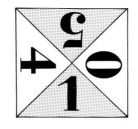

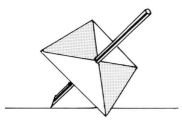

Fig. a _____ Fig. b Teetotum _____

For two players

Equipment
A teetotum. See fig b.
Each player has seven pieces of his
or her own colour and a number of
counters for the payment of fines.

Suggested rules

To enable the game to be played on these pages a simple teetotum has been devised to take the place of the pyramidal dice and this is shown in fig. b.

1. Each player contributes to a pool which becomes the winner's prize. (In one of the finds there were twenty-one small white balls which may have been tallies.)
2. One player spins the teetotum, the other calling a number while it is still spinning. If called correctly he has the choice of colour, side of the board and first move.
3. Both teams start off the board. The direction of movement is shown in fig. a.
4. The opening player spins the teetotum and the possible scores are:

    > 5 and another throw
    > 4 and another throw
    > 0 and the turn finishes
    > 1 and the turn finishes

5. A piece can only be entered on the board on a throw of 5 and then it moves forward by the number on the additional throw or throws.
6. If a piece moves on to a marked square, the opponent pays a fine into the pool.
7. When a piece moves onto the central rank it is exposed to enemy attack, and if an opposing piece lands on the same square, it is sent off the board and must start again with a throw of 5. There are twelve 'fighting' and four 'safe' squares on the board for each player.
8. An exact throw is needed to bear a piece off the board.
9. A player may have any number of his seven counters on the board at once but only one piece is allowed on each square.
10. The first player to bear all his pieces off the board wins the pool.

RACE TO THE GOLD DIGGINGS OF AUSTRALIA

VOYAGE TO THE GOLD DIGGINGS (England)

An Amusing and Instructive New Game

The board consists of a hand-coloured lithograph 19 inches by 13 inches (47cm x 32cm) mounted in eight sections on linen and folded. The rules are printed on a white card. The race-track, rules, ivory totum and six lead ships are housed in a mahogany box with a sliding lid on which is a coloured print showing two fully-rigged ships sailing past the Cape of Good Hope. The gold rush to Australia was from 1851 to 1853, and this game would have been marketed between these years. The publisher is unknown. The rules are taken from the card in the box.

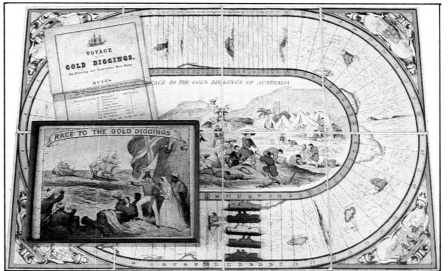

Rules

Select your ships and place them on the line marked 0. Spin the teetotum and bring the ship as the number indicates. Who exceeds or gets 80 first wins the game.

If you get on line   3 Plymouth ———— add 3 more
,,   6 Lizard Light ———— add 1 more.
,,   13 Madeira ———— add 3 more.
,,   15 Canary Islands ——— add 1 more.
,,   18 Cape Verdi *(sic)* Isles — add 1 more.
,,   on lines   24, 25, 26, Sierra Leone— add 7 more.
,,   28 Ascension ———— lose 1.
,,   32 St. Helena ———— add 3 more.

At the Cape of Good Hope add 10 for the trade wind.

If you get on line   43 Madagascar ———— lose 2.
,,   46 Maritius ———— add 3 more.
,,   on lines   68, 69 Batavia ———— lose 5.

At 65 the ship is wrecked, and the player is thrown out of the game. You cannot be placed on any of the tenth lines, and the turn that brings you there is forfeited.

For two to six players

Equipment
One dice
One token for each player.

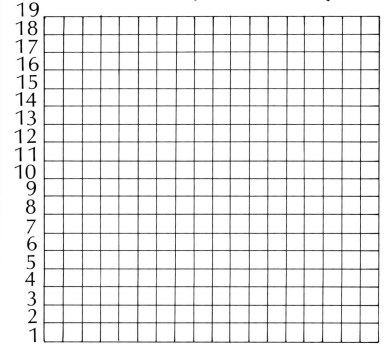

GO (China and Japan)_____

In this game for two, each player has a wooden bowl containing his 'stones' which are dicoidal in shape and some 7/8 inch (2cm) in diameter, Black having one hundred and eighty-one and White one hundred and eighty. In the best sets the white stones are made of shell from the provinces of Hitachi and Mikawa while the black are a form of slate from the Nachi cataract in Kishiu. Cheaper 'stones' may be made of glass, or over the last few years, of plastic. The players sit on the floor facing each across the board.

The diagram of a *Go* board in fig. a. shows the Korschett system of notation. Black moves are odd and White even, unless Black receives a handicap. Thus 8F14 means that on the 8th play White placed his stone on F14 or 67B6+2 means that on the 67th play Black put his stone on B6 and captured two white stones.

For two players

Equipment
One hundred and eighty-one
black counters
One hundred and eighty
white counters
(Small buttons can be used).

A B C D E F G H J K L M N O P Q R S T

Fig.a_____

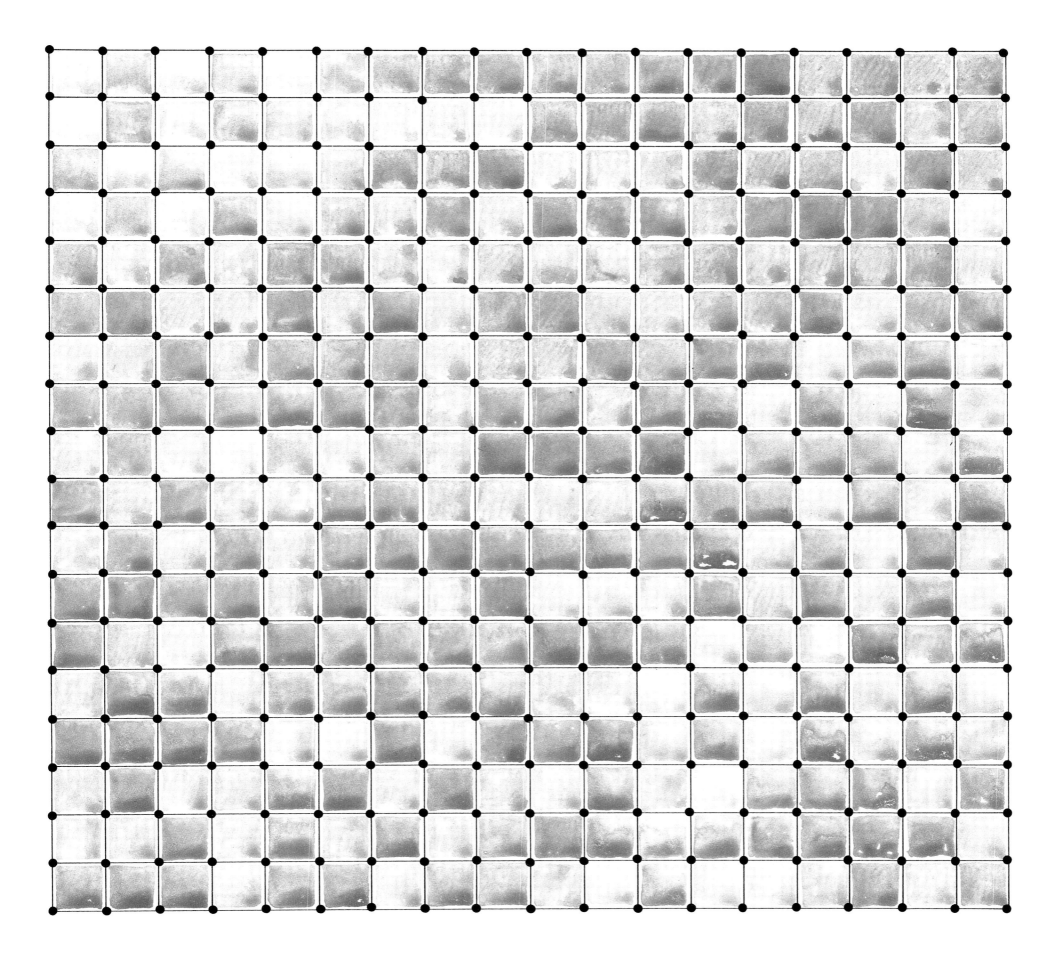

Rules

1. The board is empty at the beginning of the game unless one player has been given a handicap advantage.
2. There is a slight advantage in playing first and this is granted to the weaker player, Black, who begins by putting one of his stones on any point on the board. Play then alternates, only one stone being placed in each turn. Once positioned a stone cannot be moved and remains on the same point until the end of the game unless it is captured when it is removed from the board.
3. The object of the game is to control vacant points in such a way that they cannot be occupied by the opponent. The player controlling most empty points or 'Territory' at the end of the game is the winner.
4. Stones completely surrounded by those of the opposite colour, and without any empty points orthogonally adjacent (at right angles) to them, are captured and removed from the board. However, the primary objective of the game is not the capturing of pieces but the winning of territory. Similarly in chess, the primary objective is not the capture of the opponent's pieces but to checkmate the opponent's king. In both games it is possible to win without making a single capture.
5. If a stone is surrounded orthogonally by enemy stones, it is captured and removed from the board, figs. b & c. Stones arranged orthogonally on adjacent points are considered to be a single unit and, however large, if surrounded by enemy pieces and without contact with an empty point, are captured.

Multiple captures.
A White stone placed as arrowed
would capture the Black stone.

Positions of single capture.

Fig. b

Fig. c

6. A stone cannot be placed on a point completely surrounded by enemy stones unless it makes a capture in doing so. Figs. d and e. Nor can a stone occupy the last free point of one of its own groups, unless enemy stones are captured, fig. f.

Black cannot play onto X
as it would be captured immediately.

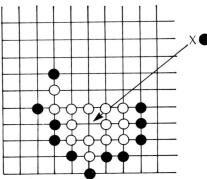

Fig. d

A Black stone on X leaves the
White formation without a vacant point.
They are captured and removed and
Black remains on X.

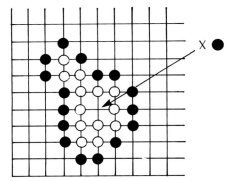

Fig. e

7. Vacant points completely controlled by stones of one colour are called EYES, and as an eye can only be occupied by an opposing stone when it makes a capture, a group with two eyes is safe from attack, fig. g.

A White stone on X captures the Black pieces, but if one of the encircling White pieces were missing, the play would be illegal as the White formation would be captured.

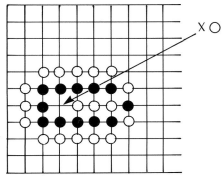

Fig. f

Safe formation with two eyes.

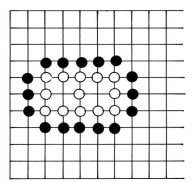

Fig. g

If Black plays onto X he captures three stones and on the next turn a stone on Y will capture the rest. A false eye.

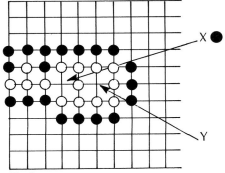

Fig. h

8. A group of stones not in orthogonal contact may contain empty points, but the disconnected stones can be attacked and the formation 'Killed', the stones being captured and removed from the board. These empty points are known as 'False' or temporary eyes, and are often constructed by beginners in mistake for real eyes, fig. h.

9. The player may place a stone on any vacant point except to make an illegal play, rule 6, or when his opponent has just captured a stone in a repetitive position known as a *ko* when he must make one play elsewhere on the board, fig. i.

10. If there are three *kos* on the board at the same time the game is declared drawn.

11. Sometimes opposing formations of stones are interlocked so that neither player can attack the opponent's pieces without losing his own. This impasse is known as *seki*. These positions are left alone until the end of the game when they are neutralized and all the empty points within it are ignored and do not count towards either player's score, fig. j.

12. At the end of the game there will be isolated vacant points between opposing formations which are neutral and useless to both players. These are filled up to help in calculating the final scores.

13. Stones which, while not actually surrounded, can inevitably become so, are dead and are removed at the end of the game without further play.

14. When the profitless points have been filled in and the dead stones removed from each player's territories, each player places his opponent's captured stones on vacant enemy points, thus reducing the opposing score by the number of pieces held.

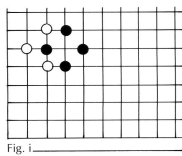

Ko or repeating position.

Fig. i

X. Seki position.
Either player placing a stone on X will lose his own formation.

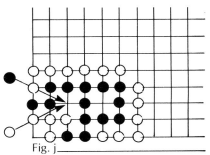

Fig. j

Casual games last one to three hours and professional matches up to three days. Beginners are advised to play on a quarter of the board and to concentrate on fundamental corner problems. Corner play analysis, called *joseki*, is described at length by most Japanese writers on *Go*.

For two to four players

Equipment
A teetotum. See fig. a.
Each player has a token of his or
her own colour and a number of
counters for the payment of fines.

The Journey or Crossroads to Conquerors Castle An entirely new game (England)

The original race games were spiral and players usually travelled in an anticlockwise direction (see the Royal Game of Goose on page 74) but from 1836 the firm of William Spooner of 250 Regent Street, London, invented a new style of track in which the contestants move across the board from junction to junction, their progress determined by the spin of a teetotum which sends them forwards, backwards, right or left, fig. a. This is a game for two to four players.

Rules:

1. Each player starts the game with a token of a different colour and an agreed number of counters of which he pays 3 to the pool.

2. The order of play is determined by drawing lots or by throwing dice.

3. The first player spins the totum and moves either forwards (F), left (L), or right (R) according to the direction indicated on the teetotum. If the totum indicates backwards (B) the turn is lost and play passes to the next player.

4. The second player spins and moves and is followed by the other players in turn. Should the circle to which he is directed be occupied he may remove that token and that player must return to the starting point and begin again.

5. As play proceeds, should the player land on an occupied circle he and the occupant must transpose their tokens.

6. If a player is directed to a 'No Thoroughfare' he cannot move and the turn is lost.

7. Each time a player passes along a road that requires a fine, he must pay the demand.

8. When a player is displaced he neither pays any fines nor receives any rewards from the pool.

9. The player first passing through any of the gates to Conquerors Castle wins and takes all the counters remaining in the pool.

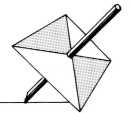

Fig. a

THE SNAKE GAME
(Ancient Egypt)

The Snake Game was popular in early dynastic Europe. The boards were flat discs with a snake carved on the upper surface, its head in the centre and its tail along the rim. The body was divided by cross lines into segments. These varied from as few as twenty-nine to over five hundred, the more segments to travel over the longer the game lasted.

No gaming equipment has been found with the boards, but a wall painting in the tomb of Hesy shows a games' box with six sets of six marbles and six animal figurines, three lions and three hounds wearing collars. The tomb of Hesy at Sakkara was built at the beginning of the Third Dynasty, c.2686-2613 BC, just after the Archaic Period. See fig. b..

The six sets of marbles suggests that the game was for up to six players and that they formed two teams, the lion team and the hound team. The animal figurines appear to have been placed on the spaces of the snake and moved towards the head with each score made by the player owning them. No description of how to play the game has survived, but a suggestion is offered below.

For two to six players

Equipment
Each player has a token of his or her own colour and one set of six marbles.

Possible Rules

1. If there were only two players, A and B, each had six marbles of his own colour.
2. Assuming A had the first turn of play, he decided how many marbles he would hold concealed in his left hand and held them out towards B.
3. B then guessed at the number held and placed this number of his own marbles on the table. The other player then opened his hand and showed the marbles held in it. If the numbers were the same, A scored nothing, but if they were different, A scored the difference and moved his figurine on by this number of spaces on the snake.
4. B then chose and concealed a number of marbles in his left hand and placed the number of his marbles he thought B had chosen on the table. B scored the difference in the two groups of marbles; and if they were the same, he scored nothing.
5. The first player to move his figurine onto, or beyond, the snake's head won the game.
6. If four players were taking part they formed two teams, A and C against B and D; if there were six players, A,C, and E played against B,D, and F with the turn of play alternating between members of the team.

   Another early representation of a game is in the tomb of Rashepsis, a scribe of the king of Tat-Ka-ra of the Fifth Dynasty. See fig. a. The drawing by Prof. Lepsius in 1861 shows a series of concentric rings, though these were probably a spiral.

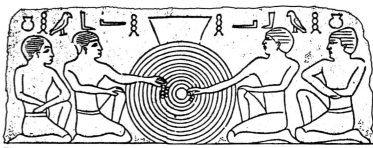

Fig. a

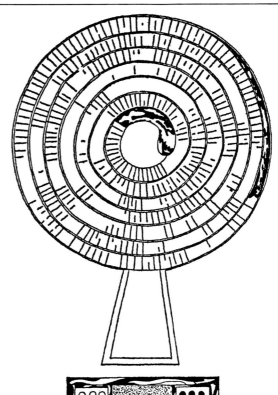

Fig. b

References: Hoerth, A.J. *Gameboards of the Ancient Near East*, a thesis for an M.A. degree, Chicago University, 1961. Flinders Petrie, Sir W.M. *Objects of Daily Use*, Aris & Phillips, 1974 (First published 1927). Emery, W.B. *Archaic Egypt*, Penguin, 1961 pps. 248-251.

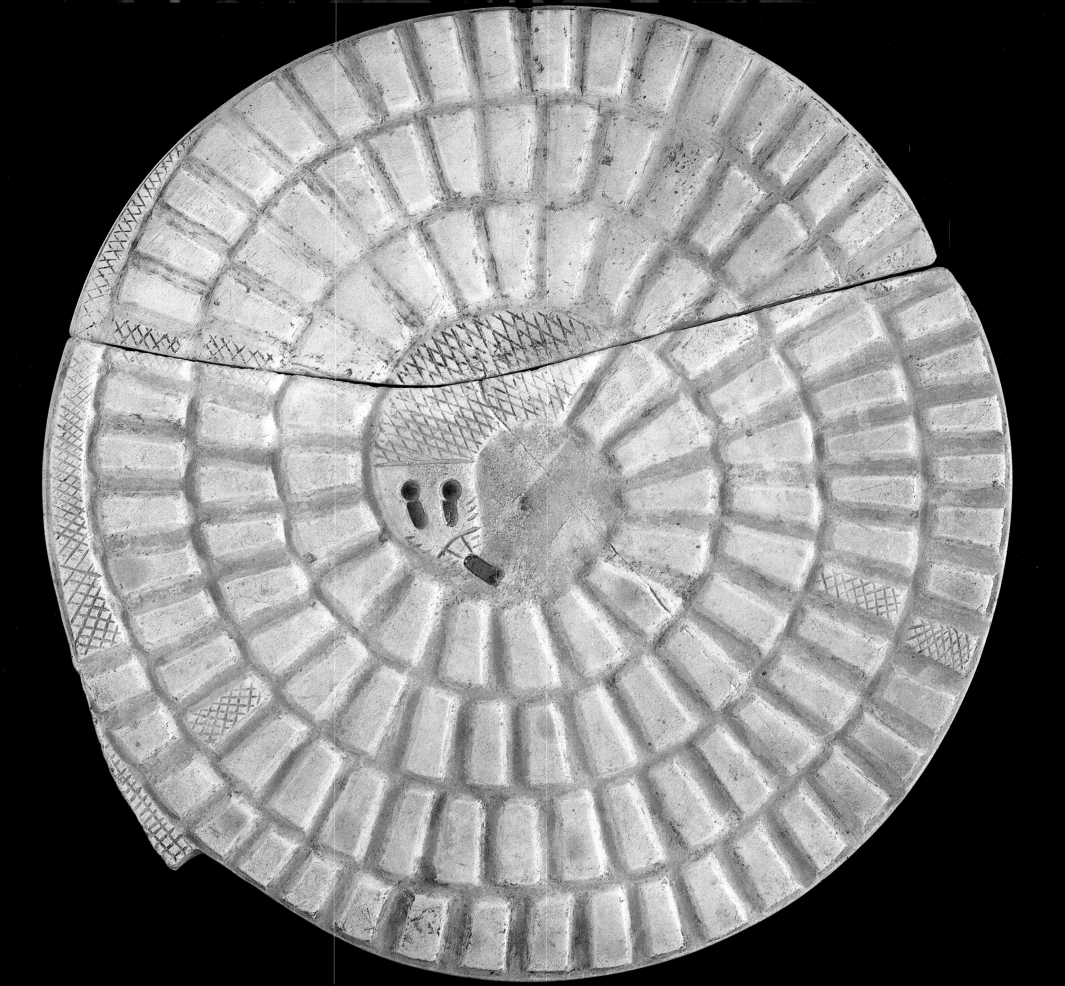

Dealer

BLACK JACK

must
draw to 16
and stand on

★ **BLACKJACK PAYS**

Equipment
A fifty-two card pack of
playing cards
A number of gaming counters or
coins.

BLACKJACK

Originally the old card game *Vingt-et-un* or Twenty-one, the game was adapted to meet the needs of the casino and its patrons. Any number may play.

Rules

1. Before the deal is made the punters place their bets on the rectangles on the cloth.
2. The dealer deals two cards face downwards to each player at the table.
3. The object of the game is for the player to hold a hand totalling 21 points, or as near to it as possible. All court cards count 10 points, all other cards the *pip* value, except for the Ace which can count as 1 or 11 points as the player chooses.
4. Starting from his left, the dealer issues additional cards to the players who wish to 'draw', passing by those who wish to 'stand'.
5. A player may draw as many cards as he wishes to improve his hand, but if the total of points held exceeds 21 he goes 'BUST' and discards his hand face up onto the table and the dealer takes his bet.
6. A player drawing an Ace and a 10 or a court card holds a BLACKJACK and is an automatic winner, receiving 3 for 2 on his stake. All other bets are even money.
7. If the dealer gets a BLACKJACK at the same time as another player the hand is a 'standoff' and is abandoned, with no-one winning or losing.
8. If the dealer holds a BLACKJACK all players lose including those holding a hand of 21 points, except those who have taken INSURANCE.
9. Any time the dealer deals himself an Ace on his first card, players may 'insure' themselves against the possibility that his second card will be a court card or a Ten which would give him an automatic BLACKJACK. To insure, the player places an amount equal to half his bet on the insurance line. If the dealer does obtain a Blackjack, the player does not lose, even if his hand is beaten, and holds his bet and the insurance money. If the dealer does not turn up a Blackjack he takes any insurance money on the line and play continues in the normal way.
10. A player may DOUBLE DOWN on his first two cards. This means doubling his bet and taking an additional card.
11. All cards are dealt face downwards, except the dealer's which are dealt last and face upwards. The dealer must stand on 17 points or more, and must draw another card on 16 points or less.

SOUTH SEA ADVENTURES
England_____

This is a simple race game for children and was first published by J.W.Spears & Son Ltd. in 1929. This description and rules were printed on the inside of the box-lid.

'Have you already heard of the wonders of the South Sea, of the fairy-like gardens of the Coral Islands, of the splendid deep blue of the sunlit Ocean, and of the strange brown children who live on the beautiful isles of those romantic lands? Numerous dangers lurk there for men, in the sea the voracious sharks, on the land the no less bloodthirsty crocodile and, in addition, the hostile natives. This game should give you the opportunity of living through all the excitement and events of a South Sea Adventure.

'We take our passage in one of the modern Steam ships, which will carry us many thousand miles over the wide Ocean. On route we are caught in a fearful storm, and have to save the crew of a wrecked ship. Finally the ship lands us on a settlement. Here we await the schooner, which is take us to the Coral Islands to find pearls. Our journey brings us to hostile tribes. In an inhabited village we must land in order to replenish our food. Only too easily can it happen that a passenger falls overboard and only with great difficulty be saved death through the waves or through the man-eating sharks. On the broad Ocean we lose our way and have to put back to one of the islands to enquire further, until at last after many adventures, we arrive at the Coral Islands. This gives great joy, not so much on account of the worth of the pearls, but because we had the patience, the strength and pluck to overcome the numerous perils.

'Only in this way could we reach the Islands and win the treasure.

1. All Players start the journey on No.1. Each player throws the dice in turn and moves the number thrown.
9. A fearful storm hinders further progress. Miss a throw.
13. Another ship has suffered shipwreck, the crew is saved, and we go on with it at once to No.26.
17. Coalling of the ship and taking on of mails causes a short stop. Miss a throw.
25. On account of a difficult storm miss a throw.
33. Favourable wind and good weather make it possible to advance to No.45.
41. Safely landed in South Sea haven, go on board a schooner, and have an extra throw.
46. Owing to lack of drinking water go back to No.40.
50. Wrecked off a lonely island, is taken back by a steamer going to No. 40.
56. Man overboard, is wounded by a shark, must go back to No.1 whence he must start the journey again.
64. Has lost his course and must go back to No.55 to enquire.
72. Landed at a native village, in order to replenish food, must therefore miss 2 throws.
79. Owing to lack of wind must lost one throw.
86. Is so badly wounded in fight with natives, that he must withdraw from the game.
90. Luckily escaped from the fight with the natives, advances to No.95.
94. Having taken the wrong channel owing to the shallows, must go back to No.89.
98. The ship cannot find her way through the Shallows and must, therefore, go back no No.91.
100. Here all perils are happily overcome. Whoever arrives at No.100, or beyond first find the pearls and wins the game.'

For two to six players

Equipment
One die
Each player has a token of his or her own colour.

MANCALA

Mancala games are some of the oldest two player strategy games in the world, yet they are still largely unknown outside Africa and Asia. Traditionally, *Mancala* is played on a board carved out of a piece of wood but, in some rural areas, it is played simply by scooping pits out of the ground.

The rules are quite simple but the strategy involved in the winning the game is challenging and the board reproduced on this page is intended as an introduction to this intriguing and absorbing game.

As the *Mancala* games will be new to many readers the following terms will be defined.

Definitions

LIFT Lifting all the shells from a hole ready to begin sowing.
SOWING Placing one shell in each consecutive hole in the direction of movement. In some games this is clockwise, in others anti-clockwise, and in a few in either direction.
LAP This may involve several lifts and sowings and ends when the last shell of a lift falls into an empty hole.
ROUND This lasts from the setting out of the shells in the holes until no more play is possible. A game may consist of a single round, although more commonly of several, until one player is no longer able to fill even one hole with pieces.
GAME When a decision has been reached and one player emerges as the winner.

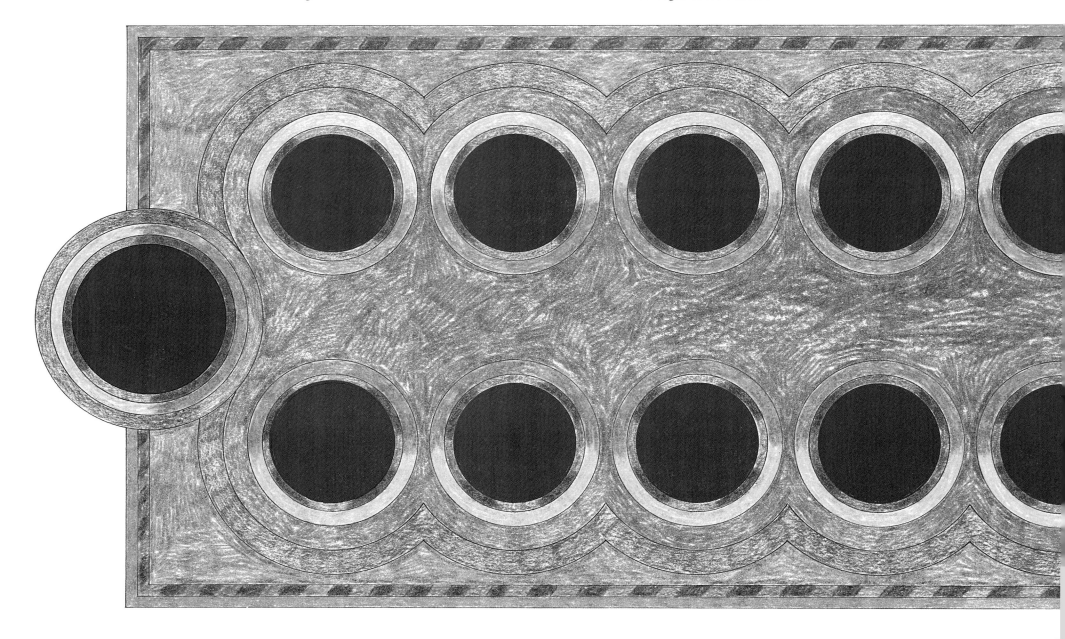

For two players

Equipment
Each player has forty-nine small shells, buttons or stones.

SUNKA (Indonesia)

In *Sunka* the players play the first lap simultaneously. This prevents any analysis of the opening moves as is possible in chess.

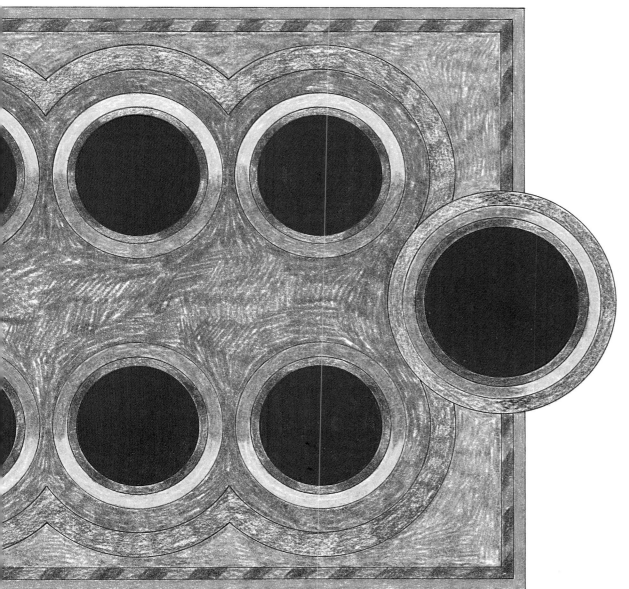

First Phase

1. The players place seven cowrie shells in each of their seven holes, leaving their store hole at the left end of the line empty.
2. Movement is clockwise around the board, starting towards one store hole and, in passing, a shell is sown into it, but a shell is not deposited in the opponent's store hole in passing.
3. In the first phase, both players start together by picking up all the shells from any one of the holes on their side of the board and sow one shell into each hole in a clockwise direction, including their own store hole.
4. When the last shell of a lift is dropped into a loaded hold, all the contents of the hole, including the shell just sown, are lifted and the sowing continues, one shell to each hole (but not into the opponent's store.)
5. When the last shell of a lift drops into an empty hole the lap ceases and the player must wait until his opponent has also finished the lap.
6. Every time a lap ends in one of the player's empty holes, he wins any shells in the opponent's hole opposite and these are put in the player's store hole. If the lift ends in an empty hole on the opponent's side of the board, the lap ends without gain.
7. Whenever a player ends a lift in his store hole, he continues the lap by lifting the shells from any hole on his own side of the board.
8. When a player has no shells left in any of the holes on his side of the board the round ends. His opponent gathers up any shells on his side of the board and adds them to his store. When all the shells are in the two stores the second phase begins.

Second Phase

9. Each player takes the shells out of his store and places seven into as many of his holes as he can. If a player cannot fill a hole with seven shells the hole is left empty and is marked with a little stick. It is out of use for that round. Any shells left over are put back into the player's store.
10. When the holes on each side of the board have been 'dressed' with seven shells each, the player who finished last in phase one begins in phase two and the players start laps alternately.
12. The game continues in this way, possibly through many rounds, until one player is unable to dress even one hole with seven shells, when the game ends and he has lost.

Résumé

Holes: 2 x 7 plus 2 store
Pieces: 7 per hole
Direction of play: Clockwise
Lap: Ends when the last shell of a lift falls into an empty hole.
Capture: Shells from loaded opponent's hole opposite at end of lap.

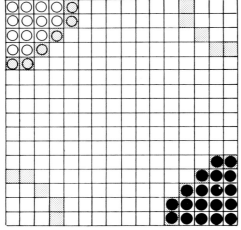

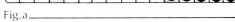

Fig.a

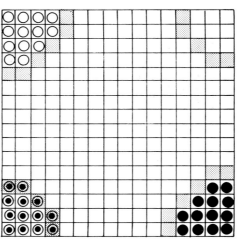

Fig.b

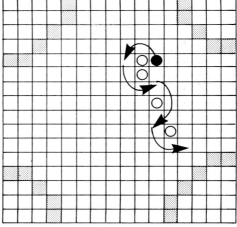

Fig.c

Halma (USA)

Halma was invented in America in about 1880 when it was extremely popular, Its name is derived from a Greek word meaning jump. When played by two players each has nineteen pieces of his own colour arranged in a CAMP on his own side of the board, the walls of which are marked by a thicker line, fig. a. In a three or four-handed game each player has thirteen pieces, fig. b.

Rules

1. Only one piece may move during a turn; either as a single step in any direction on to an adjacent empty square; or by leaping over a piece of either colour in any direction, including diagonally, onto an empty space immediately beyond. A number of leaps may be made over his own or hostile pieces and each player tries to make 'ladders' (fig. c) to help his pieces to move several squares across the board in a single turn of play. Each player also makes use of his opponent's ladders when he can, or alternatively, tries to block them to frustrate the latter's progress.

2. The first player to manoeuvre all his pieces across the board into the enemy camp wins the game.

3. In a four-handed game each player has thirteen pieces arranged in his own corner of the board.

4. Each player plays for himself, and the turn of play moves clockwise around the board.

5. The first player to marshall his pieces in the camp immediately opposite his own wins the game. Each player plays for himself. There are no partnerships.

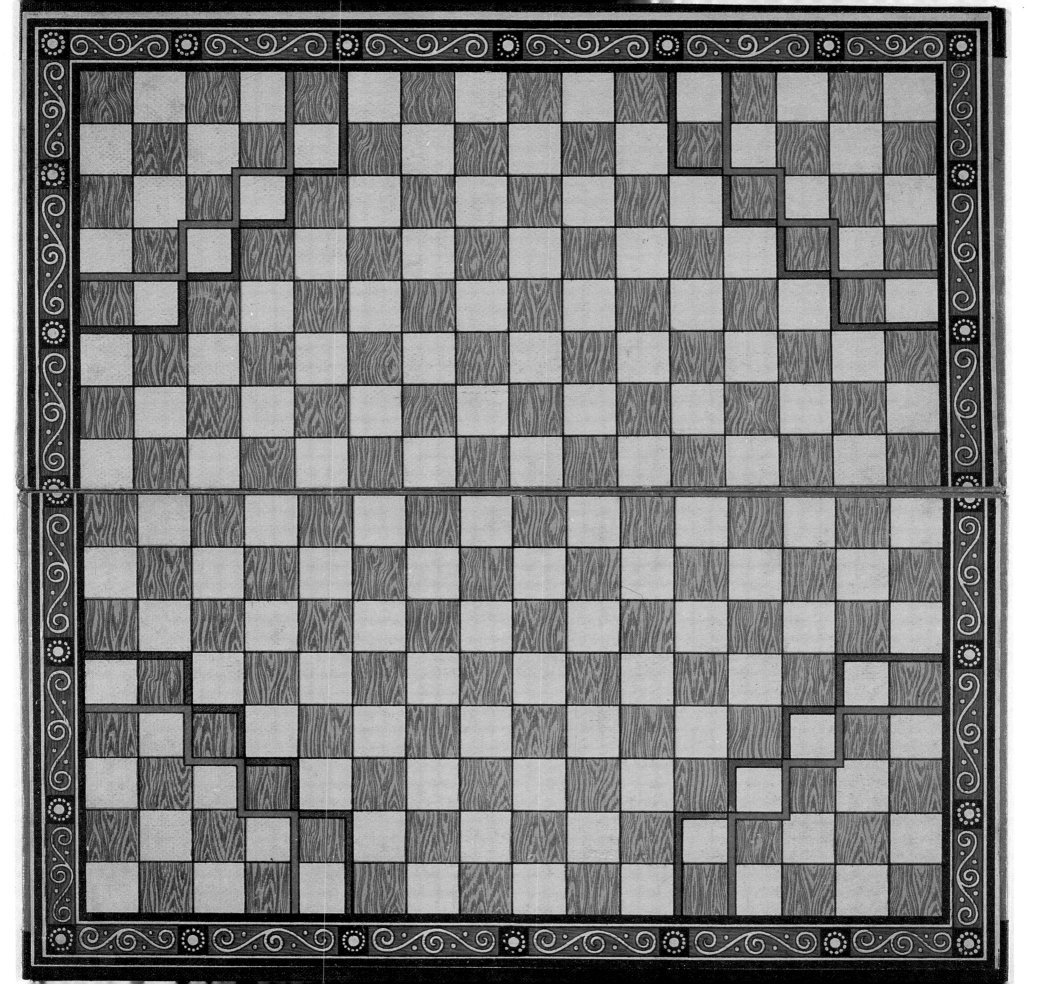

POCH (Germany)

This German variant of Pope Joan *(156)* has a long history. The oldest *poch* board in the Bavarian National Museum in Munich is dated 1527, while the earliest reference to the game appears in the work of the famous Nuremberg Meistersinger, Hans Sach, 1558. *Poch* boards may have eight or nine holes. Old ceramic or wooden boards were often decorated with superb paintings.

For Four players

Equipment
A thirty-two card pack comprising Ace, King, Queen, Jack, 10, 9, 8, and 7 of all four suits.
A number of gaming counters or coins for each player.

Method of play

STAGE ONE

1. A thirty-two card pack is used in this game for four people, comprising the Ace, King, Queen, Jack, 10, 9, 8 and 7 of all four suits. Ace is high.
2. Each player puts a chip into each of the eight pockets on the board.
3. The dealer shuffles the pack and deals eight cards face downwards to each player. The dealer looks at the last card he dealt himself and names its suit as trumps.
4. If a player has the value in trumps of any of the cards or card combinations shown on the board, i.e. the 7-8-9, the 10, the Jack, Queen, King or Ace, or both King and Queen, he takes the chips from the appropriate pockets. A player with both King and Queen of trumps collects from the King, Queen, and joint King/Queen pockets. If no player has King and Queen, or the 7-8-9 sequence, the chips remain in those pockets for the next game.

STAGE TWO

5. The second stage involves the pocket marked *POCH*. The player on the dealer's left 'bids' one or more chips into the *poch* compartment. Any player who wishes to stay in this stage of the game must match the bid. A player with a poor hand may 'pass', losing the opportunity to win the Poch stakes, although still having a chance to win the third stage. After the other players have bid or passed, the first bidder may raise the stake.
6. When bidding ends, each player lays out his best combination of cards and the highest score wins the stake in the *poch* pocket. Scoring combinations are pairs, three of a kind, and four of a kind. The greatest number of the same face value scores highest, i.e. four 7s score higher than three Kings. If two players have the same number of cards in their combinations; i.e. three Queens against three 9s, the higher rank wins. Aces count above Kings. If two players each have a pair of the same value, i.e. two pairs of Jacks, the pair that includes a trump scores higher. After the *poch* counters have been won all the players take back their cards and the third stage begins.

STAGE THREE

7. The winner of the *poch* stakes lays a card face upwards on the table. Any player follows with the next card up in the same suit and cards continue to be played in ascending order by the player holding them until the Ace of the suit is played. This is a 'stop' card and the player of the Ace may then follow playing any card he wishes, either in the same suit or another. Play continues up to the next 'stop' card and the process is repeated until one player lays down his last card, calling 'FINISH'.
8. The first player to play his last card wins this third 'race' stage of the game, and the other players pay him one chip for each card left in their hands.
9. The player on the left of the last dealer then gathers up the cards, re-shuffles, and deals them out, eight to each player, looks at his last card and announces the trump suit. Each player dresses the board by placing a chip into each of the eight pockets and a new game begins.

CHAPTER 7

DOMINOES

Until the raising of the sixteenth-century English ship, the *Mary Rose*, from the waters of the Solent in 1982, European dominoes were thought to have appeared first in Italy during the early years of the eighteenth century and to have spread throughout Europe, reaching England from France in about 1790. These ideas are now under review with the finding of a bone domino, a 4:3, in the *Mary Rose*. This piece is now on view at the Mary Rose museum in Portsmouth and in the catalogue on sale there is a statement on page 35, that King Henry VIII lost £450 playing dominoes.

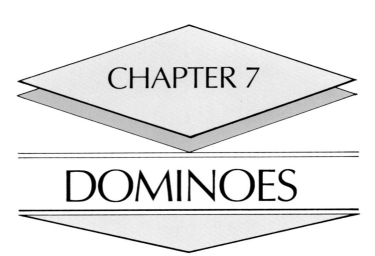

135

The origin of the name domino is uncertain, but it was accepted in 1798 by the *Académie Française* as the name of the pieces and also the game. During the nineteenth century, dominoes became popular in Coffee Houses, and in 1820 an exposé of the methods of cheating at dominoes was published in Dutch at the Hague by C. Van Greeven. Dominoes are not mentioned in *Hoyle's Games Improved* (1814) and even in *Hoyle's Games Improved and Enlarged* (1853), the game is only given a page and a half starting with: 'Domino [note the singular] is played by two or four persons with twenty-eight pieces of obling *(sic)* ivory, plain at the back, but in the face divided by a black line in the middle and indented with spots from one to a double-six'. (All the early dominoes seen by the author have been made of bone, not ivory.)

The account contains the comment, 'Sometimes a double set is played, of which the double-twelve is the highest'. The game described is the Block Game. See page 117.

Many of the earliest dominoes were made by French prisoners of war, using beef bones from their meals as a source of material for sale to supplement their meagre allowances. The dominoes were small rectangles with a length twice their breadth, divided by a groove across the middle of the face and each half marked with drill holes, often coloured black. Some of these sets were housed in novelty boxes, including the well-known 'Birdcage' sets *(135)*.

Suitable thick pieces of bone became scarce and soon thinner pieces were being used, fastened to a wooden backing with glue and a central brass sprig. Ebony to contrast with the white of the bone became popular or other hardwoods stained to imitate ebony were used in cheaper sets and the central sprig was reinforced with two smaller sprigs.

In 1855 Charles Lepage of Paris invented *bois durci*, a substitute for wood made of rosewood or ebony sawdust and albumen from eggs or blood. The sawdust was soaked in albumen and water the mixture was dried, placed in a steel mould and subjected to pressure and heat in a hydraulic press. *Bois durci* was used for many small articles, including dominoes, but sets, or even single pieces, are rare today and desirable collectors' items.

Early in the twentieth century cheap domino sets were made of tinware for use in public houses, often being provided at cost price or even free by tobacco companies as advertisements *(136)*.

(135) Bone birdcage, drum and a mahogany box, sets of miniature double six dominoes. The pound coin is included for size comparison.

136

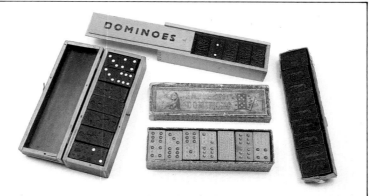

137

(136) Two black plastic advertisement sets (Will's Star and Will's Woodbine), and a white metal domino (Franklyn's Shagg).

(137) Four sets of embossed dominoes.

In 1913 Bakelite appeared, named after L.H. Baekeland, the inventor of a synthetic resin formed by the condensation of phenols and formaldehyde and used as a plastic material for electrical equipment. It was also used for making dominoes.

In the 1930s cheap domino sets (137) were made of wood stained black with white painted pips and with the backs impressed with a wide range of attractive designs. Today, many dominoes are made of modern fire-resistant plastics in a variety of attractive colours.

THE BLOCK GAME

Using a double six set (138) with twenty-eight dominoes.

This is best played by two teams of two partners who sit opposite each other and each team tries to be first to score two hundred points.

Rules

1. The dominoes are placed face downwards on the table; the four players shuffle the 'bones' and then each draws one. The player with the highest number of pips on his bone becomes the first dealer.

2. The four dominoes are returned to the table face downwards and the complete set is shuffled again by the dealer. Each player in clockwise direction from the dealer takes seven dominoes, the last seven becoming the dealer's.

3. Each player places his dominoes on a rack or holds them in his hand in such a way that their faces cannot be seen by the other players.

4. The player holding the double six begins the hand by placing it face upwards onto the table.

5. If possible the player on his left follows by playing a domino to match one of the two open ends by placing a 6: end of a domino against the centre of one side of the 6:6 on the table. If he does not have a 6: he calls 'PASS' and the next player has a chance to match the double-six, fig.58.

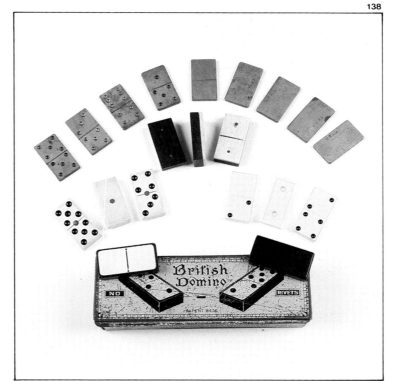

138

(138) A selection of dominoes. From back: nine brass dominoes made of shell casing (Second World War): three bone and ebony dominoes with two sprigs: three bone and ebony dominoes held with one sprig: three all plastic dominoes. In front: Tinware dominoes. Note 'No Rivets' on the box.

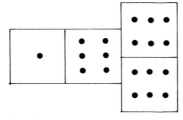

Fig.58

Rules

6.   If the second player has played a domino, the third player then plays on to the other side of the 6:6 or matches the free end of the bone played by the second player. The fourth player then follows in the same manner, playing on to an open end of the layout.
7.   If the layout is running off the table, the newly added bone may be placed at right angles to the open end. All doubles are placed across the direction of progress, fig. 59.

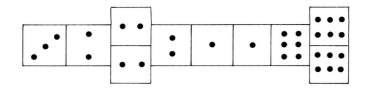

Fig.59

8.   If a player is unable to match the free ends, he calls 'PASS' and waits for his turn to come around again.
9.   When one of the players plays his last bone he calls 'DOMINO'. The pips on the dominoes in the opponent's hands are added up and score for the winning team.
10.   If no player can match an open end, the hand is *blocked* and the team holding the least number of pips on its bones wins the hand and is credited with the total pips in its opponents' hands.
11.   The new hand is started by the player who called 'DOMINO' in the previous hand or by the partner with the lesser number of pips of the winning team in a blocked hand. He can start with any one of his seven dominoes. If he starts with a mixed number the higher end is placed nearer to him.
12.   If both teams have equal scores in a blocked hand, it is a *Washout* with no scoring and the same dealer shuffles the dominoes for the next hand.
13.   If the previous hand has ended as a *washout*, the holder of the double-six leads.
14.   The player on the right of the winner of the previous hand becomes the dealer in the next and shuffles the dominoes; the winner takes his seven dominoes first and the dealer his seven dominoes last.
15.   The score for each hand is written down and also the running total until one team reaches 200 points.

TWO-HANDED BLOCK GAME

The rules are the same with the following exceptions:
1.   The player drawing the higher domino becomes the first starter.
2.   Each player draws seven dominoes and the fourteen dominoes remaining stay face downwards on the table to form the 'Boneyard'.
3.   The starter may begin by playing any domino.
4.   When a player cannot match either end of the layout, he draws from the boneyard until he is able to do so or until only two dominoes remain in the boneyard when he passes. His opponent then plays on until either he goes out or cannot play, when the hand ceases and the player with the lower number of pips wins the hand and scores the number of pips held by his opponent.

Penalties

If a player draws too few dominoes in a two-handed game, he must complete the hand from the boneyard as soon as the error is discovered.

If he draws too many dominoes, he must keep them in his hand.

If a player plays a domino that does not match, he must correct the error on request, but if the error is unnoticed until another bone has been played, the faulty matching stands.

If a player in a two-handed game takes one or more dominoes from the boneyard when he has a bone in his hand that he could have played, he must declare that he has overdrawn and ten points are deducted from his score. But if he fails to announce an overdraw and it is pointed out by the other player, he is penalized twenty points.

If a domino is exposed before the game starts, the dominoes must be reshuffled.

In any four-handed game, no information must be exchanged between players. Any player doing so loses his team the hand.

If a player makes a move to play on to a particular domino, he must complete the play if possible.

ALL FIVES

This game is for two or three players or for four playing as two teams. The players try to be first to score *exactly* sixty-one points. A cribbage board is often used for keeping score.

Rules

1.   Each player draws a domino. The player with the highest number of pips starts.
2.   The dominoes are returned face downwards to the table and after a reshuffle each player draws five dominoes. The remainder forms a boneyard.
3.   The starter of each hand may play any domino. The first

double played is open to play on all four sides, no matter when it is added to the layout.

4.   Points are scored by winning hands as in the block game, but points are also scored during play by forming multiples of five. After each player's turn the total of the pips on the open ends are counted, and if the total is five it earns 1 point, if ten 2 points, if fifteen 3 points, and if twenty 4 points. See fig. 60.

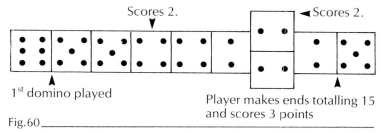

Scores 2.   ◀Scores 2.

1st domino played

Player makes ends totalling 15 and scores 3 points

Fig.60

5.   The number of pips on the free end of the domino just played may be *subtracted* from the total of the other ends of the layout instead of being *added*, if this helps to make a multiple of five.

6.   The first player (or team if four are playing) to reach exactly 61 wins the hand. If the score overshoots 61, the points causing the overshoot are lost. For example, if a player's score stood at 58 and he scored 4 points for making a layout with ends totalling 20 pips, his score would remain at 58, and the hand continues. If he managed to score 3 points with a total of 15 pips at the ends of the layout, his total would be 61 points and he would win the hand, and in addition win a point for every pip still held by his opponents.

7.   Game is usually the first player (or team) to reach 200 points.

DOMINO POOL

A pool is created by four players, each putting a stake on the table. Each player is on his own and, after the dominoes have been shuffled face-downwards in the centre of the table, each takes five dominoes. The holder of the highest domino leads and the player on his left tries to follow, but if he is unable to do so, the turn passes clockwise around the table.

Method of scoring

1.   When one player has no dominoes left in his hand, the other players' pips are counted on their remaining bones and each player's total is scored against his name.

2.   If all the players are blocked, the scores are recorded in the same way.

3.   When a player has 100 points he is OUT. The player

139

(139) Two double nine and a double six domino sets and three embossed dominoes.

surviving his opponents wins the game and the pool.

4.   By prior agreement, *starring* may be permitted. If a player is out, he may star by paying another stake into the pool. He then re-enters the game with the same score against him as the player in the worst position. Players are not compelled to star and can only do so once. The last two players in the game are not allowed to star, although they may have done so before they reached this position.

GAMES USING A DOUBLE-NINE SET
THE MATADOR GAME

In this game, using a double-nine set *(139)*, the bones are added to the layout to form sums of ten instead of in matching pairs; the sum of the two approximating bone ends must add up to ten unless one of the special MATADOR bones is used. A nine is added to a one, an eight to a two etc. Only a matador may be played on to a blank. There are six of these: 9-1, 8-2, 7-3, 6-4, 5-5, and the 00. A matador may be played at any time, fig. 61.

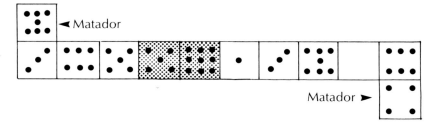

◀Matador

Matador ▶

Fig.61

Method of play
1. After shuffling, each player draws a domino, the player with the highest double, or failing a double, the bone with the greatest number of pips, becomes the leader.
2. The dominoes are returned to the table and re-shuffled. If there are three to six players each draws seven dominoes. If there are more, then each player draws only five.
3. The leader plays a double if he has one, if not, then his highest domino. If a double nine is led, it must be joined at either side with a 1 by the next player. If he hasn't a 1 he must play a matador or draw from the pool until he obtains a 1 or a matador. If he played a 1-5, the end spots would then be a 9 or 5. The next player must play a 1 to the 9, or a 5 to the 5.
4. When a player cannot make a TEN and does not wish to play a matador, or hasn't one, he must draw from the boneyard until he can play or until only two dominoes are left in it. If he has failed to draw a playable domino he must play a matador if he has one.
5. When one player has drawn all but the last two dominoes from the pool, and cannot make a TEN, nor play a matador, he calls 'PASS'. If no other player can play, the game is BLOCKED and the player holding the lowest number of pips scores the pips held in his opponents' hands.
6. If a player plays his last domino he cries 'OUT', and scores all the pips held in his opponents' hands.
7. A game is usually for 200 points.

(140) A double twelve set of dominoes, USA c.1947.

CYPRUS

This game, for any number of players up to ten, begins by the dominoes being shuffled face downwards on the table and then the players draw their bones:

Number of players	Number of Dominoes
4	13
5	11
6	9
7	7
8 or 9	6
10	5

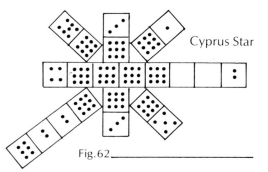

Cyprus Star

Fig.62

The remaining dominoes are left face downwards on the table and are not used.

Method of play
1. The holder of the double-nine puts it face up on the table. If no one has the double-nine, the dominoes are reshuffled and redrawn.
2. In clockwise order the players may play 9s to form a star, see fig. 62, or match the ends of 9s already played.
3. The first player to play his last bone calls 'DOMINO' and wins the hand.
4. If no player can play a 9 or match an end, the game is BLOCKED and the player with the least number of pips wins and scores the pips held in his opponents' hands. If two players have the same low count, the game is drawn and no one scores.

140

GAMES WITH DOUBLE-TWELVE DOMINOES

TIDDLE-A-WINK

Double-twelve sets are scarce *(140)* but they are manufactured by the Milton Bradley Company of Springfield, Massachusetts, U.S.A. A set contains ninety-one bones.

Rules

1. Six to ten players can take part.
2. The dominoes are shuffled and each player starts with an equal number. Any left over are discarded for the round but are shuffled in again for the next.
3. The player holding the highest double leads; double-twelve is called for and if no one holds it, double-eleven, or in its absence the next highest double which is placed face up in the middle of the table.
4. The player on the starter's left then tries to match the opening bone. When a player is unable to match he calls 'PASS'.
5. When a player plays a double, either when leading or during the game, it is placed at right angles to the direction of the layout *and he has another turn.*
6. The first player to play his last bone calls 'TIDDLE-A-WINK' and receives a point for every pip held in his opponents' hands.
7. If the round becomes blocked and no one is able to match an open end, the player with the lowest number of pips in his hand wins and scores the number of pips left in play. If two hands are equally low, then a hand with the lower number of pieces wins but if this is also equal, then the hand is drawn and is abandoned with no one scoring.
8. Game is usually 200 points but may be more or less by agreement.

References: Bell, R.C. *Discovering Dice and Dominoes*, Shire Publications Ltd, 1980. Berndt, F. *The Domino Book*. Thomas Nelson Inc. New York, U.S.A. 1974. Leeflang, K.W.H. *Domino Games and Domino Puzzles*, Hamlyn Publishing Group, 1976.

CHINESE DOMINOES

Cubic dice were imported into China from India in the distant past, but the Chinese are credited with the invention of little tablets which represented the throws of two dice. The tablets we now know as dominoes.

Chinese dominoes *(141)* differ from those of the west in several particulars. They are usually much larger; a set consists of thirty-two bones instead of twenty-eight and there are no blanks. Several pieces, however, are duplicated. These form the Civil Series. Unpaired tiles form the rival Military series. In some games the distinction is important, although not in *Disputing Tens*, the game described here. Chinese dominoes are made of ivory, bone, wood, or more recently, and now most commonly, or plastic. They are still known however, as *Kwat p'ai* (bone tablets). These incised spots of 1s and 4s are red, and the rest are white if the pieces are black, or black if the pieces are white. The pips of the double six tile are usually half red and half white.

Most games start with the tiles stacked in a woodpile, fig. 63. Only one of many games using Chinese dominoes will be described.

(141) Three sets of Chinese dominoes, two plastic and one wooden; with a set of bamboo tallies in a bamboo box.

A wood pile of 4 x 8 tiles

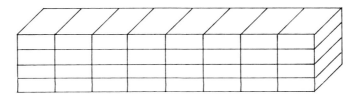

Fig.63

DISPUTING TENS (China)

One set of dominoes is used in this game for two players.

Rules

1. The tiles are shuffled face downwards on the table and then stacked, still face downwards in a 'woodpile' four high and eight long.
2. The players divide the pile between themselves, each taking four of the stacks.
3. The first player draws the top piece from the first stack at the right of his pile and lays it face up on the table.
4. The second player then draws a piece from his pile and lays it face up alongside the piece played by the first player.
5. They continue to draw and place the pieces on the table at either end of the row of upturned tiles.
6. If a player puts down a tile which is a duplicate of one of the pieces at either end of the row, he takes both pieces to make a PAIR. At the end of the game they count ten for each spot on them.
7. If a player puts down a domino and its spots make a multiple of ten when added to those of the pieces at both ends of the row, or with the two tiles at either end of the row, he lifts the three pieces and at the end of the game each spot on them counts one point.
8. If there are only two pieces on the table and a player takes them, he piles them on top of each other to make a sweep, which counts forty points. He then draws from his pile and lays out another piece.
9. If a player fails to take up a scoring combination of two or three tiles, his opponent may take them, and then lay out a piece from his own stack, and the game continues.
10. The game ends when one of the players has laid out all his tiles, and the player with the highest score wins.

MAH-JONGG

The history of *Mah-jongg* is uncertain but is appears to have originated among boatmen living on the great rivers of China, and was played with a special pack of cards *(142)*.

As cards were liable to be blown overboard by the wind, pieces of bamboo were glued to the backs of the cards and later bamboo faced with bone or ivory replaced the paper. The game does not have a long history. The first western report of *Mah-jongg* seems to be the description by Stewart Culin in his 'Chinese Games with Dice and Dominoes' contained in the *Report of the National Museum*, 1893. He describes a set of pieces in the Museum of the Long Island Historical Society, Brooklyn, New York. To quote:

'There are 141 marked pieces and two blanks. They are made of bamboo with a bone or ivory face, which is skilfully mortised to the wood, and measures ⅞ by ⅝ by ⅜ inches [22 by 16 by 10mm].'

There are important observations in Culin's early account of the game. What we now call *Mah-jongg* was then regarded as a variety of dominoes and the sets varied considerably in different parts of China. *Mah-jongg* is now one of the world's great gambling games, especially among the Chinese and, as played by them, permits quick exchanges of money, a hand lasting between five and six minutes and four whole rounds being finished in two to two-and-a-half hours.

The introduction of the game into the clubs of Canton, Shanghai and other foreign settlements in China led to the addition of Arabic numerals to the tiles to help quick identifications by the ex-patriots a practice continued for sets being exported to America and Europe. The sets for home use have Chinese characters only. Fig.63a.

Fig.63a

Mah-jongg is unusual among gambling games in being an excellent game in its own right without the stimulus of a money interest. The elaborate preliminaries described below have been devised to make cheating difficult but if the game is being played within the family or with friends for fun, most of the intricacies can be set aside.

Equipment

The basic *Mah-jongg* set consists of one hundred and thirty-six tiles of three suits Bamboos, Characters and Circles each suit consisting of four tiles of each number from one to nine. The Ones and Nines of the suits are major tiles and scoring formations of these tiles are worth twice

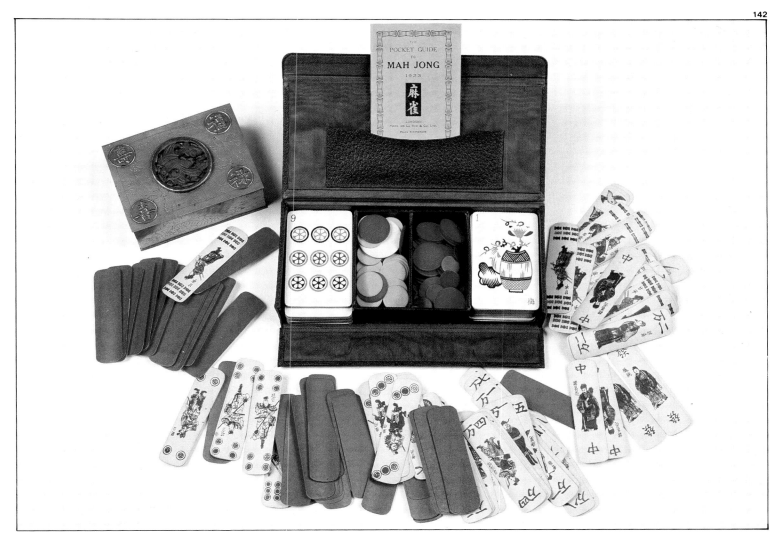

(142) Chinese *Mah-jongg* cards in front with a brass and jade box; provenance unknown. Behind are western *Mah-jongg* cards, rule book and counters.

the amount of the minor tiles numbered from two to eight. There are also three sets of Honour tiles, with four of each kind of Dragon, Red, Green and White and there are four sets of Cardinal tiles, each consisting of four tiles of East Wind, South Wind, West Wind and North Wind. These honour tiles in scoring formations are worth twice the value of the minor tiles.

In addition to the basic one hundred and thirty-six tiles described above, there are four Flower tiles which are numbered from One to Four in green and four Season tiles which are numbered One to Four in red. The designs on these tiles differ from set to set, the red or green numbering alone being significant. Many players ignore them and a description of their use will be deferred until the end of this account.

Traditional Chinese *Mah-jongg* sets (143), are made of thin plates of bone or ivory dove-tailed into a backing of bamboo. The thicker the bone, the more expensive the set. Some sets are housed in richly carved or lacquered caskets. In recent years, cheap sets have been made in composition or plastic materials, though even these will cost £20 or more. Players should buy the best set they can afford; a good set is a delight to handle and adds greatly to the enjoyment of the game.

With the set are one hundred and twenty-eight bone tallies, two pairs of dice, a tong box to hold four wind indicators and, as an optional item, four tile stands, one for each player's tiles. Four blank tiles are included to replace any that may be lost. The bone tallies are some 3 inches (7.5cm) long. In some cheaper sets the tallies are narrow strips of bamboo. At the beginning of each game each player takes:-

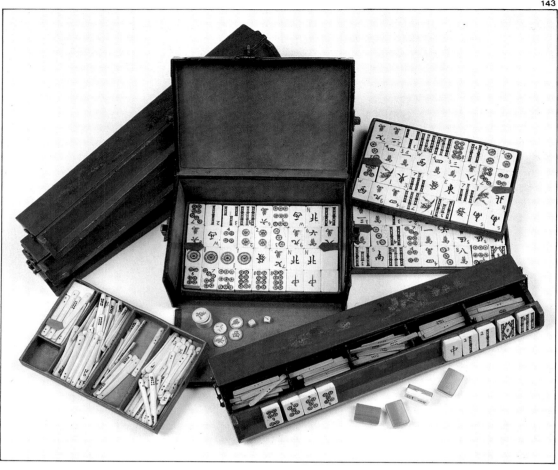

(143) Bone and bamboo *Mah-jongg* sets in a leather case, with red lacquered racks, *c.*1930.

Two tallies with five red spots each end, value 500 points —————————— 1,000

Ten tallies with one red spot each end, value 100 points each —————————— 1,000

Ten tallies with ten black spots each end, value 10 points each —————————— 100

Ten tallies with two black spots each end, value 2 points each —————————— 20

Total 2,120

There are two other less common ways of marking the tallies but equivalents for these can be worked out in line with the scoring given above.

Position of players

In home games this is unimportant but when money is involved the order of play may be crucial. The standard method in clubs is for the four players to stand around the table and one of them casts a pair of dice. The sum of the pips is noted and the caster starting with himself counts each player around the table in an anticlockwise direction, placing the tong box in front of the player where the count ends.

After placing the tong box, the caster shuffles the four round direction discs face downwards on the table and then piles them on top of each other face downwards. He then throws the dice again and counts out the number thrown around the four players starting with himself. The player indicated by the count draws the top disc from the pile and the other players take a disc in turn anticlockwise from the player who lifted the top disc. The player drawing the East Wind disc sits in front of the tong and the other players take up their positions, South on his right, West opposite and North on his left. The players place their direction discs into the tong with North at the bottom, then West, then South and finally East on the top. This indicates that East is the prevailing wind for the round. (See later.) The first East remains banker for the complete game and distributes the tallies. See fig. 64. Note that these positions do not correspond with the positions of the points of the compass.

East retains the tong until he loses a hand, when it moves

to the player on East's right who was South, but becomes the new East for the hand. The East wind indicator remains on the top of the tong to show that the prevailing wind is East. This round ends when the fourth player to the East loses the hand. He takes the East Wind indicator out of the tong, exposing the South indicator, signifying that the South Wind is prevailing for the round and hands the tong to the original East who becomes the first East of the South Wind round. A game consists of four complete rounds, each round with a different prevailing wind. The tong indicates the Wind of the Round and who is East in that particular hand. Chinese players generally play four to eight games in an evening.

The deal

At the start of each hand, East places the tiles face downwards on the table and they are shuffled by East and West. Each player then builds a wall seventeen tiles long

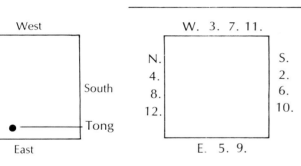

Fig.64

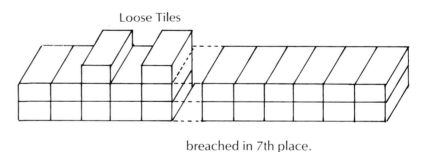

Fig.64a

than seventeen, the player's throw alone is used in deciding where the wall should be broken. The two displaced tiles are known as LOOSE TILES and have special importance, described later. East lifts the first two pairs of tiles from the wall at the breach away from the loose tiles. South takes the next two pairs, West the next two and North the next two pairs. East then takes two more pairs until all the players have twelve tiles on their racks. East then takes the top piece of the next pair and the top piece of the next pair but one. South takes the bottom tile of the first pair, West the top tile of the second pair and North the bottom tile of the second pair. If the end of the wall is reached during this procedure, the lifting continues from the adjacent wall, meeting it at the corner. As each player takes his tiles from the wall, he places them on his rack with their faces towards him, but out of the view of his opponents. East starts with fourteen tiles and the other three players with thirteen each. At the end of the 'deal', seven pairs of tiles including

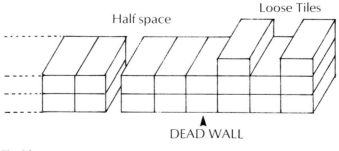

Loose Tiles

breached in 7th place.

Fig.65

and two high, face downwards in front of himself, unless the Flower and Season tiles are being used when the wall are eighteen tiles long. The completed square represents the walls of a city and the corners should meet accurately to prevent mistakes when drawing tiles from the wall during play.

When the walls are finished East casts the two dice again. Starting with himself the score is counted out anticlockwise on the walls, 5 or 9 indicating East's wall, 2, 6 or 10, South's wall; 3, 7 or 11, West's wall, and 4, 8 or 12 North's wall. See fig.64a.

The player whose wall is to be breached takes the dice and casts again. He adds the number that he has thrown to that thrown by East and counts this total number clockwise, starting from the right-hand end of his wall and he breaches the wall by removing the two tiles at the end of the count, the lower tile of the pair being placed face downwards on the pair of pieces to the left of the breach and the upper tile on the pair next but one to the left, fig.65.

If the total of the player's throw and East's throw is more

Half space

Loose Tiles

DEAD WALL

Fig.66

the loose tiles are moved a little away from the rest of the wall to form a DEAD WALL, fig. 66. These tiles are not used in play, except when a *quong* is formed.

When each player has sorted out his hand by placing tiles of the same suit into groups and arranging similar Winds and Dragons together, he closes any gaps to prevent his opponents guessing the number of tiles of individual suits or Honour tiles he holds.

The aim of the game

The object of the game is to collect four sets of three identical tiles and a pair. Sets of three tiles of a kind are known as PUNGS and the matching pair is the SPARROW'S HEAD. The first player to complete this collection calls 'Mah-jongg' and wins the hand. As an alternative to a *pung*, the hand may contain one or more runs of three tiles, each run known as a CHOW, which does not score but helps to go *Mah-jongg*. Instead of a *pung* the player may collect four of a kind known as a QUONG and scores extra points.

When the first player has completed his hand and called 'Mah-jongg' he wins the hand, reckons up his score, the other players reckoning up their scores and settlements are made between them using the bone tallies. At the end of the game the tallies are cashed for money or prizes. Many players find it easier to keep the scores on a piece of paper with a pencil.

After each hand the tiles are shuffled, the walls built, breached and the tiles distributed as already described. A complete game consists of four rounds of at least four hands each, but by agreement play may stop at the end of any hand or round.

Method of play

East begins by discarding a tile from his hand and places it face downwards on the table and within the city walls, calling out its description — Six Characters, White Dragon, Two Circles, etc. Beginners may prefer to discard the tiles face upwards and this is customary in the American form of the game. See later.

The turn of play in *Mah-jongg* passes anticlockwise to the right, from East to South, South to West, West to North, North to East etc. After East discards his first tile any player having two of the same tile may pick it up, calling 'PUNG'. He then puts his two similar tiles beside it face up on the table to his right and discards a tile from his hand on to the table within the city walls. If a discarded tile is *punged* by a player not on the immediate right of the discarder, the intervening players lose their turn of play.

If a player whose turn is next can use the tile just discarded to make a run of three consecutive numbers in the same suit with two tiles held in his hand, he may take up the piece by calling 'CHOW' and placing the sequence face up on the table at his right. He then discards a tile from his hand in the usual manner. Only the player on the right of the discarder can *chow* a discarded tile. This is a non-scoring combination.

If a player has three tiles similar to a tile just discarded, he may pick it up, calling 'QUONG' and place the four tiles face up on the table on his right. He then draws the loose tile from the wall furthest from the breach, or if that tile has already been drawn, the other loose tile. He then discards

a tile from his hand on to the centre of the table in the usual way. When both loose tiles have been lifted, the two tiles nearest to the breach are taken up and put into the loose tile positions and two tiles are moved across the half gap from the active wall to keep the sum of the tiles in the dead wall at fourteen.

A completed hand containing a *quong* will contain fifteen tiles; should there be two *quongs* there would be sixteen tiles etc. The loose tiles are used to provide these extra tiles for *quongs* and if a player forgets to take a loose tile from the wall on forming a *quong* he will not be able to form a complete hand, and his hand becomes *dead*. Any player may form a *quong* and if he is not the player on the discarder's right then the intervening players lose their turn of play. If no one *pungs*, *chows*, or *quongs* a discarded tile, the player on the right of the discarder draws a tile from the open end of the wall, examines it and may take it into his hand and discard another from his hand in its place. The turn of play then passes to the player on his right, who in turn draws from the wall if the discarded tile is not claimed. Only the last tile discarded can be taken up into a player's hand; the rest are out of play. Drawing from the wall must be from the open end and the upper tile is taken before the lower.

A player may be dealt a *pung* or may form one with a tile drawn from the wall. The combination is retained in the hand as a CONCEALED PUNG and has twice the scoring value of a similar EXPOSED PUNG.

If a player has an exposed *pung* on the table and draws a fourth tile of the set from the wall, he may add it to the *pung* making an EXPOSED QUONG; he then draws a loose tile from the wall and discards a tile from his hand in the usual way. He may decide not to declare the exposed *quong* but take the tile into his hand to make a *chow*. If this is done, he does not take a loose tile from the wall but discards a tile from his hand in the ordinary way.

A CONCEALED QUONG may occur in the player's original hand or may be acquired by one or more draws from the wall. At any time when it is his turn to play he may place the four tiles on the table, with the two central tiles face downwards to denote that it is a concealed *quong* and then draw a loose tile from the wall and discard a piece from his hand. He may not draw a loose tile from the wall until the concealed *quong* is placed on the table and if another player calls *Mah-jongg* while the *quong* is still in his hand, it scores only as a concealed *pung*.

If two players call for a discarded tile, there is an order of priority.
1. If both players require the tile to go *Mah-jongg*, the player whose turn would come first takes the piece.
2. If one player needs it to go *Mah-jongg*, even if forming a *chow* to do so, he has precedence.
3. If one player requires a tile for a *pung* or a *quong* and

the other for a *chow*, the *chow* is unsuccessful, except as under (1) or (2) above.

4. If a player is FISHING — that is only requiring one tile to complete his hand for *Mah-jongg*, he may claim the fourth tile from an exposed *quong*, a manoeuvre known as ROBBING THE QUONG. A concealed *quong* is safe from this attack.

A player can take up a discard from the table for a *pung*, *chow* or *quong*, even if the next player has drawn a tile from the wall, but the moment he makes his discard the previous discard is out of play. If a discarded tile is claimed after a player has taken one from the wall, the latter must be replaced and the player loses his turn.

When a player calls *Mah-jongg*, all the players expose their hands for scoring. A *pung* held in the hand is laid down with the central tile turned face downwards to indicate that it is a concealed *pung*, and it scores double. The player who goes *Mah-jongg* does not discard a tile and therefore has fourteen tiles in his hand and the other players having only thirteen unless they have formed a quong. In the Chinese game, the *pungs*, *quongs* and *chows* may be of any suit or Honour tiles to go *Mah-jongg*. This does not apply to the American game where the hand must be cleared, that is, contain only tiles of one suit with Honour and Cardinal tiles.

If no one has gone *Mah-jongg* before the last fourteen tiles of the dead wall are reached, including loose tiles, the hand is DEAD. There is no scoring, the tiles are reshuffled and a fresh hand is begun: East of the dead hand remaining East for the new hand, but he loses this privilege at the end of the extra hand, even if he goes *Mah-jongg*.

In the American game because of the insistence on a hand going *Mah-jongg* being cleared, there is no dead wall and all the tiles are used, the loose tiles being replaced in their original position at the end of the wall and drawn as the last two tiles in the ordinary course of play. The other major change is that a *Mah-jongg* hand may only contain one chow. Because the hands have to be cleared the games last longer and the scores tend to be much higher.

Scoring

Exposed *pung*, two points (minor tiles); four points (Major, Cardinal or Honour tiles).
Concealed *pung*, four points (minor tiles); eight points (Major, Cardinal or Honour tiles).
Exposed *quong,* eight points (minor tiles); sixteen points (Major, Cardinal or Honour tiles).
Concealed *quong*, 16 points (minor tiles); 32 points (Major, Cardinal or Honour tiles).

Sparrow's head
Pair of any Dragons; two points.
Pair of the player's own Wind; two points.
Pair of the Wind of the Round; two points. (This is optional; many players do not recognize this pair as a scoring formation)

No other pairs score, and only one scoring pair is permitted in any unfinished hand. *Chows* do not score.

Bonus scoring for the player going *Mah-jongg*
For going *Mah-jongg*; 20 points.
Winning tile drawn from the wall; two points.
Winning with the only possible tile; two points.
Winning with a standing hand; one hundred points (See below.)

All bonus scores are added to the basic score of the winner's hand before starting to double.

Doubles
The player's score is doubled if he holds:
a *pung* or *quong* of the player's own Wind (double once);
a *pung* or *quong* of the Wind of the Round (double once);
a *pung* or *quong* of any Dragon (double once);
the following doubles apply only to the winning hand:
for no *chows* in the hand (double once);
no scoring value in the hand all *chows* and a non-scoring sparrow's head (double once);
winning the last tile from the wall (double once);
winning with a loose tile (double once);
robbing a *quong* to go *Mah-jongg* (double once);
only one suit except for Honour and Cardinal tiles , i.e. cleared (double once);
hand of Ones and Nines with Winds or Dragons (double once);
hand entirely of one suit (double three times).

In settlement of scores East receives and pays double. The score is doubled for each doubling combination in a hand. If a player holds a *pung* of Dragons and a *pung* of his own Wind which also happened to be the Wind of the Round, he would double his basic score three times.

There is a special rule regarding a STANDING HAND. If a player is *fishing*, (i.e. requiring only one tile to go *Mah-jongg)* after he has drawn and discarded for the first time, he may declare a standing hand. This also applies to East after his first discard. A player declaring a standing hand is not permitted to discard from his hand but discards tiles taken from the wall until he is able to go *Mah-jongg* either with a discard, or with a tile drawn from the wall. Going Mah-jong with a standing hand is worth an additional 100 points to the basic score.

Mistakes in play
If a player's hand contains more or less than thirteen tiles after discarding, excluding the extra tiles in exposed quongs, his hand is dead and he cannot go *Mah-jongg*. He continues to play and at the end of the hand he pays the other players their due, without deducting his own score if he holds too many tiles, but if he holds too few his score is deducted before payment.

Most Chinese players recognize two special hands, both of which score a limit. As it is possible, though rare to acquire extremely high scoring hands running to over one hundred thousand points, it is usual to set a limit before a game. This is commonly two thousand points, the maximum any player can win on a single hand; East winning or losing double this amount.

The Thirteen Unique Wonders hand consists of a One and a Nine from each suit, one of each Wind, one of each Dragon and a duplicate of any one of these tiles to form the sparrow's head. Score, a limit.

The Calling Nine hand This consists of a *pung* of Ones, a *pung* of Nines, and the complete run from Two to Eight, all in the same suit with another tile of the same suit to make the pair.

Settling scores

Each player pays the *Mah-jongg* hand in turn, starting with the player on the winner's right. East then declares his total and settles with each of the other players in turn; then the two remaining players settle their scores. Should East win, South scores next and settles with West and North. West and North then settle with each other. The *Mah-jongg* hand is paid in full, but the other players pay each other the *difference* in their scores.

Undeclared *quongs* do not score. A player with a concealed *pung* may *pung* the fourth tile as it is discarded and declare a *pung* on the table, he may not add the fourth tile to the *pung* unless it is his turn to play. If another player goes *Mah-jongg* before he declares the fourth tile he cannot score anything for it; it is regarded as part of a *chow*. There is one exception to this rule: if a player draws a *quong* in his original hand and another player goes *Mah-jongg* before he has had the opportunity to declare it, it counts as a concealed *quong*.

Rounds

The first round is East Wind's Round and continues until every player has been East. The next round belongs to South Wind, starting with the original East player of the first round. The third round is West Wind's round and the last round is North Wind's. The first game ends when North has lost being East four times.

Penalties

If the wall is breached in the wrong place or if tiles are drawn in the wrong order, the tiles are reshuffled and a new start is made. A player putting down an incorrect combination as a *chow*, *pung*, or *quong* must correct it before the next player discards, or his hand becomes dead.

If a player calls *Mah-jongg*, exposes his hand completely and then finds that he has made a mistake, he pays the other three players *double the limit*. If the hand has not been completely exposed before he discovers the mistake, he may cancel his call, and take his tiles up again, unless another player has exposed any of his tiles, when the defaulter must pay the penalty mentioned above.

If a player is making a hand of all one suit and has three

pungs, *quongs*, or *chows* on the table, and another player discards a tile which enables the first player to go *Mah-jongg*, the discarding player must pay the winner the losses of the other two players as well as his own.

FLOWER AND SEASON TILES

Some players still use these tiles which increase the element of luck. The four flower tiles have Chinese characters in green and are numbered from 1 to 4; the Four Seasons are in red and are also numbered from 1 to 4. The design on these extra tiles vary from set to set.

If the original hand dealt to east contains one or more of these tiles, they are laid face up on the table at his right, and he draws a loose tile from the wall to replace each one. This is done before he makes his first discard. The other players do the same when it is their turn to play, *after* taking up a tile and *before* discarding.

If a player draws a Flower or Season tile from the wall, or as a loose tile after making a *quong*, he lays it down and draws a loose tile before discarding. Should the loose tile so drawn be a Flower or Season, the player must wait for his next turn to lay it down and draw another loose tile.

Each Flower or Season tile in a player's hand counts 4 points, but each Wind is considered to own one Flower and one Season. Number One's belong to East, number Two's to South, number Three's to West and number Four's to North. A player getting a Flower or Season of his own Wind doubles his score and a player getting a complete set of Flowers or Seasons doubles his score three times. Playing with Flowers and Seasons increases the scoring considerably because of the doubling. When playing for money and using these tiles, fixing a limit becomes important.

References: Bell, R.C *Discovering Mah-jong*, Shire Publications Ltd, 1976, 1978, reprinted 1979,1982. Robertson, M. *The Game of Mah-jong*, Whitcombe & Tombs Ltd, 7th edn, undated, *c.* 1940.

TOPS (England)

Also called 'The Number Game' *(144)* the equipment consists of six sets of plastic tiles numbered one to twenty in blue, produced by Spears Games, 1965.

Rules

1. The dealer places the tiles on the table face downwards and all the players shuffle them well. The dealer then shares out all the tiles. Note that 120 can be divided exactly by 2,3,4,5,6, the number of players that can take part.
2. The players build up their tiles face downwards into a stack in front of themselves, without examining them.
3. Play consists mainly of forming six stacks of tiles in the

stack. This can be done with the next higher number, e.g. 16 on a 15. If the player turns up a 1, he starts a new central stack.

(c)   If (a) or (b) is not possible, the top tile of the Player's personal 'face-down' pile is turned over and if possible played as in (a) or (b).

(d)   If the top tile from the personal stack cannot be played, it is placed on the player's 'face-up' stack.

6.   Whenever a player disposes of a tile, either on to a centre stack or onto an opponent's 'face-up' pile, he has another turn. The turn ends when a tile has to be placed on his own 'face-up' stack.

7.   If a player makes a mistake the other players call out 'WRONG', and each player hands him one of his tiles, which are placed on the wrongdoer's 'face-up' stack.

8.   When a player has exhausted his 'face-down' stack, he turns over his 'face-up' stack and carries on.

9.   The first player to get rid of all his tiles is the winner. Play continues, to settle the order of success of the other players.

(144) Set of 'Tops' tiles and box.

RUMMIKUB (Israel)

Rummikub appears to have been invented in Israel and marketed there by E. Hertzano. The author watched several games being played outside a café by students in a small town in Turkey in 1985.

In 1980 it was manufactured by the Pressman Toy Corporation, N.Y., N.Y. under licence. In the game illustrated *(145)* there is no maker's name on the case or tiles, but the accompanying book of rules *Playing Rummy the American Way and International Way* was printed in Taiwan, strongly suggesting the same source for the set and that it was a pirated production.

The Pressman rules for *Rummikub* and the Taiwan rules for 'The American Way' are the same, but the 'International way of Playing' in the second part of the Taiwan Pamphlet describes a much more complicated game called *Rumm-eee*. This will not be described here.

Equipment

106 engraved plastic tiles.
4 two-tier racks for holding the tiles.
A book of rules.

The suit colours are black, red, blue and yellow. The object of the game is to be first in emptying one's rack of tiles.

Rules

1.   The tiles are placed face-downwards on the table and shuffled. Each player takes a tile, and the player picking the highest number plays first, the others following in an anticlockwise direction. The lifted tiles are replaced face downwards and reshuffled.

2.   Each player in turn takes fourteen tiles and places them on

centre of the table, each stack starting with 1,2,3, etc and ending up with 20. These are known as CENTRE STACKS.

4.   The first player on the left of the dealer starts play by taking the top tile off his personal stack and turns it over. If it is a 1, he places it in the middle of the table face up, and takes the next tile off his stack. If this is a 2 he puts it on the 1 and carries on as long as he turns over the next number in sequence. The first tile he cannot place, he puts down face upwards in front of himself as the start of his personal FACE UP pile. This ends his turn.

5.   The next player on the left follows, but the play is a little different.

(a)   He looks to see if the top tile of his 'face-up' pile can be placed on any other player's 'face-up' stack. This can be done with the next higher or lower number, i.e. a 5 or a 7 can be placed on a 6.

(b)   If (a) is not possible, he tries to put a tile on a centre

his rack, arranging them in MELDS (sets) as far as possible. These may be RUNS (a sequence of at least three tiles of the same colour) or GROUPS (three or four tiles of the same number but in different colours).

3. The rest of the tiles are then arranged in stacks of seven face downwards, forming a POOL.

Play begins with the placing on the table of at least one MELD totalling 30 points. This requires a group or run or combination that totals 30 points or more. A player who does not have an opening meld draws a tile from the pool and the turn to play passes to the next player. A joker used in the opening meld will bear the face value of the tile it represents. Once an opening meld has been made, a player in his turn may add to any existing melds on the table to complete a set to MANIPULATE.

MANIPULATING This may be carried out in four ways:

a) By adding one or more tiles from the player's rack to a run; or the fourth colour to a group. e.g. 3,4,5 plus 6 or 9,9,9 plus 9.

b) By adding a fourth tile to a set and removing a tile to form a new set, i.e. there is a yellow run 6,7,8 on the table. The player has a yellow 9, a black 6 and a green 6. By adding the yellow 9 to the run, the yellow 6 may

be removed, to form a new group of 6,6,6 on the table.

c) By splitting. There is a yellow sequence on the table of 5,6,7,8,9. The player has a yellow 7 on his rack which he uses to split the sequence to form two sequences of 5,6,7 and 7,8,9.

d) There are two sets on the table, a yellow run of 1,2,3,4 and a group of 1,1,1,1 (yellow, red, blue and black). The player has a blue 1 which he uses to remove the red 1 from the group and the yellow 1 from the run to form a new group of 1,1,1 (red, yellow and blue).

As an example of manipulation, if the following melds were on the table:

Yellow_____6,7,8.
Red_____6,7,8.
Black_____6,7,8,9,10.

The player has a black 11 and a blue 6 on his rack. He may manipulate the melds to form:
6,6,6, 7,7,7, 8,8,8 and make a new run of 9,10,11. He can then add his blue 6 to form a new group 6,6,6,6.

JOKERS A joker is worth face value when melding, and 30 points when left on a player's rack as another player wins. The joker can be substituted for any other tile: and may be exchanged for the missing tile in a meld as long as it comes from a player's rack.

a) In a group of 6,6 and a joker, the joker can only be replaced by having a 6 of both missing colours.

b) A joker cannot be placed on a player's rack, but must be played in the same turn.

c) A meld that contains a joker cannot be manipulated.

TIME LIMIT Each player has a maximum of 2 minutes for each turn of play. Once a move has been completed the player should declare 'Finished'.

When a player plays the last tile from his rack he has won the game and scores the sum of the tiles on the opponent's racks, while each opponent deducts the total of the tiles on his rack from his score. A score sheet for three games might be:

Player	A	B	C	D
Game 1	+20	−10	−6	−4
Game 2	−6	−7	+18	−5
Game 3	−3	−5	−12	+18
Totals	+11	−22	0	+9

and A merges as the winner of the rubber.

PENALTIES If a player tries to manipulate the melds on the table by moving them and then fails to create new formations, he is penalized by having to take three tiles from the pool on to his rack.

To recapitulate: discarding combinations are sequences of numbers of (one colour, e.g. red 4,5,6, or sets of the same number, e.g. black 6, red 6, yellow 6.

145

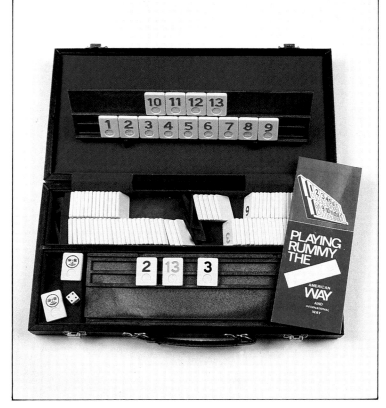

(145) Pirated *Rummikub* set, bought in Singapore, 1979.

TRI-OMINOS (United States of America)

A recent introduction of triangular dominoes made of plastic has led to fascinating problems in linkage. Made in England under licence by Ideal Toy Co. Ltd, Wokingham Berks, they were marketed under the name of Tri-Omininos *(146)* copyright 1968, the Pressman Toy Corporation, N.Y. This game for two to six players uses fifty-six triangular black plastic tiles with each corner marked with a number ranging from 0 to 5. No two tiles are alike. The rules are given on the underside of the cardboard box lid.

Rules

1. One player scores on a piece of paper with a pencil. As each play is made the scorer adds or subtracts the player's points from his total.
2. The winner is the first player to score 400 points. Players may decide on higher or lower targets for longer or shorter games.
3. Each game may consist of several rounds.
4. The tiles are turned face downwards on to the table and well shuffled.
5. Each player picks his own tiles from the pool as follows:-
   When there are two players each takes   9 tiles
   When there are three or four players each takes   7 tiles
   When there are five or six players each takes   5 tiles
   The rest are left on the table as a pool.
6. The players turn their tiles on edge with the numbers facing them, and out of view of their opponents.
7. The player having the highest tile, 5:5:5: starts the round by placing it on the table; if this is not available, then the 4:4:4: or 3:3:3:, 2:2:2:. or 1:1:1: or 0:0:0:. If the three 0's start, there is an extra bonus of 30 points plus the normal bonus of 10 points, as the player beginning a round wins 10 points for doing so, and also the sum of the three numbers on the tile. For example, if the 4:4:4: was played it would score 12 + 10 = 22 points.
8. If the player having the highest triple also has the triple zero, he has the option of playing the latter and collecting the starting bonus of 10 points plus the 30 points for the 0:0:0: tile.
9. If no player has a triple number, then the player with the highest total on one tile leads. He receives the sum of the three numbers for starting, but no bonus of 10 points.
10. The turn of play moves clockwise around the table, the player trying to match any two numbers on the exposed tile. If he can do so he gains the sum of the three numbers on his tile, fig. 67.
11. If a player cannot match, he must pick up a tile from the pool of tiles face-downwards on the table. He also loses 5 points which are deducted from his score. The turn passes to the next player on his left.
12. If a player cannot match any tile on the table and there are none left in the pool, he passes, and 10 points are deducted from his score. The turn then passes to the next player.
13. The first player to play all his tiles wins the round and receives 25 bonus points plus the total points of all the tiles left in the other players' hands.
14. If all the players have passed, the game is BLOCKED. The player having the lowest total of points on his remaining tiles wins the round and adds the total points of all the other player's hands to his score, but he deducts the total of points in his own hand. There are no bonus points. The next round starts in the usual way after reshuffling the tiles.
15. **BONUS SCORING**
    If a player is able to match all three numbers of a formation to make a closed hexagon, he adds the sum of the three numbers on his tile to a bonus score of 50 points. Fig 68.
16. If a player matches two tiles and forms a BRIDGE, he gains the sum of the three numbers plus a bonus of 40 points. Fig 69.
17. If a player matches two sides of a formation he receives the sum of the three numbers on his tile plus 40 bonus points. This can only be done after a bridge has been formed. Fig. 70.
18. When a player reaches 400 points the round being played is completed. If more than one player passes 400 during the round, the winner of the round wins the game; otherwise the player reaching 400 points is the winner of the game, irrespective of whether he wins the last round or not.

This unusual rule can leave the result of the game in doubt up to the last moment of the last round.

(146) Set of Tri-Ominoes pieces and box, *c.*1970.

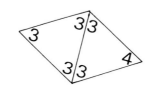

Fig.67

Fig.68

Fig.69

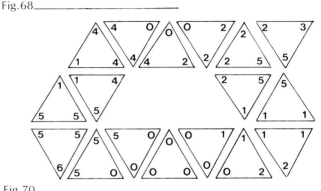

Fig.70

CHAPTER 8

CARD GAMES

REQUIRING BOARDS OR MARKERS

CRIBBAGE (England)

Cribbage is usually a game for two players and a board is used to keep their scores.

Method of play

1. The players cut the pack, low card becomes the dealer and high the *pone* or non-dealer.
2. Each player has two pegs with which he records his score on the board.
3. If a player's first score was two, a peg is placed in the second hole on the outer row of his side of the board. If the next score were 6, the second peg would be placed in the sixth hole beyond the first peg. On the third score, the player would lift his first peg and place it the required number of holes beyond the second peg. Scoring continues in this 'leapfrog' of the pegs.
4. The first player to pass a peg along the sixty holes of the board twice (i.e. score 121 or more) wins the game.
5. The game begins with the cards being shuffled by the dealer and *pone* cuts, leaving the pack divided into two parts on the table, face downwards. The dealer lifts the undermost part and deals six cards to his opponent and then six to himself. The remaining cards are placed on top of the pile.
6. In the first hand of a game, *pone* pegs three holes at the start as compensation for the dealer owning the crib.
7. The players examine their hands and both discard two cards face downwards on to the table.
8. *Pone* again cuts the pack and the dealer turns over the top card of the cut pack and exposes it face upwards on the heap. *Pone* places the cut cards beneath the heap.
9. The exposed card and the four discarded cards form the crib, which belongs to the dealer. The exposed card is also used in making up both players' scores, as well as the crib.
10. If the first card is a Jack, the dealer gains a bonus of two points 'for his heels'.
11. *Pone* leads the first card, calling out its value: court cards and tens count as ten, and the other cards according to the number of their pips. There is no suit preference. Aces count low as one.
12. When the first card has been placed on the table and its value declared, e.g. EIGHT, the dealer will try to win points either playing a SEVEN to make *Fifteen*, or play another EIGHT to make a pair. Either combination earns him two points. If he has neither of these cards he plays something else, e.g. a FOUR and would call out 'Twelve'

147

(147) Three cribbage boards. Left to right: Tonbridge ware, ivory and exotic wood veneer and eighteenth century inlaid wooden board. Scattered across the boards are three shapes of Chinese mother-of-pearl counters. The cards are by Reynolds & Sons, c.1830.

13. *Pone* could then play a THREE to make *Fifteen* (and win 2 points) or a FOUR to make a pair. (2 points). Perhaps neither was possible and he played a QUEEN instead calling 'twenty-two'.

14. If the dealer then played a NINE he would call 'Thirty-one' and take 2 points for playing exactly 31.

15. If a player plays a card bringing the total too near to 31 for the other player to play, the second player calls 'go' and his opponent has to play a card or cards towards the 31, winning 1 point for a *stop*, or 2 points if the total reached is 31 exactly.

16. When 31 or the nearest possible number to it (i.e. a *stop*) has been reached, the player who played the last card leads in the next hand, scoring as before.

To recapitulate: 2 points for fifteen and *thirty-one*; 2 points for making a pair; 6 points for making a pair royal (three cards of a kind) 12 points for a double pair royal (four cards of a kind); three or more cards in sequence, regardless of suit, peg the number of cards in the sequence; 1 point for playing the last card in a stop if the total is under thirty-one.

17. Three or more cards of any suit forming a sequence (2,3,4 etc.) count 1 point for each card in it for the last player. The cards need not be played in order: e.g. if a 5 and a 4 had been played, a 3 or a 6 would form a sequence and score 3 points for the player. If the opponent could then add to this to make a run of four with a 2 or a 7, he would win 4 points. King, Queen, Jack is a sequence, but not Ace, King, Queen. In cribbage Ace counts low.

18. When all the cards have been played out, *pone* picks up his cards and counts the points in his hand.

149

(148) Silver on ebony cribbage board, hallmarked Birmingham 1898. The cards are Hanoverian.

(149) Three cribbage boards. Left to right: Mother-of-pearl and ivory, ivory and Bombay Inlaid Work and carved ivory inlays in sandalwood. The cards were made by C. V. Faulkener & Co London, and were printed in Germany. The court cards are Shakespearean characters from original paintings by John H. Bacon.

(150) Norse ivory cribbage board.

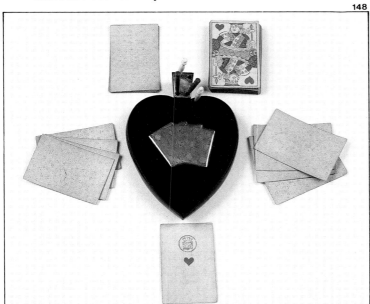

148

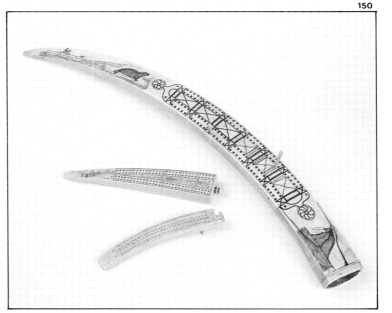

150

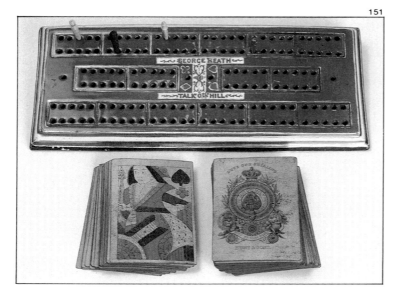

151

(151) Pottery cribbage board and pack of cards, c.1850.

(152) A triangular three-handed cribbage board, c.1890; flanked by three advertisement boards, two for Wills Woodbine cigarettes and the other for Double Diamond beer.

Three combinations are given below to show how the scoring is calculated.

Four fives: Four fifteens = 8; a double pair royal = 12, total = 20 points.

Two sixes, a four and a five: Two fifteens = 4; a pair = 2 and two runs of three = 6, total 12.

A five and three court cards in sequence: Three fifteens = 6; a sequence of three = 3, total 9.

FOUR HANDED CRIBBAGE (England)

In this game the scoring board is used, North and South being partners against East and West. Each player receives five cards and puts one into the crib which belongs to the dealer. The player on the dealer's left leads and has first scoring hand. One partner scores on the board for both. Usually game is one hundred and twenty-one points.

152

Scoring

For a sequence of three, four or five cards	3, 4, or 5 points
For every fifteen, e.g. 7 & 8 or 10, 4, & 1	2 points
For every pair	2 points
For three of a kind, e.g. three 8's (Pair royal)	6 points
For four of a kind (double pair royal)	12 points
For the Jack of the exposed card, 'His nobs'	1 point

19. The exposed card is counted as part of both players' hands and if a player had a sequence of 5,6,7 and the exposed card was 7, this would form two separate sequences and a pair, scoring 3+3+2=8 points.

20. Although all court cards count 10, a pair must be the same card, i.e. two Kings. A King and a Queen are not a pair.

21. *Pone* always counts his score first and at the end of the game it may be important as he may reach 121 and win before his opponent has counted his score. The dealer may also have 121, or even a higher score than his opponent but his score is not counted if the game has already been won by *pone*.

22. In reckoning the value of a hand, the fifteens in it are counted first, then the pairs, pair royal, or double pair royal, followed by the sequences; and if three cards are in sequence and there is a duplicate of any one of them, this makes a double run scoring 6 points, and 2 points for the pair. If three are in sequence and the other two are duplicates of one of them, this constitutes a triple run of three (9 points) and a pair royal (6 points) totalling 15 points.

23. If all the cards in the hand are of the same suit the player scores a *flush*, worth 5 points, and if the exposed card is of the same suit, then 6 points. If the cards in the crib are all the same suit the flush is worth four points, and if the exposed card is also the same suit, 5 points.

THREE HANDED CRIBBAGE (England)

A triangular board *(152)* is used for this game, or a board with three tracks. The players receive five cards from the dealer and the crib one card. Each player places one card face downwards in the crib. The player on the dealer's left

leads, and has first scoring hand. He deals in the following hand.

The first Number '29' cribbage boards *(154)* were made by Mr. Edward N.Hirst of Burnaby, British Columbia, in 1953. When he was twenty-eight, Mr. Hirst was paralysed from the hips downwards by poliomyelitis, and confined to a wheelchair. He turned to woodworking to earn a livelihood for his young family. Among several items he designed and made was the '29' cribbage board which proved popular and sold well. However, many who wanted a board were unable to obtain one because of the very limited quantity which Mr Hirst was able to manufacture personally. Following his death in 1960 no further supplies were available until early in 1962, when production of the now famous '29' board was undertaken by another Vancouver manufacturer.

The board on the right is made of thick plywood, each of its three layers being just over ⅓ inch (8mm) thick, and is probably one of Mr Hirst's original boards. The board on the left is made from a single thickness of red cedar and dates from after 1960.

POPE JOAN (England)

A Georgian Pope Joan board is shown in *(155)*. There are many variations of this game but that described is one of the best. Any number of players can take part and each begins with thirty counters. A fifty-two card pack is used without jokers and with the EIGHT OF DIAMONDS removed. The special board consists of a circular tray revolving around a central pillar and divided into eight compartments marked:
POPE, MATRIMONY, INTRIGUE, ACE, KING, QUEEN, KNAVE and GAME
POPE is the nine of diamonds.
MATRIMONY is the King and Queen of trumps in the same hand.
INTRIGUE is the Jack and Queen of trumps in the same hand.

(153) Perlite three-handed cribbage board simulating the Haida Indian Argellite carving, with a pack of western type cards made in China. Both bought in Chinatown, Vancouver, 1977.

(154) Two '29' three-handed cribbage boards and a pack of cards from the 1901 Pan American Exposition.

(155) Georgian Pope Joan Board, George III pack of cards, early Victorian porcelain card holder and late Victorian metallic counters.

The dealer *dresses* the board by placing fifteen counters from his own store into the compartments of the board as follows:

POPE _____ 6 counters
MATRIMONY___ 2 counters
INTRIGUE_____ 2 counters
THE REST_____ 1 counter in each.

Hands are then dealt to each player, with an extra hand in the centre of the table and any cards left over are added to this. The last card of the pack is turned up to decide the trump suit. If the turn-up is the nine of Diamonds (Pope), or an Ace, King, Queen, or Jack, the dealer wins all the counters in the appropriate compartment on the board.

The player on the dealer's left leads, naming the card as he does so. The holder of the card in the same sequence immediately above it, follows and this continues. The play comes to a halt when no one can continue either by the playing of the King of the suit, or the wanted card is in the hand on the table, or the card has already been played or it is the seven of diamonds. (The EIGHT of Diamonds was removed to form a stop before Pope, the nine of diamonds).

When the Jack, Queen, King or Ace of trumps are led during the game the player wins the counters in the appropriate compartment, and if he can play the Jack and the Queen, or the Queen and King of trumps, he wins as a bonus the counters in INTRIGUE or MATRIMONY respectively.

The first player to play all the cards in his hand wins the counters in GAME and also one counter from each player for every card they hold in their hands. The holder of an unplayed Pope card, however, is exempt from this payment.

Tactics

When no one can follow a card led, the same player leads any other card he wishes. Therefore, players should remember the stop cards and also the cards which cannot be led to and these should be played as soon as possible.

Sequences are valuable as they enable a player to dispose of two, three or more cards at a single turn of play; alternate sequences are almost as useful, e.g. a six, eight and ten of a suit. The lowest is led, and whether a card proves a stop or not the leader can continue the sequence as long as some other player does not go 'out' on an intermediate card.

Pope can only be played when the holder has the lead; it is usually wise to play Pope at the first opportunity after playing any known 'stops'.

The unclaimed counters in each compartment are left to accumulate, and sometimes MATRIMONY and INTRIGUE may not be claimed in a whole session. Any unclaimed counters at the end of the game may be disposed of by dealing a final round, face-uppermost, without the

surplus hand and the holders of Pope, Ace, King, Queen and Jack of diamonds receive the counters in the respective compartments, the holder of the Queen also taking half the counters in MATRIMONY and INTRIGUE; the other halves are taken by the holders of the King and Jack.

The illustration on page 182 shows a beautiful mid-nineteenth century Pope Joan set of eight lacquered trays replacing the eight compartments of the round board, four five-sided lacquered boxes holding mother-of-pearl counters, three square lacquered boxes for three packs of cards and four storage counter-trays, one for each player, all housed within a large lacquered box.

POCH (Germany)_____

This German variant of Pope Joan (*156*) has a long history. The oldest *poch* board in the Bavarian National Museum in Munich is dated 1527, while the earliest reference to the game appears in the work of the famous Nuremberg Meistersinger, Hans Sach, 1558. *Poch* boards may have eight or nine holes. Old ceramic or wooden boards were often decorated with superb paintings.

Method of play_____
STAGE ONE
1.   A thirty-two card pack is used in this game for four people, comprising the Ace, King, Queen, Jack, 10,9,8 and 7 of all four suits. Ace is high.
2.   Each player puts a chip into each of the eight pockets on the board.
3.   The dealer shuffles the pack and deals eight cards face downwards to each player. The dealer looks at the last card he dealt himself and names its suit as trumps.
4.   If a player has the value in trumps of any of the cards or card combinations shown on the board, i.e. the 7-8-9, the 10, the Jack, Queen, King or Ace, or both King and Queen, he takes the chips from the appropriate pockets. A player with both King and Queen of trumps collects from the King, Queen, and joint King/Queen pockets. If no player has King and Queen, or the 7-8-9 sequence, the chips remain in those pockets for the next game.
STAGE TWO
5.   The second stage involves the pocket marked *POCH*. The player on the dealer's left 'bids' one or more chips into the *poch* compartment. Any player who wishes to stay in this stage of the game must match the bid. A player with a poor hand may 'pass', losing the opportunity to win the Poch stakes, although still having a chance to win the third stage. After the other players have bid or passed, the first bidder may raise the stake.
6.   When bidding ends, each player lays out his best combination of cards and the highest score wins the stake in the *poch* pocket. Scoring combinations are pairs, three

of a kind, and four of a kind. The greatest number of the same face value scores highest, i.e. four 7s score higher than three Kings. If two players have the same number of cards in their combinations; i.e. three Queens against three 9s, the higher rank wins. Aces count above Kings. If two players each have a pair of the same value, i.e. two pairs of Jacks, the pair that includes a trump scores higher. After the *poch* counters have been won all the players take back their cards and the third stage begins.

STAGE THREE

7. The winner of the *poch* stakes lays a card face upwards on the table. Any player follows with the next card up in the same suit and cards continue to be played in ascending order by the player holding them until the Ace of the suit is played. This is a 'stop' card and the player of the Ace may then follow playing any card he wishes, either in the same suit or another. Play continues up to the next 'stop' card and the process is repeated until one player lays down his last card, calling 'FINISH'.

8. The first player to play his last card wins this third 'race' stage of the game, and the other players pay him one chip for each card left in their hands.

9. The player on the left of the last dealer then gathers up the cards, re-shuffles, and deals them out, eight to each player, looks at his last card and announces the trump suit. Each player dresses the board by placing a chip into each of the eight pockets and a new game begins.

NAIN JAUNE (The Yellow Dwarf) (France)

A *Nain Jaune* board is shown in *(157)* and there are no less than four *Nain Jaune* boards illustrated on one page of *La Samaritaine* Catalogue for 1909. The prices are also of interest. *Acajou* means mahogany. The description of one of the boards reads:

'*Nain Jaune* (imitation mahogany) with cardboard lining
without cards _____ 1.95FF
with lining of wood _____ 2.95FF
Mahogany throughout _____ 3.90FF'

The board illustrated here and also for the jacket of this book was of the best quality!

BONANZA (United States of America)

The equipment in this game for two to nine players consists of a wheelboard, a standard pack of cards with one joker and a quantity of chips *(158)*. Each player has a share of the latter and at the beginning of the game dresses the board as in Pope Joan or *Poch*. The dealer then deals a

(156) A *Poch* board, *c.*1880 and twentieth century German cards.

(157) *Le Nain Jaune* board, bone counters and recently reproduced playing cards, originally designed by Gilbert in Paris in 1850.

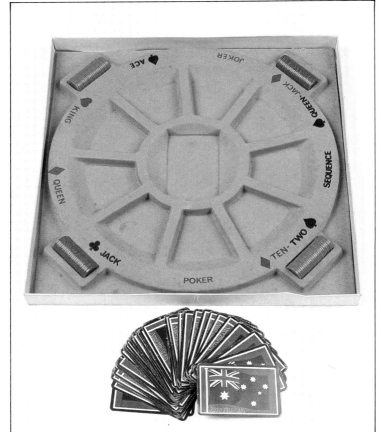

158

159

(158) A Bonanza board and Australian pack of cards.

(159) Blackjack layout, cards and coins, Reno, 1978.

hand to each player and one extra hand, known as the WIDOW. The cards in this hand are dead and out of the game.

Bonanza is said to be based on a form of Michigan Rummy, but as a copyright was taken out in 1965 by a British manufacturer on permit from the National Broadcasting Company of America, c.1964, only a brief description will be given here, but it is interesting to look at four countries' variants of the same basic game — Pope Joan, *Poch*, *Le Nain Jaune* and Bonanza.

The play falls into two stages; the first taking part on the upper half of the wheel (Joker, Queen-Jack, Sequence, Ten-Two and Poker), and the second stage on the lower half, (Ace of Spades, King of Hearts, Queen of Diamonds, Jack of Clubs and Centre section).

Play on the upper half of the wheel is a modified poker game, and on the lower half a form of Pope Joan, but with many more stop cards owing to the dead hand (Widow) on the table. The first player to get rid of all his cards calls 'Bonanza' and wins the chips in the central section.

BLACKJACK

This hyped-up version of the old card game *Vingt-et-un* has been designed to meet the needs of the casino and its patrons. This is a fair game with the expenses of the house being met from the advantage of the dealer (croupier) playing last, and the dealer is relieved of all responsibility of choice by the rigid rule No.11.

The use of the board or 'Lay-out' brings the game, within the scope of the present work and a board has been reproduced for play on page 106 together with the rules.

THE ROYAL HURDLE RACE GAME

This is a variant on *The Game of the Race*, mentioned in Chapter 1, using a pack of cards instead of a die or a teetotum and the board has been reproduced to playable size, along with the rules, on page 86.

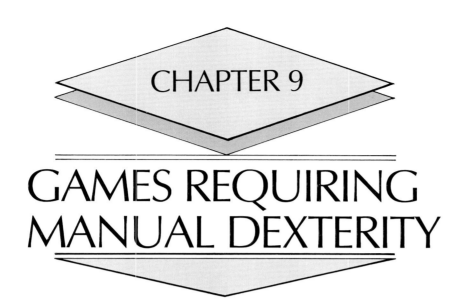

CHAPTER 9

GAMES REQUIRING MANUAL DEXTERITY

SHOVE HA'PENNY

Shove Ha'penny has been derived from Shoffe-grotte, played in English taverns at least as early as the fifteenth century, when the usual coin used for counters was the Edward IV groat. (Shoffe-grotte = shove groat).

The original boards were marked out on a table-top with chalk, but most modern boards are made of hardwood with the grain running lengthwise, and with a strip of wood beneath the board at the near edge to prevent the board slipping on the table. Ten narrow grooves cut across the board divide it into nine beds, each 1¼ inches (3cm) wide and 9½ inches (24cm) long. Two lines 1¼ inches (3 cm) wide from the long edges of the board limit the playing area, and three holes in each of the 1¼ inch (3cm) squares receive pegs for keeping the score, one player using the right-hand side and the other the left. Alternatively, the squares may be marked with three lines with a piece of chalk and rubbed out at the end of each game.

Five small coins can serve as counters. They are placed one at a time protruding over the near edge of the board and are then struck with the palm of the hand, the ball of the thumb or the tips of the fingers at the choice of the player, who tries to propel them along the board to rest in one of the beds. Those lying within a bed score, but those cutting a line are 'dead' unless they are knocked by another counter clear of the lines. The first player to score three times in each bed is the winner. If several players are taking part, three times may be reduced to twice.

The players take turns to shoot the five counters. Any passing beyond the beds are 'dead' and are immediately removed. Some players permit counters to rebound from the ridge at the back of the board into play. A decision on this should be made before the start of the game. Counters more than half-way over the side lines are also removed; those less than half over the line remain on the board but cannot score unless they are knocked back into a bed by another counter.

At the end of each player's turn all counters lying within a bed score and corresponding pegs are inserted into the marker holes or appropriate chalk marks are made in the squares. The beds may be filled in any order, but once three of the player's counters have come to rest in a bed, any further score in the bed is credited to his opponent if the latter still needs a score in this bed, otherwise the unwanted score is ignored; the final point in a game, however, must be scored by the winning player himself.

Cannoning and striking one counter with another is allowed and no points are scored until the last counter of the turn has been played. If one counter lies on top of another, neither scores. If a counter stops short of the first line, the shot is taken again, but if it touches the line, it is in play and must be left. It can be tapped on by another counter, but if the latter thereby stops short of the line it may not be lifted. It in turn can be knocked on by another counter.

As a change from the standard game players may like to try 'Thirty-one'. The nine beds are numbered consecutively from one to nine with the lowest number nearest the striker. The object is to score exactly thirty-one. If, for example, the player had scored twenty-six and needed five to finish, if he scored more, the turn ends and he remains at twenty-six and must try again at his next turn.

Powdered chalk is often used as a lubricant on the playing surface. Alternatively, soft beeswax furniture polish achieves the same purpose. Pre-1971 halfpennies are treasured as counters for the game. It may be difficult to decide whether a counter is free in a bed or cuts a line. If a coin on edge is passed along the groove and it touches the counter the latter is 'dead'.

The value of a piece depends upon its quality, rarity and the number of collectors who would like it. Illustrated in (160) is a shove ha'penny board which is modern, perfectly adequate for playing the game, and priced at £15-£25/$27-

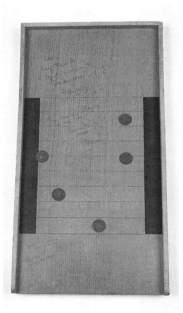

(160) Shove ha'penny board used in *Collectors World* TV programme in Bristol with the late Athur Negus, c.1976. The board is signed by Hugh Scully and two members of the studio team.

$46. The match-play board, *(161) c*.1890 is from a public house in the Ipswich area and is labelled Gaskell & Chambers Ltd. Bar Fitters, 109-114 Blackfriars Road, London, SE1. It is made of mahogany and the grooves separating the beds contain brass strips which are hinged at the left hand side. If, on lifting the strip, the counter was disturbed it was 'on the line' and didn't count. The rebound arc at the far end of the board is of brass and the separation line between the playing and scoring areas is an inlay of mother-of-pearl. The scores are recorded by little white cylinders viewed through small round windows, the four quadrants being mark one, two, three and blank. At the beginning of a game all the cylinders are set at blank.

Four of the five counters are original, ¾ inch (20mm) in diameter with a ¼ inch (6mm) hole in the centre. They are made of silverplated brass, are plain on one side and have an inscription 'ST GEORGE SERIES. MADE IN ENGLAND', between concentric circles on the other. Such a board is a collector's item and would be worth around £150 to £200 ($270-$364).

(161) Shove ha'penny Match board. Late nineteenth or early twentieth century, from a public house near Ipswich. Four out of five of the counters are original.

(162) Set of boxwood Squails with a lead target, *c*.1890.

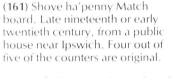

161

SQUAILS (England)

Squails *(162)* can be played on any round polished table by two to eight players. A loo table, as illustrated on page 186, is ideal. Each player has an equal number of coloured wooden discs called squails, the players are divided into teams and a partner from each team alternately strikes a squail towards the small lead target placed in the centre of the playing area. The squail is placed over the edge of the player's segment of the table and propelled with the palm of the player's hand, a similar movement to that in shove ha'penny. The object of the game is to place the greatest number of squails near the target and it is part of the game to knock opposing squails away from the target as well as trying to leave one's own close beside it. If the target is moved more than 6 inches (15cm) from its original position which is marked, it is replaced, but if less than 6 inches (15cm), it remains in position and all measurements are taken from it. The squail furthest from the target scores one point, and the squail nearest, sixteen points. A tape

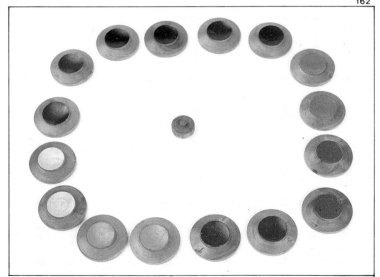
162

measure is required to decide disputed positions.

Squails was popular among cabin passengers on the long nineteenth-century voyages to India, Australia and the Far East. The movement of the ship adding to the difficulty of accurate calculations!

CARROMS (India)

Carroms has been a favourite game in India and Burma for over a hundred years and a variety of it, *Kairam* is popular in the Yemen. The rules below are taken from the official regulations of the All India *Carrom* Federation

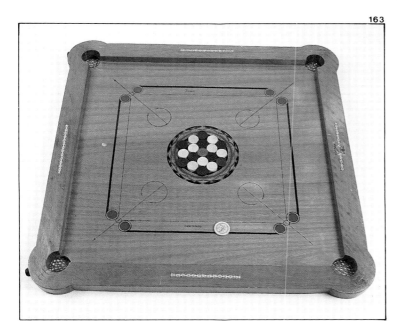

163

8. If a disc falls on the striker, the striker is removed and the disc left in place.
9. The red Queen may be pocketed any time after a player has pocketed his first disc. See rules 10, 11, 12.
10. If the Queen is pocketed before the player has pocketed one of his discs his turn ceases and the Queen is replaced in the Centre, or as near to the centre of the inner circle as possible.
11. If the Queen is pocketed by a stroke but is not then covered by one of the player's discs before the end of his turn, the Queen is lifted at the end of the turn and placed back in the central circle.
12. If the Queen is pocketed by a stroke and then the player pockets one of his own discs at the next stroke, the Queen remains in the pocket for the rest of the board.
13. A BOARD is finished once one of the players has pocketed all his discs. He scores a point for each of his opponent's discs still in play, plus 5 points if sometime during the board he has pocketed the Queen. The Queen only scores for the winner of the board; she then scores 5 points, *unless* he already has 24 points or more, when she scores one point.
14. There are several boards to a 29 point game.
15. A match consists of the best of three games.

Important measurements For those making their own carroms board and pieces.

The standard *Carroms* board is made of plywood 29 inches (71cm) square. Adjoining the playing surface are wooden borders made of hardwood. The borders are 1 inch (2.5cm) high and 2-2½ inches (5x6cm) wide. The pockets at each corner are 1¾ inches (4.5cm) wide.

There are two parallel lines on each of the four sides of the board called base lines. The outer line is 4 inches (10cm) from the border and ⅛ inch (0.3cm) thick. The inner line is 1½ (3.7cm) inches from the outer line. The two lines terminate on two red circles 1½ inches (3.7cm) in diameter. In all there are eight red circles. The red circles of the lines on one side are separated from the red circles of the adjoining lines by a circle ¾ inch (1.9cm) in diameter. From the centre of each such circle an arrow points towards the centre of the centre circle.

The centre circle is 1¼ inches (3cm) in diameter in the centre of the board. Concentrically outside the centre circle is the inner circle 6⅜ inches (16cm) in diameter and outside that is the outer circle 7⅜ inches (18.7cm) in diameter.

The circular *carromen* are of hardwood and are coloured white, black and red, with a diameter of 1¼ inches (3cm) and are ¼ inch (0.6cm) thick.

The striker is of ivory, plastic or wood but not of metal. Its diameter must not exceed 1 inch (4cm), and its weight 15 grams. The board is placed on a table or stool between 25-

(163) A *Carroms* board, counters and striker, 1975.

created on 4th March, 1956. The board and pieces illustrated are standard match equipment.

In this game for two players each has nine discs, black or white. A red Queen disc, a larger Striker disc and the board, completes the equipment. The pieces are arranged in the centre of the board as shown in *(163)* the stem of the Y formed by the white discs facing the opening player who is White.

Rules

1. White shoots first by placing the striker anywhere within the rectangle on his side of the board and flicking it towards the cluster of discs in the centre of the board. He tries to knock one of his own white discs into a pocket. Only the fingers may cross the front line and only the fingers and the hand are allowed over the base line. If a player infringes these rules, he must return one of his pocketed discs to the inner circle. If he cannot do so, he must as soon as he can.
2. The first player's turn continues as long as he pockets a white disc with each shot, the player returning his striker to his rectangle (known as his box) after each shot.
3. The striker may cushion from the walls to strike a disc, or it may hit an opposing disc to pocket one of the player's discs.
4. If a player pockets one of the opponent's discs it remains in the pocket and his turn ceases.
5. If the striker lands in a pocket, the player owes a penalty and his turn ceases.
6. If a disc flies off the board, the turn ceases and the opponent replaces it as close as possible to the centre of the central circle.
7. If the striker falls on to a disc, it is removed without

disturbing the disc.

27 inches (63-68cm) in height and is made level. The players' stools or chairs are without arms and of normal size and 21 inches (53cm) in height. Boric powder is used on the board and the striker as a lubricant. In singles the players sit opposite each other. In doubles the two pairs of partners sit opposite each other, that is a player occupying each side of the table.

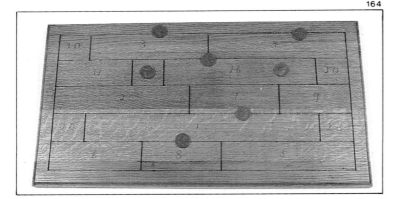

(164) Reproduction Brother Jonathan board with pre-1971 halfpennies for counters.

(165) Three bagatelle boards.

BROTHER JONATHAN (United States of America)

Any number of players took part in this eighteenth century American game of pitching copper coins on to a board marked with spaces, taking turns to toss five coins, usually large cents *(164)*. (Pre 1971 halfpennies are a handy size.) When a coin landed in a compartment the player scored the number of points marked on it but if the coin touched a line it was 'dead' and did not score. The winning total was decided by the players at the beginning of the game. The scores were calculated at the end of each player's turn of five throws.

BAGATELLE

The delightful board shown in *(166)* is quite small measuring 16½ by 8 inches (42 by 22cm). The original balls are missing and have been replaced with steel ball-bearings.

The basic equipment for bagatelle consists of a rectangular shaped board made of painted wood which is roughly twice as long as its is wide. One end is curved in the form of a semi-circle; the rim is raised to keep the balls within the playing area, and the curved end of the board is raised on a block some 1 inch (2.5cm) higher than the squared end.

There are ten balls, either of steel, glass or plastic and when not in play they are housed in a gutter along the base of the board. The balls are pushed along a channel on the right hand side of the board with a stick. (But see rule 10.)

A number of small nails are driven into the board and the exact arrangement of these varies, *(165)*. Some of the nails form semicircles called CUPS, other nails are free standing and act as barriers to the balls. There are also several depressions just large enough to hold a ball. A number is painted alongside, ranging from five to one hundred and fifty. The board is placed on a table for play.

Rules

1. Any number of players can take part.
2. Each in turn takes a ball and places it at the bottom of the guide channel on the right-hand side of the board and propels it up the slope to the curved end of the board. In the follow through, the tip of the stick must not pass beyond the end of the channel. (See rule 10).
3. If the player does not push the ball hard enough for it to escape into the playing area he may push the ball again.
4. If the ball is pushed too hard and leaves the board it is 'dead' and the player scores nothing for the turn.
5. The number of balls each player propels in a turn is decided between the players at the start of the game. Usually it is about five.

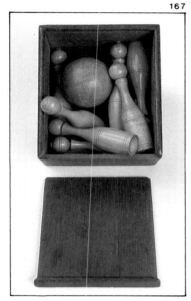

(166) Bagatelle board with Chinese decorative theme, c.1920.

(167) Table-Top ten-pin bowling set in boxwood. Late nineteenth or early twentieth century.

6. All balls are left in position on the board until the end of the turn.
7. Each player's score is recorded at the end of every turn. Balls finishing inside a cup or in a hole score the corresponding number of points.
8. There is no score if a ball enters a cup or hole and then rolls out again, rests against the outside of a cup or hole or ends up in any non-scoring area of the board.
9. There are three posssible ways of winning:
    a) being in the lead when a set time has elapsed;
    b) being the first player to reach a pre-determined score;
    c) by having the highest score at the end of an agreed number of turns.
10. On many boards the balls are fed to the front of a spring-loaded trigger. By modifying the pull on the trigger the balls are propelled at different velocities and take different courses on the board.

TABLE TEN-PINS

Ten small wooden pins are arranged on the top of a long table, if possible allowing about six feet (two metres) of playing surface. The players in turn roll two or three balls towards them and score one point for each pin knocked down. The winner is the first player to reach an agreed total. The set shown in *(167)* is probably incomplete; there is only one ball whereas two or possibly three would be expected. The box containing the set would only hold one more ball, but this box may not be the original, although it

is of the same period. The ball and skittles are beautifully turned in boxwood and polished.

There are several modifications of this game using ten or nine pins and the latter may be set up in a diamond formation or in a circle.

Down the Kaiser (168) is interesting for its historical associations. Dating from the time of the First World War, the poor workmanship reflects the scarcity of raw materials and skilled craftsmen at a time when the country's energies were concentrated on the war effort.

Very different in quality is the Georgian tenpin set of ivory *(169)*. The ivory pins are 2½ inches (6cm) high and instead of balls there are two small ivory tops with serrated edges. Considerable skill is required to spin the tops accurately down the table, which needs to be smooth and polished.

SKITTLES WITH FIFTEEN SLICED SPHERES

The game illustrated in *(170)* is incomplete, but is a strange variation on the common theme of 'Skittles'. There are ten balls which have a flat side and each flat is engraved with a number. These are 1,2,3,4,5,9,11,12,14 and 15, suggesting that five balls are missing. How the game was played and the significance of the numbers on the truncated spheres is not known, but so unusual a variant deserves recording. The skittles are turned in elm and the balls in a hard close wood, possibly pear or apple.

(168) 'Down the Kaiser' skittle game, c.1915.

(169) Table-top ten-pin bowling set of ivory with tops instead of balls, c.1830.

(170) Incomplete set of pins and truncated spheres for table-top bowls game.

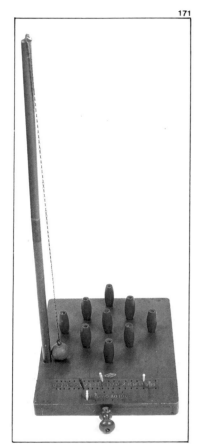

TABLE SKITTLES

Yet another form of table skittles is shown in *(171)*. In this game for two to eight players each player has three 'pitches' with the ball suspended from a gallows at the nine pins placed on their marks on the platform. The player scores one point for each pin knocked down. If they are all downed at one go they are reset and the player has another turn. The maximum score is twenty-seven, three pitches in which all nine skittles are downed each time. A game consists of three 'chalks' or set of pitches, with a maximum score of 27 x 3=81.

By pulling on the red handle which is attached to every pin by a separate cord, the pins can all be set simultaneously in a second or two.

(171) Gallows skittle board and ball, with pegs for scoring, *c.*1935.

(172) Hooplah set, 1987.

(173) Blow Football set, *c.*1930.

(174) A Tiddley Winks set.

TABLE QUOITS (Hooplah)

This game is derived from the outdoor variety although in table quoits there is only one hob and each player has four quoits. The players cast all their quoits in each turn of play and RINGERS (a quoit over the hob) count one point. Game is usually 15 or 25 points. See *(172)*.

BLOW FOOTBALL

Two players or two teams take part *(173)*. The goals are placed at the ends of a table, and a table-tennis ball is placed in the centre. At a signal the players blow through drinking staws at the ball trying to guide it into the opponent's goal. A wall around the edges of the table lessens the frustration of the ball falling on to the floor. If the ball does leave the field, it is replaced by the opponent at the spot where it left the table and he has free blow. At half time the players change ends.

This is an excellent game for asthmatic children, encouraging them to take big breaths and to expel air from the depths of the lungs.

PING-PONG OR GOSSIMA (England)

The name ping-pong appears to have been used for the first time in 1900, when the game was described as a parlour game resembling lawn-tennis, played on a table with bats and celluloid balls. The design on the lid of the early ping-pong set, *(175)*, would do credit to a scene from *A Midsummer's Night's Dream* with two elves on the right waving battledores and on the left sprites sheltering under toadstools, while a plethora of print informs us:

'The New Table Game of Ping Pong or Gossima causes

immense excitement and healthy exercise and is the nearest approach that can be to the Game of Lawn Tennis as played out of doors. Sole Publishers and Manufacturers J. JAQUES & Son LTD & HAMLEY BROS (Jointly concerned) Wholesale 102 Hatton Garden, London. Proceedings will be taken against anyone infringing the Registered Titles of this Game.' On the underside of the lid is the label:

'**CAUTION TO THE PUBLIC**

The only genuine PING-PONG Games are those which bear the Registered Trade Marks. "PING-PONG and GOSSIMA" and the Public are requested to observe this on the Box Labels, Rules and other implements.

'**ALL IMITATIONS** sold under other spurious titles should be refused, as they are NOT Ping-Pong at all, and have no right to be sold as such.

IMPORTANT NOTICE

'To prevent the original Battledores sent out with the sets being substituted for others of inferior quality, in order to cut the prices at which they are offered, The Public are requested to note that the catalogue Nos. of the sets under which they are sold are stamped on the faces of the battledores themselves.

'Every set also bears the Sole Publishers' names — J. Jaques & Son Ltd, & HAMLEY BROS (Jointly concerned) to be obtained at all the leading sports and Games Dealers throughout the World.'

Note that the racquets are known as battledores. An illustration *(176)* taken from the April edition of *The Royal Magazine* in 1901 shows a lady and gentleman playing Ping Pong with equipment similar to that in *(175)*.

The difference between Ping-Pong and its modern equivalent is that, originally, the scoring was the same as in Lawn Tennis.

The name Table Tennis was adopted in 1926 by the International Table Tennis Federation (ITTF) which was founded in January of that year in Germany. Through the 1930s international competitions were dominated by Europeans; during the Second World War they were abandoned and by 1952 the Far East, in particular Japan and Communist China were producing the men's singles champions.

(175) An early Ping-Pong set, *c.*1900

(176) A game of Ping-Pong, 1901.

(177) A Rings board.

RINGS

This game requires a wooden board often made in the shape of a shield, but rectangular, circular and diamond-shapes are also found. Usually there are thirteen numbered hooks arranged on its surface, although pubs on the Isle of Wight have boards with fifteen hooks. The numbering of the hooks also varies from board to board. That shown in *(177)* differs from both described by A.R. Taylor in his *Pub Games*.

The board is suspended on a wall with the central hook 66 inches (1m 68cm) from the floor. The players throw rubber rings at the board from a distance of about 8 feet (2m 45cm) and any rings landing on a hook score the appropriate number of points. There is no uniformity in the positions of the numbers, or indeed in the number of hooks which vary from twelve to fifteen. The players throw three rings each. Two popular games are — One Hundred and Fifty-One and Twice Round the Board.

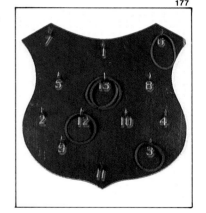

ONE HUNDRED AND FIFTY-ONE

The players throw three rings each and only one ring is permitted on any one hook in a turn; if two rings land on the same hook they cancel each other out and score nothing. The third ring can score separately. The game must end with an exact score of one hundred and fifty-one, an overthrow finishes the turn with the score reverting to what it was before the turn began.

TWICE ROUND THE BOARD

In this variant from Lanacashire the players have to ring the number in sequence from one to thirteen and then repeat. Doubles are counted in this game if they are achieved with *consecutive* throws on to the same hook. For example a player scoring a 'double four' would next throw for a nine.

EIGHTYONE

In this form of Rings *(178)* the board is placed on the floor or on a table and in turn each player throws five rubber rings on to its surface from a pre-determined distance. Handicapped players throw from further away. The winner is the first to score eighty-one or over. The unmarked centre counts as ten, while any ring touching a line scores nothing. Two or more rings are permitted in the same compartment.

Bought several years ago from a dealer in Alston, the board came from a village pub in Cumbria, and may be indiginous to that part of the country.

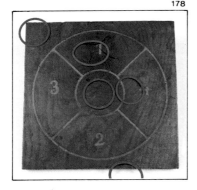

(178) A public house Rings board. Provenance and date unknown.

(179) Darts board, London pattern, c.1950.

DARTS

The origin of darts is uncertain and the game is only given a scant mention in Joseph Strutt's *Sports and Pastime of the People of England*, 1801. The board shown in *(179)* is a standard dartboard with an outer ring counting double, the middle ring treble, the outer bull twenty-five and the inner bull fifty. This board is known as the 'London' board to distinguish it from regional variants, among them being those of Manchester, Yorkshire, the Fives board, the Burton board, the Target or Norfolk board, and the Tonbridge board. For further information refer to Taylor's *Pub Games* pp. 14-21, Mayflower Books, 1976.

Dartboards are made of bristle, cork, or wood and are fixed to a wall with the centre of the board 5ft 8in (1.73m) from the floor. The 'Toe-line' is 8ft (2.44m) from the board though this is flexible and long narrow rubber mats are sold which are marked at 8ft (2.44m), 8ft 6in (2.60m) and 9ft (2.75m). There are several different games played with darts, only two will be described.

179

THREE HUNDRED AND ONE

The object is to score three hundred and one exactly. The scoring must start with a double and finish on a double or the inner bull. A contest is the 'Best of three'.

As a team game with eight players on each side the total is increased to 501, 801, or 1,001 with members of the two teams playing alternately. Three darts constitute a 'set' and there is considerable individual variation in players' preferences for large heavy darts, small, light minidarts, and every shade of weight and size in between.

ROUND THE CLOCK

The players progress numerically around the board from one to twenty, starting with double one and finishing with treble twenty and then the inner or outer bull. Some players dispense with the bull requirement as the dart flights are more likely to be damaged when concentrating on so small an area.

CARPET BOWLS

This game is based on the well-known game played on the bowling green. The indoor variety requires a stretch of carpeted floor 10 to 20 feet (3-6m) long and not less than 6 feet (1.84m) wide. The carpet should be a little rough to provide a slight drag — a Wilton carpet is ideal. On a smooth surface the bowls describe too marked a curve *(180)*.

Equipment

a) Eight bowls a pair with red spots, a pair with white spots, a pair with blue spots and a pair with yellow. The bowls are weighted to produce bias on the opposite side to the spot, causing them to roll in a gentle curve away from the spot instead of in a straight line, thus enabling the jack to be approached from either side according to how the bowl is held in the hand. This allows the avoidance of an opponent's bowl lying in the direct line of approach. Bowls must be rolled and not thrown.

b) An all-white jack approximately half the diameter of the bowls.

c) A small 3½ inch (9cm) rubber mat behind the front edge of which the bowler's toe must remain.

d) A tape measure.

Rules

1. Each player has one pair of bowls with his own coloured spots. If there are only two players each has two pairs.

2. If there are four players they may play individually; or as two teams of two players who then play alternately, separated by the play of one of their opponents.

3. The first player or team to reach 21 points is the winner, although other targets can be set before play begins.

4. The option of starting is decided by the spin of a coin, the winner of the toss having the choice of playing first or second. The first player in each round rolls the jack and follows with his first bowl. The others follow in an agreed order from the same spot marked by the rubber mat. The winner of each round starts in the next.

5. If the jack rolls off the carpet it should be replaced 12 to 18 inches (30-45cm) from the edge nearest to where it went off; but if the jack is knocked off by a bowl during play the round is dead and is started again from the opposite end.

6. Any bowl leaving the carpet, or being obstructed by any object is considered dead, and if necessary may be removed.

7. The player or team whose bowl is nearest to the jack at the end of a round counts one point but if two or more bowls belonging to the same player or team are nearer than the nearest of the opponent's each of these bowls will score 1 point. It is therefore possible to score 4 points in one round if all a partnerships' bowls are nearer the jack than any of the opponent's.

8. If two players tie for the nearest position, both scores a point.

9. If a bowl is played out of turn, it may be re-played in its proper order, but if it has touched the jack or another bowl, the opponent has the choice of declaring the round dead or if it is to his advantage, accepting the play which continues in the new order.

10. At the end of a round the players go to the other end of the playing area, collect their bowls, put down the mat and the winner of the last round starts the new one by rolling the jack and then his first bowl.

Carpet bowls is based on outdoor Crown Green Bowling. The green of the Southampton Town Bowling Club is said to have been laid down in the reign of Edward I (1272-1307) and has been used ever since. Certainly the game dates back to the thirteenth century and was popular in summer on open greens and turfed alleys during the fourteenth century. Nearly every Elizabethan country house had its bowling green. At first a cone was used

(180) Carpet bowls set, c.1980.

instead of a jack. Biased bowls were introduced in the sixteenth century. Robert Recorde wrote, 'A little altering of one side maketh the bowl to run biasse waies'.

Outdoor bowls were universal by the end of the eighteenth century, but faded in the nineteenth, enjoying a revival at the turn of the twentieth. In 1950 there were two thousand clubs affiliated to the English Bowling Association.

(181) Royal Billiard Bowls set with mahogany inclined plane, measuring cord and original box, c.1950.

(182) Trench Football game/ puzzle, c.1920 or a few years earlier.

ROYAL GAME OF BILLIARD BOWLS

The set of bowls *(181)* was supplied by Burroughs and Watts of 19 Soho Square, London. Inside the box are two inked stamps: 'BURROUGHS & WATTS LTD BILLIARD TABLE MANUFACTURERS ATHENAEUM BUILDINGS SUNDERLAND, and a similar stamp but with the address 'VICTORIA BUILDINGS 15 NEW BRIDGE STREET NEWCASTLE ON TYNE'.

There are eight *lignum vitae* bowls 2 inches (4cm) in diameter marked in pairs: 1,2,3,4, indicating the amount of bias, and two white jacks. There is also a sloped mahogany gutter down which the bowls were rolled. The rules are the same as those described under carpet bowls except that the inclined plane is used instead of bowling from the hand and a billiard table is used as a green instead of the floor.

TRENCH FOOTBALL (England)

This solitaire game *(182)* dates from the time of the First World War and is an early example of a host of similar games/puzzles requiring the negotiation of balls past holes. As interesting as the game itself is the description on the back reproduced below:

'Trench Football
By the makers of the Sensationally Successful
War-Game "THE SILVER BULLET"

MODE OF ATTACK
'You have a feeble opponent in "Little Willie" at "Outside Right". Loot Ball is his speciality, and passing the outsider with the contempt he deserves, you negotiate the skulker Von Tirpitz, (notorious for his foul play) on his first appearance *in the open* as "Centre Forward".

'Having downed (or Drowned) him you pass to your "Outside Left" and although Von Kluck is now used to being "Left Outside" he is an honest thruster but is not clever, and in an important match of recent date he lost his nerve and broke down badly when within shooting distance of goal.

'Von Bulow at "Inside Left" talkative and tricky, can be swept aside with an honest rush.

'Von Hindenburg at "Inside Right" has not been played regularly of late, the Grand Duke having badly shaken his confidence. Competent critics are of the opinion that he was greatly overrated, and is not likely to re-gain his form or to give trouble on this or any future occasion.

'Von der Goltz, stiff and stodgy at "Right Half" has never been able to think clearly since the Belgian International outwitted him.

'Von Moltke, a poor imitation of the Great Von Moltke has greatly subsided since his quarrel with the goal keeper, and it is unlikely that he will in any way retard the attack.

'Enver Pasha of doubtful sanity, at "Left Half" is, on a pinch more than likely to attack his own colleagues.

'Von Sanders at "Left Back" is a comparatively new man of unproved merit.

'Count Zeppelin at "Right Back" is the gasbag of our opponents, he has been badly pricked of late, and is far less dangerous than he appears on paper.

"Lord High Everything, Canting Bully Bill" in "GOAL" you must keep your eye on, he holds the record for mouth, and foul play.

'To obtain a goal you must *dodge his mouth*, it is the chief difficulty. He has proved himself mentally incapable of understanding the rules of the game or the meaning of fair play. Many complaints have been lodged against him, and it is probable that he will in the near future be *"Suspended indefinitely"*. Vigour and decision is necessary in dealing with him.

R.F. & S.'

So far the firm R.F. & S. has not been traced. The author remembers playing this game at school in 1929. It makes an interesting pair with 'Down the Kaiser' shown on page 143.

'Games are products of the periods in which they were played. The simple table skittles game 'Down the Kaiser' is a modification of the board game shown on page 144, *(171)* but instead of a ball suspended on a string from a gallows, three narrow wooden cylinders are rolled towards the targets, one of which is painted red, placed in the centre of the board and designated as the KAISER and earning the highest score for being knocked down. This game belongs to the years of the First World War; the skittles are crudely turned and unvarnished, the wooden cylinders are more easily made than wooden balls and the cardboard 'board' tells of a country at war, with little time, money or craftsmen to spare for the creation of pastimes. Such items have a place in the Museum of Mankind.

Incidentally the unvarnished pieces had a few woodworm holes with fine sawdust at their edges indicating active infestation. Such pieces are a danger to any other wood in the vicinity and should be soaked in a reliable pesticide. Only when such articles have been made safe should they be permitted to join a collection.

TI RAKAU (The Stick Game) (New Zealand Maori)

Ti Rakau, (183) is one of the best of the musical rhythm games and is taught to New Zealand school children as part of their cultural heritage.

Originally the players assumed a circle formation. To their own chanting they threw sticks from one to another, either across or round the circle, using set patterns and exchanging sticks on key words. If a player dropped a stick he was out of the game, which continued until only one player was left — the winner. The game required considerable dexterity and quick eyesight and was played by girls and young Maori women as well as men.

Today the game is played with the players kneeling in two lines, facing each other and sitting back on their heels. Each player has two sticks, 1-2 inches (2.5-5cm) in diameter and 10-18 inches (25-46cm) long. At the beginning of the game the sticks are laid flat on the ground, one on each side of the body. Each movement is repeated to the end of the tune and the chorus is repeated after each movement. For further information, including tunes used, see *Games and Dances of the Maori, A Guide Book for Teachers.* Curriculum Development Division, Department of Education, Wellington, N.Z. 1979.

The Stick Game sticks are made of honeysuckle.* They were used by a member of the New Zealand contingent at the Scouts Jamboree in Melbourne, Australia in 1933 and are part of the set of sticks presented as a gift to the team by Princess Tapui. These particular ones were used in the demonstration by Stewart Frame and the bottom of the sticks are marked S.F.

*New Zealand Honeysuckle is not the same as English honeysuckle. It belongs to the *Proteacae* and is called *Rewarewa* and grows to a height of 100 feet (294m).

183

(183) Maori *Ti Rakau* sticks with two postcards showing games in progress, 1933.

CHAPTER 10

NORTH AMERICAN INDIAN GAMES

North American Indians were compulsive gamblers and their games were used for this purpose. Pre-Columbian Amerindian games fell into three groups, each with many variants. Only one game from each group will be described.

(184) West Coast Indian in full feather-rosette regalia at a pow-wow, Mission City, 1986. *R. C. Bell.*

To many Europeans, an American Indian is a 'Plains' Indian complete with warbonnet *(184)* and living in a teepee. In reality, the West Coast Indians, the Indians of the Prairies and the Indians of the Eastern Woodlands lived very different lives, in very different environments and eating very different foods. For an early account of the Coastal Indians of the Far West we are fortunate in having the record of John Jewitt, a Boston seaman who was captured by the Nootka Indians in the early years of the nineteenth century. He was kept as a slave for three years but was well treated in return for his services as a blacksmith. In his *Narrative of the Adventures and Suffering of John R. Jewitt*, Edinburgh, 1824, he has left us a fascinating account of the longhouses and life in them, of the Coast Indians. The commonest article of furniture was a cedar chest used for storing possessions and as containers for dried foods.

People squatted around the fires and sat or lay on platforms in order to keep below the level of the smoke. Most of their evenings were spent in discussing the day's affairs, exchanging stories or gambling. The latter depended upon variations of the hand game and were accompanied by special gambling songs and drumming with frequent shouts of jubilation over opponents' discomfiture.

Jewitt's description of a longhouse is worth repeating:
'... the top is covered with planks of eight feet broad, which form a kind of covering projecting so far over the ends of the planks that form the roof, as completely to exclude the rain. On these they lay large stones to prevent their being displaced by the wind. The ends of the planks

are not secured to the beams on which they are laid by fastenings ...

'...The houses are without a chimney, nor is there any opening left in the roof, but whenever a fire is made, the plank immediately above it is thrust aside by means of a pole, to give vent to the smoke...' Picture *Slahal* being played in such surroundings.

184

SLAHAL (The hand game of the Salish Indians) (British Columbia)

In its original form for two players, one held a piece of bone from the foreleg of a deer behind his back in one hand and nothing in the other. The opponent tried to guess which hand held the bone. Later two bones were used, one plain and the other marked. The guesser tried to identify the marked piece. *(See 187.)*

For at least fifty years *Slahal* has been played as a team game and using two sets of bones. Today the teams are often from different reservations. It is even on a national basis, Canadian Indians playing against those of the United States. Each team has a leader who collects the bets from his players to form a pool equal to that of their opponent's, although the individual players may contribute varying amounts, according to their wealth. The teams line up with the players in front and their supporters behind. Only the team members are permitted to hold the bones.

Each *Slahal* team starts with five sticks or markers, which are stuck into the ground in front of the leader. In the first phase of the game each leader takes a pair of bones, one marked and the other plain, mixes them behind his back and then holds out his closed hands while his opponent tries to guess which hand holds the PLAIN bone. The leader who guesses correctly wins both pairs of bones and a King stick which is larger than the ordinary markers. If both guess correctly they continue until one makes a mistake, while if both are wrong, guessing continues until one is right. The winning leader's team starts the second phase with the King stick stuck into the ground beside its other five sticks.

The team with the bones begins to sing a gambling song *(185)* and fig. 73. Each team has its own repertoire of songs, and some players have a personal song designed to raise the morale of their own team and lower that of the opposition. Songs are considered to put life into the bones and confusion into the minds of the opponents. The latter remain silent. Teasing and heckling of the guessing side is an essential part of the game.

The leader of the mixing team rubs both pairs of bones in his hands and then tosses a pair to two of his players. The bones are hidden behind these players' backs, mixed and held out towards the opposition with the bones concealed in the palms. The leader is usually the guesser for his team but he may take advice and if he is doing badly may delegate the duty to another player.

Guessing is done by signs, as words would be lost in the singing and chanting, or at least open to argument. The signs for the four possible combinations that the plain

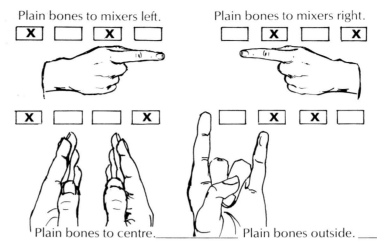

Plain bones to mixers left.   Plain bones to mixers right.

Plain bones to centre.   Plain bones outside.

Fig. 72

HANDGAME of the KIOWA, KIOWA APACHE, & COMANCHE   IH 2501

(185) Sleeve of recording of the singing during a Hand-game.

bones may assume are shown in fig. 72.

If both sets of bones are guessed correctly, they are tossed over to the opposing team; if one set is guessed, it is handed over but the other is retained and one of the guessing team's sticks is taken and added to those of the mixing team. If both guesses are incorrect, both sets of bones are then mixed again and the game continues until the mixing side has lost both pairs of bones.

If the guesser chooses wrongly, the bones usually remain with the same mixers, although occasionally the leader will call them back and pass them to new mixers. One of the mixing team has two slats of wood which he beats together to accompany the gambling songs and hold the rhythm.

When both pairs of bones have been guessed, the team's roles are reversed and the new mixing side starts up song, while its opponents fall silent. A winning team usually keeps to the same song but if losing, will switch to another to change its luck. When a team has won the opponent's five sticks and has ten stuck into the ground in front of its leader, for the next five points it lays one of the captured sticks on the ground for each point. When they are ten points ahead with all the captured sticks lying flat, the game is over, unless the losing side holds the King stick which must be won in the same way. The side holding the King stick thus has eleven lives against its opponent's ten.

At the end of the game, which may last for several hours, the winners collect the money in the pool and each player in the winning team takes double his individual stake. Throughout the game the onlookers may place side bets on the results of individual mixings. These bets are at straight rates, which may or may not be accepted, although it is usual to do so as a point of honour. The side bets are settled immediately the guess has been made.

The Carnegie Roadrunners and Billy Goat Hill are two of the biggest and best sounding teams in southwest Oklahoma and a live recording *(185)* of one of their hand game contests was made at Carnegie, Oklahoma on 24 November 1968. The Carnegie Roadrunners is an all Kiowa team and Billy Goat Hill is a Kiowa-Apache team with a number of Kiowa and Comanche members. For the recorded contest the Carnegie Roadrunners hosted Billy Goat Hill for an afternoon and evening of hand games. In the afternoon they played three games. Billy Goat Hill won the first and the Roadrunners the second and third. Following supper, the two teams played a very close and outstanding game. The first part of this game is presented in the album, unedited, exactly as it was played. Recorded on high fidelity equipment compatible with both mono and stereo record players. INDIAN HOUSE, BOX 472, TAOS, NEW MEXICO 87571.

The four 'Bones' shown in *(186)* were made on the Blood Indian Reservation near Fort Mcleod in Alberta, for sale to tourists and were bought by the author in a back-street shop in that town in 1977.

Fig. 73 records *Slahal* songs transcribed by W. Stuart at the Cultus Lake Indian Festival, held at Cultus Lake, British Columbia in June 1969 with the participation of players and supporters from Vancouver Island and the lower British Columbia Mainland against Northwest Washington Lummi Indians.

The author has adapted this outdoor game into one played on a table *(187)*. Each team starts with five sticks, marked red and green respectively and there is one yellow King stick. The sticks are placed in holders shaped as a war-canoe for the Haida (red), a northern tribe, and a whaling-canoe of the Nootka in the south (green). One set of bones is made from a sheep's femur and the other is of lilac, a hard white wood simulating bone. The markings are traditional.

Reference: Maranda, Mrs L. *Coast Salish Gambling Games*, National Museum of Man, Mercury Series, Canadian Ethnology Service, Paper No. 93, 1984.

Fig.73

THE DICE GAME (Amerindian)

The dice game was considered to be a woman's game and was played by two players kneeling or sitting opposite each other, although sometimes there were two or three players on each side, with, on occasion, additional supporters placing side bets. Between the players was a mat or blanket. Commonly four beaver teeth were used as dice marked on one side only, two with lines and two with circles. One of the latter had a cord tied around it and was known as the *Kes*, *(188)*. All four dice were held between cupped hands by one player, shaken and thrown on to the mat in front of the players.

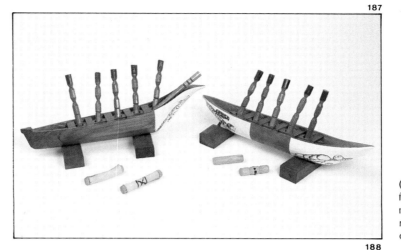

(186) Set of Hand-game 'Bones' from the Blood Indian Reserve, near Fort McLeod, Alberta and reproduction set of gambling sticks of the Coastal Indians.

(187) Reproduction *Slahal* set with 'bones' of sheep's femur and holly.

(188) Set of beaver teeth dice and reproduction counting sticks, chair dice and leather dicing tablet.

Scoring

4 sticks.——When the *Kes* was uppermost and the other three dice were plain, or when the *Kes* was plain and the other three dice had their marks uppermost.

2 sticks.——When all marked faces were either up or down.

1 stick.——When both lines were up and circles down, or both circles up and lines were down.

No other throw scored. When a score was made, the caster continued throwing but when she failed to score the dice were passed to her opponent.

Scoring was kept by counters or sticks. The counters were usually made of wood and were about 3 inches (7.5cm) long. Between ten and forty were placed in a central pile on the mat. Each time a player scored she took the appropriate number of sticks from the pile and placed them by her side. When the central pile was finished, the players won and lost counters to each other until one player had won all the sticks or until a previously agreed total had been reached by one player. She then took the stake which might be money, clothing, mats, basketry or dried fish.

The rules of the Dicing Game varied a little from tribe to tribe. As played by the squaws of the Makah Indians, Neath Bay, Washington State, USA, the two longer of upper teeth were called *laki* (male) and the pair of lower and shorter teeth *gule* (female). When all the teeth fell marked side uppermost the player won two tallies. If both female or both male teeth fell marked sides up they won one tally. Any other throw scored nothing. The players cast the dice alternately. The game ended when one player had won all the tally sticks (188). The beaver teeth were shaken in cupped hands and cast down on to a blanket.

Replicas of a Norse ivory and a wooden die, as used by the Tlingit Indians of Alaska, are also illustrated. They are shaped like a chair and called *Ket-chii*. Only one die was used in this woman's game.

Scoring

Either side up	0
Back or front up	1
Bottom up	2
Top up	No score but another turn

The die is thrown on to the leather tablet. If it rolls off the tablet, there is no score. The painting on the tablet represents a beaver, identified by its cross-hatched tail, here painted yellow. The art of the North West Coast Indians is unique and its interpretation difficult without considerable guidance.

153

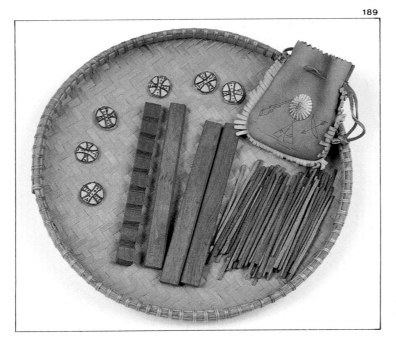

189

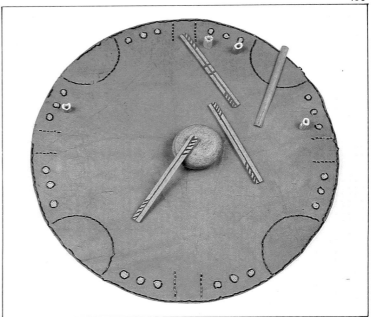

190

(189) Reproduction bowl, dice, counting sticks and leather bag for the Bowl Game.

(190) Reproduction leather and bead-work board, sticks, *Ahl* stone and bone markers used by the Kiowa Indians, Oklahoma, USA, for playing *Zohn Ahl*.

THE BOWL GAME. WER-LAR-DA-HAR-MUN-GUN (Penobscot Indians, Maine)

Several tribes of Indians living in the east of America played variants of the Bowl Game. The variety described here was popular among the women of the Penobscot Indians in Maine, Eastern USA. The requirements were a set of counting-sticks, six thin flat discs of bone carved and painted on one side and plain on the other for dice and a bowl, either of wood or basketware *(189)*.

The dice were cut from the shoulder-blade of a moose, the fifty-five counting sticks were of cedar, fifty-one being splits about 6 inches (15cm) long, three flats a little longer and one cut into a zig-zag shape. A folded blanket was put on the ground or on the floor for the dish to be thumped down upon. Two players sat opposite each other; the dice were placed in the dish and were tossed up and then brought down hard on to the cushion.

Scoring

Five dice with the same side up won three sticks.

All six dice with the same side up was called a DOUBLE and the player took one of the large flat sticks and had another turn.

The game continued until all the sticks had been drawn. The player with most points won, the small sticks counting one point and the large sticks six points. The notched stick was the last large stick to be won and when it had been

taken the game was over, even if there were unclaimed small sticks still on the blanket.

Onlookers often took part, wagering side bets on the state of play or on the next score of the dice.

THE STAVE GAME (Se-tich-ch) (Bounce-on-the-stone) (Amerindians)

Se-tich-ch is one of many similar stave games and is played by the women of the Navaho and Apache in the south-west of the USA.

Equipment

Two sets of three sticks of hazel wood were used 8 inches (20cm) long, ¾ inch (2cm) wide and about ⅜ inch (0.9cm) thick. They were flat on one side with a diagonal black band across the middle, the other side was rounded and plain.

Four or six women took part forming themselves into two teams. The board consisted of forty small stones in a circle on the ground, divided into four divisions of ten stones each. Fig. 74.

The players knelt outside the circle of stones, each team with its own set of dicing sticks. The first player took her team's sticks in one hand, curved sides outermost and slammed them end first on to the central stone, an action giving rise to the name of the game, *Se-tich-ch* (Bounce-on-the-stone).

Scoring of the sticks

3 plain round sides up	10 and another turn
3 marked flat sides up	5
2 round sides up and 1 flat	3
1 round side up and 2 flats	2

Each team had two sticks to mark their count, leap-frogging in a similar manner to the pegs in cribbage and the markers of the two teams travelled in opposite directions around the circle. The first team to guide its marker home won the game and the stake. This quick game was ideal for gambling and also had the merit that cheating was difficult.

Zohn Ahl *(190)* is a similar game and is played by the Kiowa Indians, Oklahoma. Four dicing sticks are used: the flat stone in the centre is known as the *Ahl* stone and the breaks in the circle at the cardinal points are hazards. At the north and south they represent rivers in flood and a marker landing in them is swept away and has to start again. At east and west they represent dry gulleys and a marker landing there is held up for one turn. This game is derived from *Nyout*, illustrated on page 8, of North East Asia and is thought to have been taken by the first inhabitants of North America across the Bering Strait. The torrents and gulleys at the cardinal points are vestigial remains of the Cross, with the Circle surviving intact. In *Patolli* of the Aztecs *(191)* the opposite occurred; the cross survived and doubled, while the circle vanished.

PATOLLI (Aztec) (Mexico)

Father Diego Duran in his *Antiguallas e Historia de los Mejicanos*, written about 1560, describes Mexican gamblers walking about with a *patolliztli* mat rolled up under an arm and carrying a little basket containing coloured stones used as markers. The dice were five large beans called *patolli*, each with a hole drilled in one side to act as a white pip. The score for a throw depended upon the number of white pips uppermost. The markers were moved along the divisions according to the throws and the game seems to have been similar to modern Ludo, see page 10.

The last of the North American Indian Games to be described is the simplest.

GAMBLING STICKS (Amerindian)

The Haida of British Columbia used sticks 4 to 5 inches (10 to 12cm) long, each stick having different marks on it, and representing a warrior in the tribe. One stick was entirely coloured and one entirely plain, the latter being the winning stick. Each player had a bunch of forty or so of these sticks.

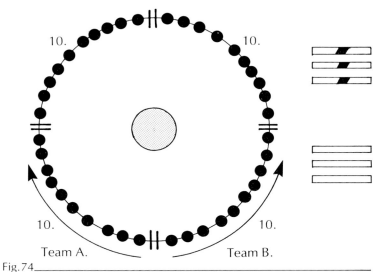

Fig.74

191

(191) Reproduction *Patollitzli* mat, onyx pieces, and five patolli beans.

The Indian about to play put down his stake, matched by his opponent and then took up his sticks and put them under shredded cedar bark which was as fine as tow and, under this concealment, divided them into two parcels, wrapped these up in a piece of bark and passed them from hand to hand to confuse his opponent. The opponent then pointed to the bundle he thought contained the plain (winning) stick. The player then shook the sticks amid mounting excitement out of the bark one at a time on to the blanket on the ground until the plain stick appeared or, if it was not there, the opponent had lost. See page 153.

The winner took one or more markers from his opponent's store and when one player had won all the markers, the game was over and the winner collected his prize. Onlookers wagered side bets on the outcome of each concealment.

The oldest known gambling sticks are in the Museum of Man (British Museum) and were taken to England by Captain Vancouver in the 1790s. They are stored in a cedarbark woven bag.

CHAPTER 11

FORTUNE TELLING

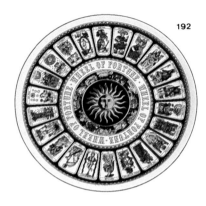

(192) A Wedgwood 'Wheel of Fortune' plate, c.1978. Arranged outside the wheel are the twenty-two cards of the major Arcana comprising a series of mystical symbols representing life. Inside the wheel are the twelve signs of the Zodiac and in the centre, the Sun.

(193) *Chi Chi* sticks and booklet, 1959.

CHI CHI STICKS

The games-playing section of this book began with a reference to fortune-telling as being the probable *raison d'etre* of race games, and it seems appropriate to close with it. Among the numerous methods of divination one of the oldest is using *Chi Chi* sticks (193). The set produced by Pacifico of San Francisco, Copyright 1915 consists of a box of bamboo sticks numbered from 1 to 78. The box is shaken with a continuous snappy downwards motion without stopping until one stick drops out. If more than one stick falls they are replaced and the shaking repeated. The number on the stick holds the clue to the enquirer's fortune for the day, which is read off from an accompanying booklet.

In the preface to the booklet the author states that, while touring China, he had his fortune told in a Chinese Joss House using the sticks. After considerable time and expense he secured a translation of their fortune telling book. A native son of China, he tells us, never thinks of entering business for the day without first having his fortune told from these mysterious sticks. First is the luck for the day, then future events, the answer to a wish and a word of advice.

When the sticks were being photographed No.4 fell from the box. On referring to the booklet:
'No. 4 YOUR LUCK FOR TODAY —
It's only fair, don't wish for more.

'YOUR FORTUNE
Your mate in life will bring you luck
And be your guiding star,
So cherish either him or her
Or success you'll surely bar

'Beware of fatal extravagance.
Your wish is doubtful.'

THE TELEPATHIC SPIRIT COMMUNICATOR

Produced by 'The Two Worlds' Publishing Company Ltd. 18 Corporation Street, Manchester. Not dated. (195).

The directions for using the planchette are given on the lid and are reproduced below:

'DIRECTIONS:- When sitting for investigation into the subject of Spirit Return, try to take all possible precautions against outside interference. Quietude is a valuable aid. Place the fingers of one or both hands lightly on the board, and sit passively until movements take place. When that occurs, ask the unseen operators to try to spell out a name or message. Should our first attempt result in failure, do not get discouraged, as it often requires a few sittings before the power can be sufficiently controlled to ensure reliable results. Take care that mistakes do not occur on your part and always remember that errors are quite possible on the part of the communicator. Spirits are only human beings and do not possess more knowledge or goodness than they have acquired by their own efforts, and if any should try to impose upon you chasten them kindly. Ignorant spirits will sometimes attempt to flatter and deceive. Always exercise judgment and discretion

concerning all messages received. Be kind and sympathetic towards your unseen communicators. They may need your friendship. To obtain the best results, maintain a tranquil condition of mind, and cultivate a habit of sincerity and honesty. You should not sit more than an hour at a time, and not oftener than twice a week. Two persons can use the instrument by placing one hand each lightly upon the board. After a little practice the person sitting at the board may be blind-folded, a second person recording the messages.'

This device seems to be similar to the Ouija board which was eventually outlawed in some countries because of adverse psychological effect on some of its addicts.

TAROT CARDS

A few games are played with tarot cards *(196)* but their main use is in fortune-telling. Their origin is unknown. The standard modern tarot pack has four suits Swords, Cups, Coins and Batons with an extra court card in each suit. These are: King, Queen, Knight, and Page, with the numbered cards running from Ten down to Ace.

There are also 22 extra cards known as the Major Arcana, having their own names and numbers. They are:

0 The Fool	9 The Hermit	18 The Moon
1 The Juggler	10 The Wheel of Fortune	19 The Sun
2 The Female Pope	11 Strength	20 The Day of
3 The Empress	12 The Hanged Man	Judgement
4 The Emperor	13 Death	21 The World
5 The Pope	14 Temperance	
6 The Lovers	15 The Devil	
7 The Chariot	16 The Tower	
8 Justice	17 The Star	

Large books have been written on the use of these cards and nothing will be attempted here except to quote from a small booklet supplied with a pack:

'Tarot cards are used for placing the past into more meaningful perspective, understanding the present, and revealing the alternatives which exist in the future. Whether you use the Tarot cards for divination, or as a game, you will find them entertaining and fascinating.'

Many of the modern packs are very ugly, but some of the early cards are miniature works of art.

Reference: Cavendish, R. *The Tarot*, Michael Joseph, London. 1975.

(194) Six porcelain fortune-telling cups. All twentieth century.

(195) The Telepathic Spirit Communicator, c.1930.

(196) Two packs of Tarot cards and an *I-Ching* pack with three counters.

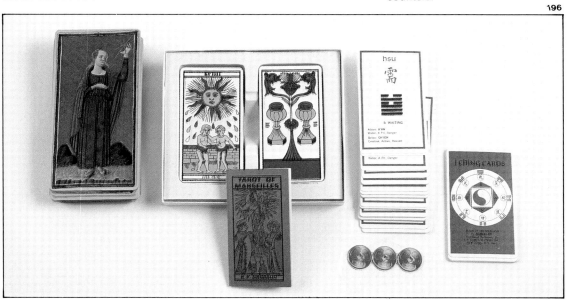

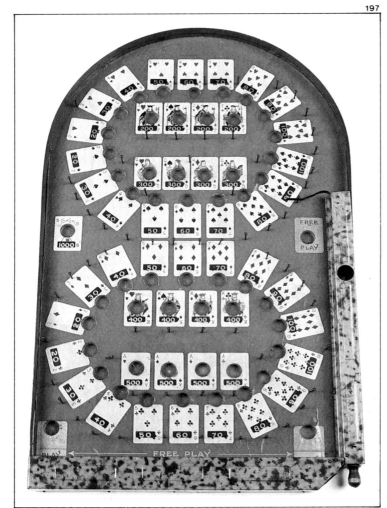

197

(197) Fortune Telling Bagatelle board, c.1930.

(198) The Fortune Teller, c.1930.

(199) *Poh-Kam* and two good-luck talismen with the Chinese domino pairing recorded on them, late nineteenth century.

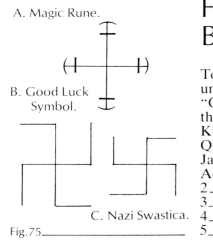

A. Magic Rune.

B. Good Luck Symbol.

C. Nazi Swastica.

Fig.75

FORTUNE TELLING BAGATELLE

The board *(197)* was produced by the Lindstrom Tool & Toy Co, Bridgeport. Conn. 1934. The rules are on the underside of the board. 'Hearts and Diamonds are "GOOD" cards, Clubs and Spades are "BAD" cards. Of the picture cards, red are blonde and black are brunette.'

King_____ a married man
Queen_____ a woman
Jack_____ an unmarried man
Ace_____ a letter
2_____ a divorce
3_____ the health card if red, good; if black, poor)
4_____ a surprise (if black, a disappointment)
5_____ a change
6_____ pertaining to business
7_____ marriage
8_____ travel
9_____ love
10_____ money

For example:
Ace of Diamonds, Jack of Clubs, 4 of Hearts — you will receive a letter, from a dark young man, which will be a pleasant surprise.
Queen of Diamonds, 5 of Spades, 9 of Diamonds, King of Spades — a woman will cause a change in the affection of a dark man.
10 of Diamonds, 6 of Hearts, 5 of Hearts — You will receive a sum of, money, you will travel, and make a change for the better.
Jack of Spades 9 of Clubs, Jack of Hearts — two young men are in love with you, one is blonde, one dark and both are unhappy.
Ace of Hearts, 6 of diamonds, 10 of hearts — you will receive a business letter which will result in money for you; the entire transacton being a fortunate one for you.
8 of Diamonds, 3 of Hearts, 5 of Clubs, 6 of Spades — you will travel, your health will improve, there will be a change in your busines affairs (to the worse).
The balls — steel ball bearings — are propelled by a spring mechanism which is still in working order.

THE FORTUNE TELLER

Produced by Milton Bradley Co. Springfield, Mass. USA Copyright 1905, this game *(198)* can be played by any number of persons with one of the company taking the part of the Fortune teller and who will read the fortunes aloud.

Rules

1. Place the Magic Wheel in the centre of the table and the player on the left of the Fortune Teller may adjust the Wand to one of the three circles and turn the Wheel around three times, calling the card to which the Wand points, when the Fortune Teller will read out the fortune from the explanation following these rules.

2. Should the Wand point between two cards, the player may turn the Wheel around until it stops at a card.

3. When the player has learned his fate he may have a silent wish while the Fortune Teller turns the Wheel around *once*. At whichever card the wand points, that card represents the answer, which will be found on the other side of this card. (Booklet)

6. The Fortune Teller must alter the wording of the fortunes to suit the sexes, substituting 'he' for 'she' or 'wife' for 'husband' etc.

Examples of cards

'EIGHT OF CLUBS You are going to attend a great banquet, but beware of the man who will sit opposite you. He is your enemy and possesses a secret about you. JACK OF SPADES There is a person of boundless effrontery who will bring great distress into your life unless you are firm and take him for a drive in a motor car and lose him. (Remember the year — 1905!) 'FIVE OF DIAMONDS Your name will one day be inscribed on the roll of fame. Why did you let your rival see you in the moonlight that night? It was your best chance of securing treasure. 'QUEEN OF HEARTS Beware of red hair. It will bring you bad luck. A very fair individual, fond of gaiety and a flirt, is your rival.'

ANSWERS TO THE FIFTYTWO SECRET WISHES

TWO OF CLUBS Hopeless. Your last letter has given too much offence. EIGHT OF HEARTS There is a mystery here. FIVE OF SPADES Not for ten years. ACE OF DIAMONDS You betrayed yourself too soon. etc.

TALISMEN, CHARMS AND GOOD LUCK SYMBOLS

Game-players and in particular gamblers place reliance on charms and good luck tokens. Three are shown in *(200)*. On the left is a small Cornish Pixie in brass, one of the little green people, bringing good luck to believing humans.

In the centre is a reproduction of an Icelandic talisman inscribed with a 'magic rune', ensuring success while playing chess or backgammon. Better known as a symbol of good luck and extending back to the days of ancient India is the *swastika,* defined as a cross with equal arms with a limb of the same length projecting from the end of each arm, all in the same direction. Fig. 75.

In Iceland there still exist old 'magical' formulas to enable a player to win at chess and others for backgammon. One of the latter runs, 'If you wish to win at backgammon, take a raven's heart, dry it in a spot on which the sun does not shine, crush it, then rub it on the Dice'.

Magical backgammon verses seem to have been fairly common at one time. Another way of winning at backgammon is mentioned by Jon Arnason, 'The backgammon player should cry "Olave, Olave, Harold, Harold, Erik, Erik". This formula should also be written in Runic letters and carried on his person, or better, placed unnoticed beneath the backgammon board. He must also

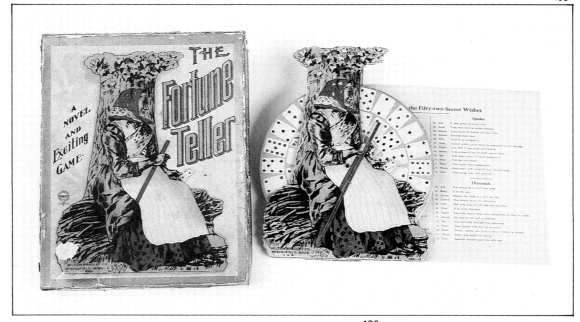

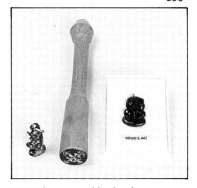

say the Lord's prayer in honour of St. Olave, the King.'

On the right in the picture is a Maori *Hei Tiki* made in nephrite jade. These were originally fertility symbols and the carving probably represented a foetus. The *Hei Tiki* is now regarded as a good luck token. This is a modern piece. Some of the old ones are very valuable, fetching $1,000/ £550 or more and have been recovered from Maori burial grounds.

On the left in *(199)* is a *Poh Kam* used in the game of Spinning Treasure *(Lien Poh)* and on the right a pair of Chinese Domino charms made of ivory, ensuring success in play, but also having the practical value of recording the scoring combinations of the dominoes in their order of seniority. It is probably nineteenth century. Provenance unknown.

(200) Three good luck talismens. Left to right: Cornish pixie in brass; reproduction Icelandic good fortune rune in holly; *Hei tiki* in nephritic jade from New Zealand (Maori).

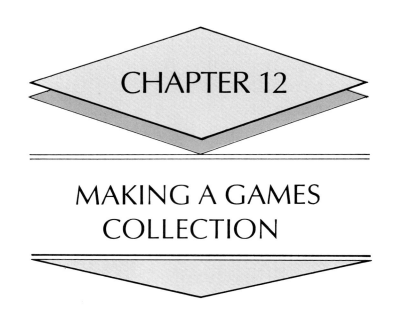

CHAPTER 12

MAKING A GAMES COLLECTION

The games player who becomes a collector passes through the portals of a new dimension, leaving the stress and excitement of competition for quieter pleasures of scholarship, the appreciation of history and a respect for craftsmen's skills. In many fields collectors may require only a knowledge of a single factory (ceramics), material (ivory), artist (paintings), country (numismatics), but a collection of games is likely to cross all boundaries of time, geography and culture. The collector will find that he has a key to open many doors and contacts with people in many parts of the world, from the Maori in New Zealand to the Eskimo of Alaska; to many religious beliefs and to all civilizations in the long history of man.

As with all of man's activities the playing of games has led inevitably to the creation of artefacts. However, the function they serve has, very early on, become subsumed by their form. As a consequence, the objects by means of which a game is played have long since ceased to exist merely as objects with which to play. The earth, stones, and bits of bone man first used became progressively transformed into tangible objects of play. Thus, for example, the throwing stick gave way to the astragalus (the four-sided ankle bone of a sheep or other animal) which in turn gave way to the die. The die is essentially a manmade symbol and, as such, the material of which it is made ceases to be of importance. It can be made of almost any material as long as the recognized form is maintained. It is essentially at this point that aesthetics come into play. The visual appeal of the game and the 'feel' of its components takes on an increasing importance. As noted by Erving Goffman in *Fun in Games* 'The game-relevant meanings of the various pieces of the game equipment are in themselves a useful disguise, for behind these meanings the sentimental, material, and aesthetic value of the pieces can steal into the interaction infusing it with tones of meaning that have nothing to do with the logic of the game but something to do with the pleasure of the gaming encounter; the traditional concern in Japan about the quality of

equipment used to play *Go* is an extreme example.' It is not surprising therefore to note that artisans of all cultures and ages have striven to produce sumptuous artefacts as a means of enhancing the 'gaming encounter'.

On a subliminal, if not a conscious level, the games buff must be well aware of this factor. Consequently, the desire to play games is supplemented for many by the desire to possess them, not only as part of a 'library' of play, but as objects in their own right. The choice as with so many other fields is exceedingly diverse. As with all specific quests, the mere act of looking for a particular item tends to uncover far more than one originally anticipated. Not only the games themselves, but also pictures, ceramics or other *objets d'art* representing the playing of games, many examples of which are to be found within the pages of this book.

The neophyte collector need not necessarily burden himself with what, at times, may appear to be a fruitless quest for priceless treasures or rare museum pieces. Exquisite as they are, many such items remain, on the whole, unobtainable, requiring a deep pocket and infinite patience. However one need not despair. We live in the late twentieth century, some two hundred years after the advent of the Industrial Revolution which spawned a whole host of innovative wonders. The greatest legacy of this was the advent of an urbanized society and the fruits of 'mass production', granting the public at large access, for the first time, to an exceedingly diverse array of manufactured products. The linchpin was, of course, the last half of the nineteenth century which saw the introduction of many of the items of daily life that we now take for granted.

It was a multiple revolution reaching into every aspect of society, not least of which was the manufacture and invention of new games, and games-related products. It witnessed the formation of many new manufacturing companies, some of which have since become household names for successive generations of games players names such as Chad Valley in England or Parker Brothers in the

United States. Among the many new games which have gained popularity since that time are to be found repackaged versions of more ancient games. Thus the latter half of the nineteenth century was to see the introduction of the perennially popular Snakes and Ladders (the original version of which was *Moksha Patamu* a traditional Hindu game), as well as another old favourite: Ludo (in essence a modified form of the much older game of *Pachisi*).

Coupled with this were radical advances in printing and marketing techniques which led inevitably to more sophisticated methods of presentation. The last hundred years or so have been a veritable golden age of game design, making use, in many instances, of the talents of a number of leading graphic artists. Even if, at times, a newly acquired, though little known, game of former times proves to be somewhat dull, lacking the essential challenge of more successful games formats, the collector can at least take an altruistic pleasure in the charm and beauty of the graphic presentation. The added bonus is that because many such items are of relatively recent vintage they are still within financial reach.

Nicholas Costa.

ADVICE TO NEW COLLECTORS

1. LIMITS Decide early on the limits of your collection and stick to the parameters chosen, otherwise a hobby and fun become a financial worry. Examples of limitation follow:

a) Boxed games. If a game isn't in a wooden box, it isn't included.
b) Only board games. No board — not accepted.
c) Cards, or card games, only.
d) Games of skill.
e) Games of chance.
f) Action games.
g) Pub games only those played in public houses.
h) Oriental games.
i) African games.
j) Games published by a specific firm; e.g. Goddard & Son; F.H. Ayres; Jaques & Son.
k) Games of a particular country.

The choice is very wide and this list only gives a few ideas.

2. RECORDS As a collection grows remembering the details becomes impossible. The author uses a simple card index system, classifying the games into main groups:

Action games (A), Calculation games (C), Dice games (Di), Dominoes (Do), Mancala (M), Games of Position (P), Race games (R), War games (W) etc.

Within any group are further sub-divisions. In Race games are: Ra — Amerindian race games, Rb — Backgammon group, Rj — Japanese race games, etc. Each item is given its own number and card. For example, the card Re (England) 24 reads:

'Re 24 Everest Mountain Climb. 20" x 14", England. Remploy product. Published about the time of Sir John Hunt's Expedition 1938-9. No pieces with it. Bought from a junk shop near Wyatt Road, Islington for 25p, June 1981.'

The card thus carries details of country of origin, manufacturer, time of production, where purchased and price paid. Any interesting information about previous owners, provenance etc. is noted.

The following pieces are taken from the author's own collection which ranges from something as simple as a Chinese print of two ladies playing *Go* and produced just two years ago, to beautiful antiques, such as the carved ivory chessmen or the games tables. The variety of pieces illustrated in this chapter also serves to demonstrate the wide range of sources available to the collector of games and games-related objects. These are as varied as the items themselves and the collector should be as vigilant over a stall selling tourist souvenirs in an African village, as in a high-class antique saleroom in one of the world's most elegant cities.

201

(**201**) A *Capo-di-monte* figurine with two Italian urchins playing cards. Note the cards are Italian with suits of Swords, Batons, Coins and Cups. Each figurine is modelled and painted by a master craftsman and no two pieces are identical.

(202) An unsigned Japanese copy of a famous *Capo-di-monte* piece, *'The Cheats'* by Cavazzin, in which all four urchins are cheating unbeknown to each other.

(203) *The Chess Players* is a puzzling piece. It carries an underglaze printed mark, fig. 76 and 'Made in Western Germany'.

Fig. 76

The word Dresden surmounted by a crown was at one time the mark of the private firm, Wolfson and their pieces were sometimes referred to as 'Crown Dresden', but this was in the late nineteenth and early twentieth centuries. This piece was made after the Second World War, *c*.1950. The stamp 'Western Germany' is also strange as Dresden is in the German Democratic Republic (East Germany).

The piece is of high quality, the rendering of the lady's lace dress being particularly pleasing. The tip of the male figure's right index finger is missing.

(204) The little figurine shows two elderly men playing cards, sustained by a carafe of wine with two tumblers alongside. The piece is signed GINO but there is no other indication of its source. The men's features are caricature.

(205) The unmarked *Famille Rose et Verte* saucer shows two Chinese ladies playing a game. The figure on the right is taking a counter out of a bowl. The lines are marked diagonally on the board and all the pieces are black. The game is probably meant to be *Wei-ch'i (Go)* but, if so, the artist has been careless. The lines should be marked at right angles, the stones should be black and white and both players should have a bowl to hold their stones. Perhaps the discrepancies can be attributed to artistic licence. The piece dates from *c*.1850.

209

206

207

(206) This plate shows two children playing *Sz Hwa* (The Game of Four Directions) in the village of Heng Chuen in South Taiwan. This was the first plate in a series entitled 'Chinese Children's Games' by the artist Kee Fung Ng (1986), issued by the Pavilion of T'sang YingHsan and sponsored by the Hwa Kang Museum. They were produced in a limited edition under the hallmark of *Artists of the World ©*.

1985. Kee Fung Ng was born in Canton, China, before World War Two and trained in the state-supported Fu San Art School. Later he emigrated to Hong Kong where he worked for several years developing a subtle mixture of Eastern and Western painting techniques. Today he lives in the USA where examples of his work are on display at the Kee Fung Ng gallery in San Francisco, and at the Lahaina Gallery in Maui, Hawaii.

(207) Bought in Singapore in 1979, this tile 12 by 9 inches (30 by 22cm) is thought to have come from Peking. The stamp is of Ch'ien Lung, and the piece is in the style of his period, 1735-1796, but it is a modern reproduction.

Similar imitations of Ch'ien Lung pieces were made in Victorian times, *c.*1850 and are now regarded as antiques in their own right but the reproductions of the twentieth century are not well known, and thus are also of interest. The design shows two ladies, one holding a fan, and playing cards lying on the table.

(208) This porcelain vase was bought in Singapore in 1978 and was made in China about a year earlier. It is marked with a Chinese seal in red and MADE IN CHINA in black. The scene shows two ladies playing *Siang-k'i* at a table in a garden watched by a third lady, while a fourth views them through a moon window in the background.

208

(209) The hard paste porcelain card-holder was presumably one of four — the kings of Spades, Diamonds and Hearts being missing. The piece bears no ceramic marks except that inside the upper portion is an eighteen in a red-brown paint, probably a workman's number. It is thought to have been made about 1870 in England.

FAIRINGS

Most early Fairings bear a caption and all were made of china. They were used as prizes at fairs in the nineteenth century. The early examples, 1860-70, were generally a little larger and of better quality than the later figures; those of the 1870s and 1880s were mass-produced and are clumsier with flat bases. After 1890 the colouring became even more garish and gilding was added to the base. They were manufactured in Germany, the two main firms being Conte and Boehme of Pössneck and Springer and Oppenheimer of Elbogen. Both companies also produced uncaptioned fairings intended primarily for sale in shops rather than as fairground prizes.

Reference Anderson, M. *Victorian Fairings and their Values*, Lyle Publications, 1975.

(211) The second fairing of chess or draughts players, who are sitting in front of an empty board, is of the later period being smaller and with a solid base. The seated lady's right hand is missing. *c.*1890.

(210) *The Chess Players*, is uncaptioned but is hollow and of the earlier period. Unfortunately two of the chess pieces are broken and also the seated lady has a hand missing *c.*1860.

(212) The Chinese figurine of two old men playing *Siang k'i* or Chinese Chess was bought in Vancouver's Chinatown in 1978. Its provenance is unknown. The faces and hands of unglazed biscuitware contrast with the glazed and coloured robes, giving a realism surprising in a low-priced piece. Similar pottery figurines are fairly common, but not of gamers. *c.*1975.

(213) This caricature piece shows two monks passing the time with a game of cards. One has an extra card tucked into the strapping of his left sandal which has been noticed by his opponent and gives rise to the title of the piece, 'Oh Brother'. Made by Naturecraft, England, of Hydrocal stoneware and bought in York in April 1976.

(214) *The Card Players*, in lead, *c.*1978, was made by a model soldier enthusiast who spent many hours making and painting this one-off model of two sixteenth-century merchant venturers passing the time on the quayside playing cards. Note the rat scampering over the planking.

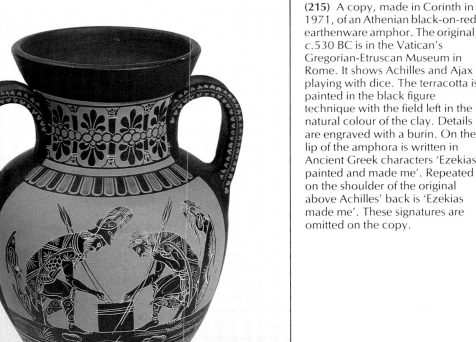

(215) A copy, made in Corinth in 1971, of an Athenian black-on-red earthenware amphor. The original, *c.*530 BC is in the Vatican's Gregorian-Etruscan Museum in Rome. It shows Achilles and Ajax playing with dice. The terracotta is painted in the black figure technique with the field left in the natural colour of the clay. Details are engraved with a burin. On the lip of the amphora is written in Ancient Greek characters 'Ezekias painted and made me'. Repeated on the shoulder of the original above Achilles' back is 'Ezekias made me'. These signatures are omitted on the copy.

(216) The Black Sambo die-holder and dicing cup (left) is carved in boxwood and stained black to simulate ebony. The top hat unscrews to reveal a small red wooden die with gold coloured pips. The hat is hollow and serves as a dicing cup. The provenance is unknown and its date of manufacture difficult to estimate but probably late nineteenth or early twentieth century.

The mahogany puzzle ball (right) has six large sets of concentric circles engraved on its surface and eight smaller sets of concentric circles interspersed between them. One of the large circles and it is quite difficult to find which, pushes out to reveal a cylinder, which itself is hollow and contains two small dice. The cylinder functions as a dicing cup. A nice example of a woodturner's skill and ingenuity.

217

218

(217) The lead chessmen are of the Rose pattern, Patent No. 546516 in their original box. The smaller set seems to have been issued, one at a time, with packets of sweets. On collecting a complete set a visit to the dentist may have been needed!

Nothing is known about the two lead draughtsman shown with them. One surface bears the word KING and the other side is plain. They appear to be rare.

(218) The Temple of Heavenly Happiness is the oldest temple in Singapore and among its treasures is a wooden statue some 5 feet (1.5m) high of How T'si Kong, the god of gambling. The sale of opium is illegal and severely punished in the city, except at the entrance to this temple where it can be purchased by gamblers to smear on the chin and neck of the god to bring them success in their calling.

The little replica is some 12 inches (30cm) high and was carved in a workshop a few hundred yards away from the temple by Lim Aik Thuan, Idol maker, No.11 Club Street, Singapore, in May 1978. It is based on the lifesize carving of the God in the Temple of Heavenly Happiness. Only three weeks were available for the carving and painting of the figure, which has suffered from this haste and the gilding has tended to flake away under the climatic change from the humidity of the island near the equator to the dryness of a centrally-heated home in Britain.

Around the neck of the original statue are strings of cash donated by worshippers and regularly removed by the priests; on the replica there is a single string of modern coins.

PAINTINGS

219

(219) These three kittens have reduced a postponed game of chess to chaos. The picture is signed *Sybil Burton*, probably an art student at the time of its execution, and is possibly a copy of a famous painting. It was bought in Newcastle, near the department of Fine Art of the University, about ten years ago. The artist's interest seems to have been concentrated on the cats, whose faces and expressions are excellent, rather than on the chessmen, two of the white pieces being of unrecognizable shape. The chess board itself is incorrect with each row consisting of four squares of one colour and three of the other. Such 'artistic licence' limits the value of many pictures of games from antiquity to modern times. Often the question must be asked; 'Is this an accurate representation or an artist's impression?'.

Painting on glass, known as *Verre Eglomé* is named after its inventor in the West, Jean Baptise Glomy, a Parisian artist, writer and antique dealer who lived at the end of the eighteenth century. In the *verre eglomisé* painting **(220)** two

Chinese ladies are playing *Wei ch'i (Go)* and the artist depicts a moment early in the game. Note the wooden bowls for holding the stones, similar to those used in the game of *Siang k'i* **(221)**. These pictures are similar in style and period (1790-1830). They were probably painted by different artists of the same school, the painter of the *Wei ch'i* game being better at depicting faces. At some time the picture had been exposed to damp and the colours had run. Even in this damaged state it is a desirable item as these pictures are rare. There is no artist's seal, but it is either late eighteenth or early nineteenth century.

Note that the two ladies playing *Wei ch'i* are using an antique form of the board with 13 x 11 squares. The tablets on the wall behind the players read, 'Under the pine-tree I asked for the master; he had gone gathering herbs among the hills'.

'Since you went away, why have I no longer bothered with the abandoned board? When I think of you, I am like the full moon whose brilliance wanes night after night. Your lover.' These are

220

221

222

quotations from well-known poems.

Chinese artists depend upon 'atmosphere' to create the illusion of distance, whereas the Western artist relies upon perspective. At the end of the eighteenth century, there was a Chinoiserie movement in Europe, with Chinese Chippendale furniture, Willow pattern plates and lacquered cabinets. An Occidental equivalent in China produced equally bizarre results. This picture is an attempt by a skilled Chinese artist to employ the unfamiliar Western technique of perspective. The curious mixture of Oriental and Occidental art displayed in this picture and the next are sufficiently rare to be of interest to a growing body of *Go* players in the West. Most Chinese pictures of this period were either religious or poetical, fortunately here a secular subject is combined with poetry.

The second picture (221) showing a game of *Siang k'i* also relies on 'atmosphere' for the creation of a sense of distance, and both have failed to understand the Western use of perspective. Painted within a vertical rectangle instead of a horizontal, it is slightly larger, 26 by 19 inches (66 by 48cm) and there were six figures instead of five. The glass is cracked in one place and the picture has also been exposed to dampness at some time, causing the colours to run. It came from the home of a warehouseman and had been in his family for many years. There is no artist's seal and the style is very similar to the previous picture.

(222) This coloured lithograph signed C. Hunt '92 is a romantic interpretation of rural life with a donkey and a horse in a cottage kitchen. In the foreground the elderly Danny is facing defeat in a game of draughts with a boy of about ten, possibly his grandson. The youngster has trapped the old man's remaining white king. The board is accurately drawn although the double corner should be on the player's right, and each player seems to have eleven pieces instead of twelve. These are unimportant details unless the picture is being used for research. Title: *Danny Puzzled.*

223

(223) A woodblock print by the Japanese artist Chikanobu, *c.*1890, depicting two ladies near the beginning of a game of *Go* being watched by a third. The lady on the left is drawing a stone out of her bowl with her right hand ready to place at her next turn of play.

224

有喜古之琴

(224) The second woodblock print, by Shuntei, 1873-1899 shows the start of a game of *Go* before any pieces have been placed on the board. These highly coloured prints were intended for sale in the West and were not regarded highly in Japan.

(225) The triptych by Chikunobu (1838-1921) was published in 1889 and shows three ladies playing *Hyaku-min-itsushu*. The man on the right is calling out half a quotation and the players have to match the rest of the quotation from a card in their hand, placing it in front of themselves or, failing to do so, have to take up a card from the pool. The first player to clear her hand is the winner, but the scores are based on the number of cards they have managed to match with the reader's quotation and place on the table. By way of explanation, if the quotation were from Shakespeare's eighteenth sonnet 'Shall I compare thee to a summer's day?', the wanted card would read, 'Thou are more lovely and more temperate'.

Readers wishing to enquire more deeply into Japanese prints are recommended to consult a *Guide to Japanese Prints and their Subject Matter* by Basil Stewart, Dover Publications Inc. New York, 1979.

226

(226) Before Europeans introduced playing cards into Japan, the Japanese used the shells of a bivalve known as *Hama-guri* for a game called *Karuta Hiyaku-nin-Ishu*. In this game the two halves of the shell were separated and the inside of one half inscribed with a poetic quotation and the other half painted with a scene relating to the quotation. As an example, if the quotation were taken from Shakespeare's

Macbeth, Out, damned spot! Out, I say! One; Two; Why then 'tis the time to do 't', the picture might show Lady Macbeth sleepwalking. The picture shells were spread on the floor, the players gathered around, and a reader read out the quotations. The player who collected the most pairs' won the game. The painted *hama-guri* shells are late eighteenth or early nineteenth century. They are scarce even in Japan.

227

(227) The three packs of *Uta-Karuta* cards are of different periods: in front c.1859; those at the sides c.1890; and those behind in unstained wooden box, 1965. These cards are a cheaper substitute for the *hama-guri* shells, but are used for the same games. The literary game of *Uta-Karuta* is only played by educated people, and only for a few days during the New Year Festivities. In the triptych by Chikunobu three Japanese ladies are playing *Hiyaku-nin-ishu*, one of the *karuta* card games.

225

228

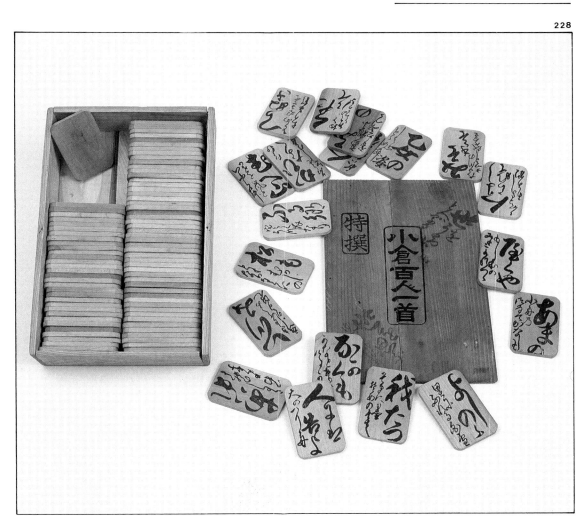

230

(228) A set of wooden cards for *Hyakumin Issu*. These have no pictures, but are for a similar literary game where two halves of a quotation are matched together. These *Ogura Hyakumin Issu* cards (a regional difference in spelling) were bought in a Japanese shop in Hastings Street, Vancouver in 1986 and had recently been brought from Kyoto in Southern Japan, from the home of a prosperous farmer with an extensive property. They are hand-painted on thin pieces of wood in an old style of script and are said to be at least a hundred years old.

(229) The perforated spoon shows a tavern scene with two eighteenth-century gentlemen enjoying a game of chess. Coach travellers on long journeys either in private vehicles or in stage coaches often took games boxes with them to help pass the time in the evenings at the hostelries where they spent the night.

The little silver and ivory dicing box is of native workmanship, does not carry a hallmark and may be of low standard metal. Its origin is unknown, although it was probably made in Asia or the Near East. The modern die inside, of imitation ivory, draws attention to the real ivory in the lid.

(230) This travelling games box has handles at both ends to help in carrying it from the coach to the inn. The three drawers held cards, chessmen and draughts, backgammon pieces, dice and dominoes. The upper surface is veneered with an 8 x 8 checkered board. The sides are veneered with walnut and the bottom is covered with a grey baize cloth. It was probably made about 1829 or earlier.

229

Reverting to the scene on the silver spoon in (229) the gentleman on the left has changed into comfortable attire and surveys the chess board with smug satisfaction, where his companion, still in his travelling frockcoat and boots, supports his brow with a hand in an attitude of concentration. One senses that he is in deep trouble and that checkmate is not far away. This piece is hallmarked London 1914 and the maker's mark is H & Co. Whether this spoon had a use or was purely ornamental is open to debate, but it is a desirable games-collector's item.

The silver case for the miniature Little Duke packs of patience cards is hallmarked Chester 1898, with the firm's mark N & H. The lid only bears the stamps of the lion for sterling and the date shield which is also for 1898.

WHIST MARKERS

Before describing some of the markers for this game, a few words about the game itself may not come amiss. Whist, once called Wisk, comes from a long line of card games belonging to the same family with common features. There are always four players, two against two in partnership. A full fifty-two card-pack is dealt out equally with each player holding thirteen cards, and the object of the game is to win tricks, each trick consisting of four cards, one card from each player, with the highest card taking the trick. Among these related games, in chronological order, were Triumph, Trump, Ruff and Honour (also known as Slamm), Whist and Swabbers, Whist, Bridge, Auction Bridge and, the most recent, Contract Bridge. These games appear to have originated in England. In a sermon preached at Cambridge in 1592 Hugh Latimer referred to Triumph, while Charles Cotton in his *Compleat Gamester* (1674) wrote, 'Ruff and Honours, and Whist are games so commonly known in England in all parts thereof, that every child almost of eight years old hath a complete knowledge in that recreation'.

Early in the eighteenth century, whist was taken up by gentlemen in London coffee-houses; and following the publication of Edmond Hoyle's *Short Treatise on Whist* in 1742, it became extremely popular in fashionable circles, soon spreading to Europe and America, and was THE card game until being displaced by its own offspring, Bridge.

There were two forms of whist, long whist with ten points making a game, with the best of three games needed to win the rubber, and short whist in which five points made a game, with two out of three games needed to win the rubber as in the long form.

The first standard laws were those published by Hoyle in 1742, revised in 1760 and again in 1864 by the Arlington and Portland Clubs. A different code of laws issued in 1893 by the American Whist League became standard for the United States. Under English laws, five points constitute a game. (The old Short Whist.)

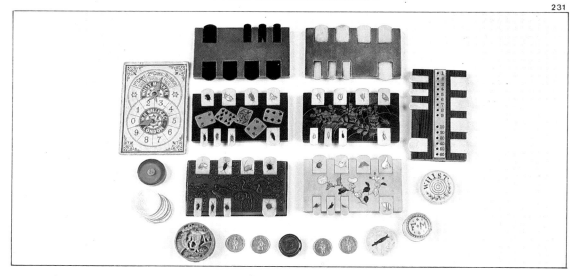

232

(232) The pair of brass markers are in the shape of a shallow round box, with a man and a woman playing whist embossed on the upper surface. Above them is a little window. The top of the box has a milled edge and revolves to show a series of numbers from one to nine and then a plus sign representing game at ten points. Below the figures is written WHIST MARKER.

Also illustrated is a pair of bone markers with a central revolving hand, of about the same date, c.1849. The brass 'hand marker' carries a registration mark on its underside of 31st January, 1860. It may have been made after this date but not before. The compartments are marked from zero to nine-ten points for the long game.

231

(231) A variety of late nineteenth century 'key' markers. The furthest pair are of silver, hallmarked 1899. One has ivory keys and the other ebony. The two middle and two nearest markers are Japanese. The bronze marker is embossed with cranes, the ivory marker has a flowering plant design and the two lacquered markers display flowers and cards respectively. Note the cards have rounded corners, indices and the Queen has two heads, all indicating a late date in the nineteenth or even early in the twentieth century.

The keys of these markers have inlays of metal or semi-precious stones, carved into the shape of insects. This form of ornamentation using encrustations of mother-of-pearl, ivory, amethyst, malachite, soapstone, coral, gold, silver etc. and set into ivory, wood, lacquer or metal was developed by the Shibayama family which was active during the An-ei era, 1722-81 onwards. First used for panels in screens about the middle of the nineteenth century, this work was employed for decorating *inro* and other small items. The whist marker faced with ivory is a good example of Shibayama work.

The four large keys on one side of the markers were used to score single points, the single large key on the opposite side represented five points and the three small keys recorded games won.

The rosewood and ivory marker is one of a pair and was made by Charles Goodall and Son, London, and both are marked on their under surface 'THE CAMDEN COMBINED CRIBBAGE & WHIST MARKER'. These are scarce.

The clock-faced carboard markers date from the beginning of the twentieth century. The rules of Long and Short Whist are recorded on the reverse.

233

(233) These markers are for *Bezique* and are not to be confused with those for whist.

IVORY AND BONE

The worldwide decline in the number of elephants and the attempts to control their slaughter for their tusks, has increased the value of ivory pieces, while bone, although readily available, has been mainly abandoned for the more easily worked-plastic materials so bone articles are also becoming scarce. Differentiation between bone and ivory should be simple with a hand lens. Tusks, being modified teeth, have a central dental canal but otherwise the structure is homogeneous, whereas bone contains a series of minute blood vessels running in Haversian canals, readily seen under low-power magnification or even with the naked eye.

The rules of chess, chess boards and complete sets of chessmen have been discussed elsewhere (See pages 27-34). A few years ago collectors were advised that they should rarely, if ever, buy incomplete chess sets or single pieces. The chances of replacing missing pieces was slight, and singletons were useless except as bric-a-brac on a mantlepiece.

Today the situation has changed. With the decline in the amount of ivory available, pieces in this material have become desirable, especially if well carved and, even more if they have anthropological associations. Indeed, sets of unusual quality are being broken up and sold for more as individual pieces than the complete set would fetch, a sad parallel to the many fine books that have been destroyed for their illustrations. Examples of single pieces are recorded below.

234

(234) Ivory Chess King. Probably nineteenth century and made in Delhi. A *mahout* sits astride the elephant's neck guiding the animal with a short goad held in the right hand. (The goad has been broken.) Inside the *howdah*, resting on richly ornamented trappings, are two princes.

235

(235) Ivory Burmese Chess Piece. This chess piece is carved as a Buddha in the *Bhumispara mudra* or earth-touching gesture, with his right hand touching the earth and the left palm uppermost across his lap. This posture was used by the Buddha to call the earth-goddess to witness his triumph over Mara the god of evil, and thus winning his right to sit beneath the tree of wisdom. Most Burmese chessmen are made of wood. See page 33.

The little ivory crocodile is from an animal chess set and represents a white bishop. Probably late nineteenth century. Provenance unknown.

236

(237)The third Indian piece is from an entirely different tradition, and was probably a knight in a lovely set made in the eighteenth century. The horse's tail and foreleg have been broken and repaired. The carving represents a participant in a Jain festival. The hat and costume are traditional, as are the horse's trappings and the special cut of his mane.

In 1960 there were over one and a half million Jains living in India. The *Digambara* in the south believe that a saint should own nothing, including clothing, and therefore they are usually naked. They also believe that salvation is not possible for a woman. The other section of the faith in the north, the *Shvetambara,* or white clad, differ on both points.

'Hurt no one' is a positive injunction of Jainism and the horseman's spear is purely ceremonial and would not be used. The Jains believe in love and compassion towards all creatures and build asylums and rest homes for old and sick animals, caring for them until they die a natural death. They are vegetarians and will not eat after dark, lest they should swallow some insects by mistake.

237

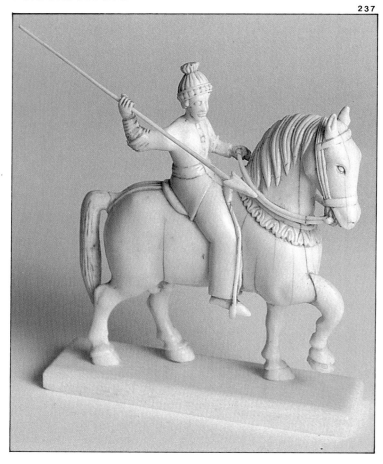

(236) A second ivory chess king is also probably from Delhi. It came from a large country-house sale a few years ago and seems to have been made in the mid to late nineteenth century. One of the foot-soldiers is missing, together with the pinnacles on the roof of the howdah and the mahout's goad. Only the stump remains in his right hand.

238

(238) Chinese Ivory Knights. The smallest piece is just under 2 inches (6cm) high and the horse stands on a simple base. The piece comes from a relatively cheap Cantonese set. The middle piece stands 3 inches (8cm) high and there are three balls within the external one. The horseman carries a sword in his right hand and is riding on a saddle with stirrups. The largest of these Knights is from a magnificent set. The piece stands 8 inches (20cm) high and there are five balls within the external one. The sword is missing, otherwise the piece is intact. Note the detail in the horseman's clothing and the horse's saddle cloth. The piece is difficult to date and could have been made anywhere between 1860 and 1920.

Mounting chessmen on puzzle-ball bases began early in the nineteenth century as a means of making simple chessmen look more impressive. The balls are carved from a single solid piece of ivory. First the outermost ball is turned on a lathe into a spherical shape, then it is drilled with a hollow-ended taper-drill to the centre; a shaped knife is used to cut free the various balls working from the centre outwards. Special tools, considerable skill and extreme patience is needed. Lastly the outer surface of the outer ball is carved with intricate designs. On this Knight the ball-puzzle base has several small figures representing immortals in the Taoist Heavens. Within the outer ball, each of the inner balls is pierced with a different design.

The ball-puzzle on the extreme left has seven balls within the outer one, which is carved with a series of intertwining dragons. Note that, unlike the dragons on the ivory cribbage board and dicing cup on page 177 *(248)*, the eyes of these dragons are not minute pieces of jet or ruby, but small drill holes touched with black ink.

SIX PIECES FROM A MYSTERY SET

239

(239) These six pieces provide a fascinating problem in possible provenance. They were purchased from an antique dealer in Durham who had no idea of their origin or age, as he had obtained them from another dealer who was unaware of their source.

The animal third from the left is a Kylin. The body of a horse supports the head of a dragon, the spirals on its haunches represent clouds and mounted on its back is a carrier decorated with a cloud pattern and containing a *T'i ch'i* or the Great Ultimate of Taoism. The Kylin passes across a base of swirling clouds, indicating its extraterrestial nature. Kylin is an anglicized form of *ch'ilin* (male) and *lin* (female). The kylin is frequently depicted on Chinese and Japanese pottery.

The Great Ultimate, fig. 78, symbolizes the interlocking elements of *yin* (female) and *yang* (male). Each contains an element of their opposite in the form of a dot. In Taoist belief the interaction of *yin* and *yang* gives rise to the Five Elements of Wood, Fire, Earth, Metal and Water, from which all objects are derived. This concept of the intermixing of male and female is popular in current western psychology where all individuals are regarded as unique blendings of female and male in varying proportions, giving rise, in

Fig. 78 —— The Great Ultimate

173

extreme cases, to masculine women and feminine men.

Liu-Hai, fifth from the left is one of the Taoist immortals, regarded as the protector of wealth and prosperity and so the patron of merchants. He was fond of fishing and on one occasion rescued a three-legged toad from a deep well. Attached to the toad was an endless string of cash. The chess piece shows *Lui-Hai* with his right foot resting on a three-legged toad, one of his attributes. In his right hand he holds up a piece of cash, an allusion to wealth, but also symbolic of the inter-dependence of the sexes, the round rim of the coin standing for heaven and male and the central square hole for earth and female. *Lui-Hai*'s third attribute, a fishing rod has surprisingly been replaced by a fly-whisk. The band around his top-knot is reminiscent of those worn by the hill tribes of North Vietnam.

The first piece on the left shows a *nat* or devil riding on the back of a Chinese carp, a symbol of scholarly success. The *nat* is holding a Malayan *kris*, while his sash is of a type worn by the Burmese. Note the distorted head of the spirit figure. The fish is swimming through swirling water representing *yin*. The *kris* is a *yang* symbol.

The two pawns, second and fourth from the left are tail-less monkeys. The red pawn is holding a dagger and the white pawn a small sword. These pieces suggest the battle between the demon king *Ravana* and the monkey allies of Rama described in the epic poem *Tamayana*, composed by the Indian poet Valniki in sansckrit about 300 BC.

The last piece is difficult to place. All the other pieces are related to religious mythology, whereas this is typical chinoiserie of the Malayan Peninsula, the headgear being west-coast Malayan. The small cannon is mounted on wheels and is being pushed by a single soldier. This piece could be from northern Thailand or southern Burma.

The multiplicity of cultures incorporated in these six chessmen suggests an origin in a large cosmopolitan centre where the various symbolisms would be familiar and appreciated. When they were examined by an oriental expert, who wishes to remain anonymous, he suggested that they were probably carved by a Chinese craftsman living in Bangkok. To support this view he pointed out that the stiff rosette pattern of the bases was more in keeping with Siamese than Chinese or Vietnamese origin. The skill and detail of the carvings suggested nineteenth-century work, and the degree of wear and polish on the head of the carp a date of about 1850, give or take thirty years. They are unlikely to have been made before 1820 or after 1880.

No records of similar pieces have been seen in any reference book consulted and they are therefore assumed to be rare and worth this detailed description. They also serve to indicate how an investigation into provenance can be conducted.

TWO MORE MYSTERY PIECES

240

241

(240) These two items belie their appearance. They are not what they seem to be; a child's money box in boxwood, and a chess rook of rosewood. Does (241) provide a clue?

In many Victorian households gambling was viewed with abhorrence and dice and dicing cups were regarded as tools of the devil; but what more respectable than a child's money box encouraging the virtue of thrift? Unscrewing the lid exposes a totally unnecessary depth of thread for the fixing of the lid, but provides a rough surface to make cheating by 'sliding' dice more difficult.

The upper third of the other piece in (241) unscrews to reveal a cavity 2 inches (6cm) deep in the larger portion and ¾ inch (1.8cm) deep in the smaller portion. This rosewood 'Rook' was used for smuggling opium. In the *Daily Telegraph* Magazine, No. 553 of July 4th, 1975 is an article by David Sears on the smuggling of hard drugs into Amsterdam, and one of the illustrations accompanying the article is a photograph of Chief Superintendent Toorenaar of the Amsterdam Drug Squad displaying a *Mah-jongg* set used to smuggle heroin.

Near the red light district of Amsterdam are the opium dens, gambling casinos and brothels of the city's Chinatown. The illicit narcotics merchants operated in relative safety, exploiting wide loopholes in Dutch law. More than half the heroin then entering Holland (1975) was believed to have been used by the ten thousand Dutch and foreign resident addicts; the rest was re-exported causing great anxiety to neighbouring countries. Looking at the little rosewood chesspiece one can appreciate some of the difficulties in suppressing this horrible trade.

242

243

(242) Backgammon was also held in some families as a dubious pastime, encouraging gambling and distracting minds from more serious pursuits. These three backgammon boxboards have every appearance of respectability and scholarship, their spines bound in leather and titled in gold leaf HISTORY OF ENGLAND and HISTORY OF AMERICA: they appear to be worthy additions to any row of learned tomes in a handsome bookcase!

(243) This backgammon board was made some forty years later than the 'History' boards but is in the same tradition and at first glance it appears to be a medieval leather bound religious volume, either a psalter or a Book of Hours.

Closer inspection shows it to be a book-shaped backgammon board, the black, green and gold embossed leathers being a clever imitation using pressed and toughened paper over cardboard. The dicing cup of the same materials also simulates green grained leather. The dice and pieces are missing.

The original booklet *Game of Backgammon* provided with the set is shown alongside the board. Its cover is of the same toughened paper but simulating a light coloured skiver. The title page includes the information: 'Printed in U.S.A. Copyright 1930 by Cutler & Saleeby Inc. Edward J. Cadigan Inc. Springfield, Massachusetts.' The booklet and the board appear to have been produced together in the early 1930s.

CHINESE IVORY BACKGAMMON PIECES

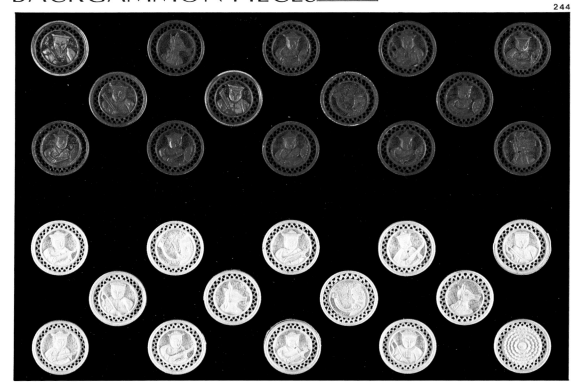

244

245

(244) The mounted display of twenty-eight tablemen was bought in an antique shop in Pitlochry in 1984. They are mounted behind glass in a shallow mahogany display case which opens at the right-hand side with a sliding catch, made about 1880. The pieces are Cantonese but the case is probably Scottish. The set had been bought by the dealer about a month earlier at a house sale in Edinburgh, together with an ornate ivory chess set of red and white pieces, which was resold within a few days. They were many Chinese items in the sale and the family appear to have had shipping connections with China at the end of the nineteenth century. This backgammon set may have come to Leith in a tea clipper. The pieces themselves are interesting. Apart from having been hand-carved and therefore with minor variations in every piece, they fall into the following categories:-

Red Pieces   7 men with daggers and shields
     1 bearded man with a quill pen
     2 men with batons
     1 man with a flywhisk
     2 horses' heads
     1 elephant's head and trunk

White Pieces   7 men with muskets
     3 men with fly whisks
     2 horses' heads
     2 elephants' heads and trunks

The reverse of all the pieces is the same, a rosette. See the right hand lower corner where a white 'Man with a musket' has been turned over to show the rosette. Why are there only fourteen pieces on each side instead of the usual fifteen, or sixteen in Thailand where the game is known as *sake*? Are two pieces missing or is there a twenty-eight piece backgammon variant played somewhere. Why the difference in the pieces? Is this merely at the whim of the carver or do the different designs have some significance, such as different powers or points values? Indeed, are the pieces meant for backgammon or some other game? Intriguing questions to which, at the moment, there are no answers.

(245) The ivory Chinese chessmen (*Siang k'i* pieces) in the right hand compartment of the carved box once belonged to Captain Jones of the Royal Flying Corps. After the end of the First World War Captain Jones went to China as an instructor for the Chinese airforce and left the country a few months before the Japanese invasion in 1931 bringing the ivory pieces with him. The chessmen were made c.1880 or earlier; the ivory dominoes in the left hand compartment also belonged to the Captain. Their date is uncertain. The *Poh Kam* in the central compartment came from elsewhere.

BONE

(246) The games compendium of bone, *c.*1815 or earlier, is thought to have been made by a French prisoner of war or by a sailor at sea. Carving bones from their food was a popular occupation of whalers and deep sea sailors becalmed on long voyages. Seafarers also engraved on walrus tusks, usually scenes of fishing or ships, but occasionally gameboards, either for cribbage, see page 133 *(150)* or solitaire, see page 53 *(97)*, which shows a modern Italian copy in a resin compound of a rare Norse ivory board in a museum. Such engraved Norse ivory is called *scrimshaw*. A word of warning: fake scrimshaw made of plastic is sometimes passed off as the genuine article.

To return to the compendium. The lid contains one hundred and twenty-two drill holes for cribbage pegs and inside is a set of double six bone dominoes and two bone dice. There is also a full pack of bone cards, the backs of which are plain and the fronts painted. The court cards only have one head indicating a late eighteenth or early nineteenth century date of manufacture.

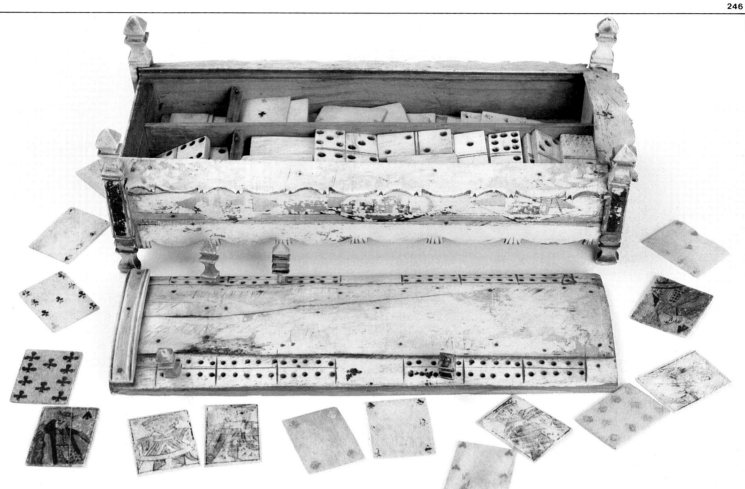

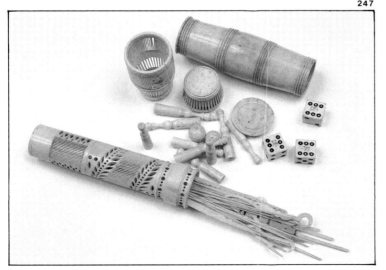

(247) Shown here is a filigree ivory container for spillikins. In the centre is a bird cage container holding a miniature set of nine ivory skittles and two balls and behind, in ivory, a dicing cup with three dice of the reign of George III, each marked with G R separated by a crown, all in red, indicating that the official tax had been paid on the dice.

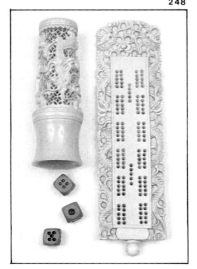

(248) The ivory dicing cup was made about 1850 and the dragon's eyes are tiny rubies. Note the similarities between this cup and the ivory cribbage board alongside, although the latter's dragons' eyes are tiny pieces of jet, *c.1880*. Such dating is only approximate and they may have been made more recently.

TINWARE GAMES

Contrasting with ivory in the cost of the raw material is tinware, popular in the 1890-1930 period for the production of cheap toys and games, which sold for a few pence. The life of most of these pieces was short and, when damaged, they were thrown away as rubbish. Hence their rarity and value today, since they are not likely to be made again as this down-grade market has been taken over by plastics.

The underside of the roulette wheel with an arrow point instead of a ball, seen on page 69 (127), carries an advertisement for 'TURF' Virginia cigarettes. There is no indication of where it was made, except that the 00 space near the 5 o'clock position suggests an American origin, c.1930.

(249) The Gee-Wiz game is no longer in working order although the principle of its action is clear. The heavy fly-wheel propelled by a length of string wound around its axle, drives a square shaft. Behind each horse was a small steel ball which was knocked forwards by the revolving surfaces of the shaft and struck the back of the tin sledge carrying each horse, pushing it towards the finishing post in little jerks. The gentle incline then directed the ball back to the revolving shaft to be knocked forwards again and the process was repeated a number of times, the horse making a 'stride' towards the finishing post each time it was struck. The front of the sledge eventually reached the bottom of the finishing flag which fell forwards towards the start of the course and there was no dispute about the order of finishing of the horses. Bets were placed on the coloured discs on the right-hand side of the course. Note that in 1930 the game was selling new for $2.29 in the United States. The square shaft of the Gee-Wiz fly-wheel and the flat-sectioned spinning top of the Alpine Hoca game, shown in (123) page 68, both use the same method to drive balls in haphazard fashion.

Behind the Gee-Wiz game is a horsehoe race track game with its original tinware dicing cup which also doubles as a holder for the little tin horses and the die.

250

(250) Two tinware games. On the left is a spinning arrow horserace game, with the inside of its cardboard box serving as a betting board, c.1930. On the right, is a combination of three games on the same tinware board: Crown and Anchor, Roulette and a horse-racing game, c.1920. The different odds on the horses are given on a folding canvas betting cloth (not shown): Maid Marion 11 to 1, Peeping Tom 8 to 1, Mr Pickwick 17 to 1, Dorothy 3 to 1, Esmerelda 2 to 1, Waverley 5 to 1. Note that there is no 00 in the roulette.

249

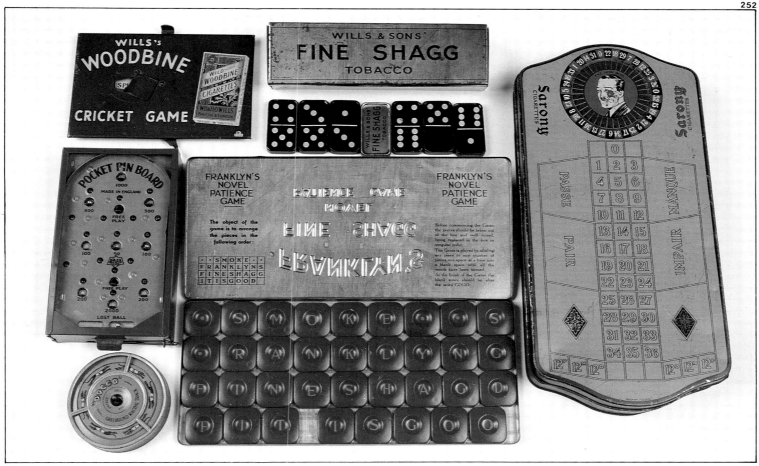

(252) A selection of Tobacco Company advertising items: a Wills Woodbine Cricket game, a Wills Fine Shagg set of Dominoes; A Franklyn's Fine Shagg Patience Game; and a Saronoy's Cigarettes Betting Board. To the left in front is a little greyhound racing game called Doggo, and behind this is a Pocket Pin board.

(253) This ingenious game seems to be an inexpensive copy of the Jaques race-game 'Ascot' shown in (**254**). In 'Ascot' the lead horses are housed in compartments within the mahogany box. When racing, each horse is pulled towards the finishing line by a thin cord which is fastened to an axle turned by a small ivory crank handle at the left hand side of the box when seen from the front. The way the cords wrap themselves around the axle determines the speed of advancement of the horse; if it spreads out equally along the axle, the progress of the horse is slow, but if it 'piles up' thus increasing the diameter of the axle, progress is faster.

Originally there would have been a considerable difference in the price of the two games but, today, the gap has narrowed considerably. Jaques' records were destroyed in an air-raid in the Second World War, but 'Ascot' probably dates from about 1910. Originally there were eight lead horses, each with a jockey wearing well-known racing colours, making them desirable to the racing fraternity and therefore raising their price.

(251) Other examples of tinware games are shown here with a solitaire board in the centre, surrounded by trump indicators. The first on the left has a flag beneath a crown on the base and S.S.Montcalm, and the third from the left, a lion with WEMBLEY beneath, and *British Empire Exhibition 1925*.

LACQUER

Lacquer has been used in China since ancient times. During the Chou Dynasty (1122-249BC) it was used for decorating carriages and harness, bows and other treasured possessions. A late Ming (1368-1644) manuscript, the *Hsui-shih-lu*, states that it was first used for writing on bamboo slips, then for utensils for food, made of black lacquer and later for black ceremonial vessels with red interiors, a tradition still surviving.

255

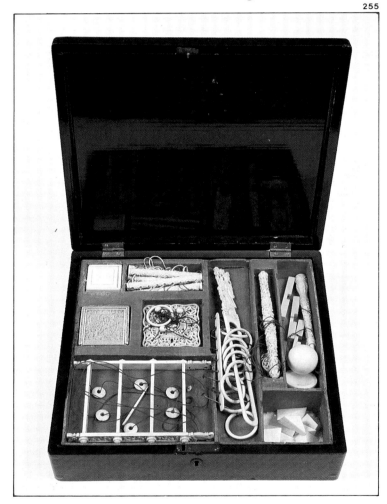

(255) Black lacquer box containing Chinese ivory puzzles.

256

Lacquer is the sap of a tree, *Rhus verniafera* which is indigenous to China and has been cultivated in Japan since the sixth century. The tree is first tapped when it is about ten years old, lateral incisions being made in the bark and the sap collected from June to September. The sap is greyish-white in colour and about the consistency of treacle. On exposure to air it turns yellow-brown and then black. Excess moisture is removed by heating over a slow fire, and then it is stored in airtight jars. The foundation of lacquer work is nearly always wood a type of soft even-grained pine is used and reduced to remarkable thinness. When lacquer is exposed to air, it becomes very hard but not brittle and will take a brilliant polish rivalling that of porcelain. Remarkably, maximum hardness is developed in the presence of moisture and after each application of lacquer, the object is placed in moist surroundings. After each layer of lacquer is applied, (there may be twenty or more) the surface is dried and polished. This preliminary work may take at least three weeks and then the artist begins the decoration, using gold or silver dust applied through a bamboo tube. Larger fragments of precious metals were applied separately by hand using a small pointed tool.

(256) A Chinese black lacquer and gold box containing mother-of-pearl counters. Every counter is engraved on both sides.

A second type of lacquer work was also popular. The lacquer was built up in successive layers until it was several millimetres thick and then carved. To increase the effect of the carving the layers of lacquer were often of different colours and, by cutting to different depths, a range of colours was exposed. The carving was carried out with V-shaped tools, kept very sharp, when the lacquer was cold and very hard. Red Lacquer *(tansha)* is the commonest variety and was coloured with cinnabar (red mercuric sulphide). Other colours used included two shades of olive green, buff, brown, black and aubergine.

Japanese lacquer work is based on the Chinese, although it has developed along national lines and the treatment of landscape and flower subjects usually uses a background of flat gold lacquer. Some of the later Japanese lacquer is of a fiery brown tint.

257

258

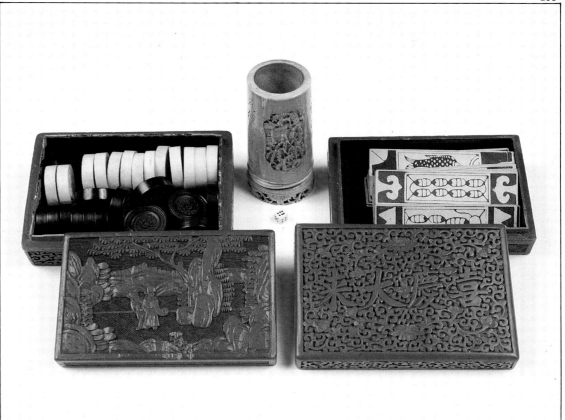

(257) Clockwise: black lacquered dice box with children playing a game in goldgilt, a lacquered card-case made of papier mâché, with an inscription in Arabic that states that it was made in Tehran in 1911, and behind, a pack of cards from Morocco, a Chinese black lacquered and gold gilt card case for two packs of cards and three sets of Chinese dice from the dicing box. The card box, *c.* 1880 or earlier, on the left, simulates a book. The front cover is ornamented with a scene of three men and a woman by a table on a terrace in a Chinese garden, seen through an ornamental window. The design is depicted in two shades of gold. The oval case of black and gold lacquer is a Japanese card holder for three packs of western cards. The aces of Hearts, Diamonds, Clubs and Spades on the lid indicates that it was made for export.

(258) The two carved red lacquer boxes holding Chinese playing cards and ivory backgammon pieces respectively are typical late nineteenth or early twentieth century carved lacquer work.

The combined chess and backgammon *(shwan-liu)* boxboard shown on page 19 is decorated externally in gold on a black lacquer base. The 'white' squares of the chess board are gold and the 'black' squares are black but decorated with a spray of leaves in gold. Around the sides of the box is a simple rustic scene. Inside the box, the backgammon points are of gold and red alternately, with the tips formed of three leaves in the opposite colour to the points, c.1890.

The Chinese filigree ivory tablemen, carved dicing cups and dice are c.1860 and are housed in the brocade-covered cardboard box resting on the side of the board. Incidentally, these boards are still being made, and the new ones are hard to distinguish from the old. Provenance is all-important. This board was bought in Edinburgh in 1949 and was said to be old then. It was bought for £3/$5, convincing evidence that it was not new at that time.

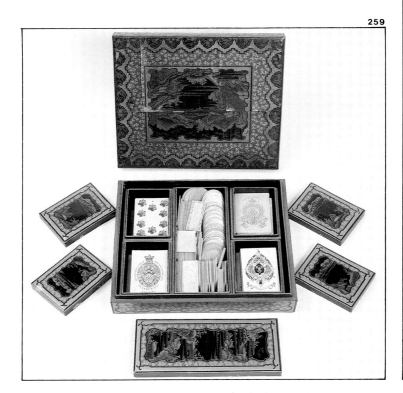

(260) This lovely black and gold lacquered box is 15 by 12 by 4½ inches (36 by 29 by 11cm) and mounted on four ornamental brass feet. The scene on the lid shows bowls of tea being served out of doors in an exotic oriental setting of pagodas and sampans on an idyllic lake. The sides of the box are similarly ornamented with further scenes of Chinese life. Inside are three rectangular lacquered boxes holding packs of cards and four five-sided boxes holding engraved mother-of-pearl counters of different shapes round, eliptical, short rectangular and long rectangular. There are also twelve shallow trays, eight marked with a Queen, King, Queen and King, Jack, Jack and Queen, Ace of Diamonds, Nine of Diamonds and GAME for use as compartments in the game of Pope Joan, c.1850. Its provenance is unknown.

(259) Less flamboyant in decoration, but still very attractive, is this lacquered cardbox with four separate smaller boxes for individual packs and a long central box for holding mother-of-pearl counters. The gold and black lacquer tops of all the boxes are displayed.

BOMBAY INLAID WORK

The fine Officers and Sepoys board reproduced on page 92 as a playable game is a choice example of Bombay Inlaid Work. This method of ornamentation was first used c.1790-1820, but the board illustrated was probably made about 1860. The 'Inlaid Work' is not a true inlay but a veneer formed by glueing together thin rods of ivory, tin, 'sappan wood', ebony and dyed samber-horn. These rods were usually triangular in section, sometimes round and frequently obliquely four-sided and were then built up further into a variety of more complex rods. These rods were then sliced to form thin decorative veneers.

In 1862 Dr Birdwood published an article on this work in the *Journal of the Royal Asiatic Society (Bombay Branch)* Vol. VII which is summarized below.

'Bombay Inlaid Work' seems to have been started in the city about 1800 being introduced from Hydrabad in Sindh, which had received the secrets of the craft about AD 1700 from Persia. The following materials were employed.

(261) Five examples of Bombay Inlaid Work.

Framework Sandalwood from Malabar, deal, blackwood or other woods and occasionally ivory.

Veneering Sandalwood, ebony, 'sappan wood', ivory, stagshorn and tin wire of varying sections. Animal glue was used for joining the framework and fixing the veneer.

The tools used:

A wheel, known as a *katt*, was used for drawing the tin wire into different cross sections for the preparation of the ornamental patterns.

A large saw was used for cutting the framework, a smaller saw for ebony, another for ivory and a fourth for cutting the prepared fasciculi of pattern.

A coarse file was used for the samber-horn and a fine one for ivory. Various chisels, drills, planes and a T-square were also used.

The patterns most commonly used in Bombay Inlaid Work are recorded below and several are illustrated in *(261)*, *c.* 1890.

Round *(Chukur)* from ¾in (20mm) in diameter to 1in (25mm).

Small round *(Teekee)* from 1¼in (23mm) to ½in (14mm).

Hexagonal *(Kutkee)* made of obliquely four-sided rods of ivory or sandalwood, and ebony, tin wire, sappan wood and stained samber-horn mixed together.

Triangular *(Teenkoonia gool)* made up of tin wire, ebony, ivory, sappan wood and stained samber-horn.

Obliquely four-sided *(Gool)* were formed as were the triangular. Both were used for central ornmanent.

The following were used only for borders and before being sawn across were like boards two to three feet (60 to 90cm) wide, a foot or two (30 to 60cm) long, and from ⅛ to ⅜ inch (0.3 to 2cm) in thickness.

a)   A compound of all the ornamental material *(Gundeirio)*.

b)   A single row of tin beads in a ground of ivory *(Ekdana)*.

Porce Lehur, Sankroo Hansio and Poro Hansio were patterns set in sockets of ivory, ebony or sandalwood, forming the framework of the article or veneered over a framework of some common material.

The similarity in technique between Bombay Inlaid Work and Tonbridge Ware is striking.

A VICTORIAN GAMES COMPENDIUM

262

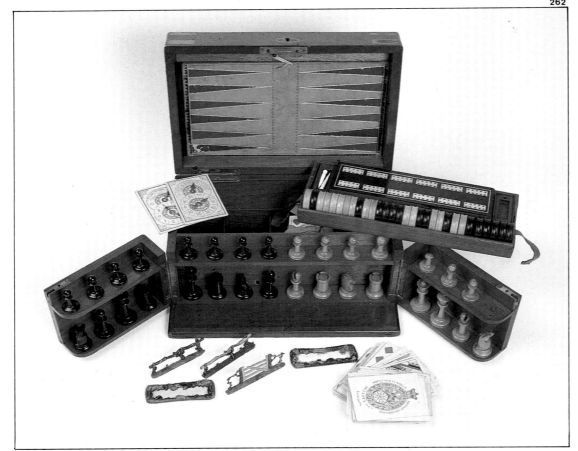

recess containing a double six domino set made of bone. The pieces are 1¾ inches (4cm) long, ⅝ inches (2cm) wide and ³⁄₁₆ inches (0.5cm) thick without any backing. These are true 'bones' and are delightful to handle. Beneath the tray containing the dominoes, cribbage board and backgammon pieces, is a well divided into five unequal compartments.

The first compartment contains three lead fences and two lead water-jumps for the race game, all that survives of eleven obstacles that originally graced the course. There are also four large and four small plain ivory counters coloured blue, red, yellow and green.

The second compartment holds a pack of cards made by De La Rue, London. The corners of the cards are square, there are no indices and the court cards have two heads, with duty paid of 3d marked on the Ace of Spades, details indicating that the pack was made after 1862 but before 1870. (Seen on the table in front of the compendium.) It is a later replacement.

The narrow third compartment contains a boxwood hammer and six of the eight special dice used for the game of *Bell and Hammer*.

The fourth compartment is divided up into stalls for six lead racehorses which are missing. The last compartment contains a dicing cup of boxwood and two glass dice. The latter are rather crude and are probably a later replacement.

Judging from the quality of the mahogany and the simple style of the brass keyhole, an antique furniture expert thought that the box was late Georgian, about 1830. The chessmen are of the Staunton pattern. His pieces were first made in 1839 and registered in 1849. The latter were marked with a registration number. These pieces are unmarked and may be pre-registration pieces.

The cribbage board is of rosewood veneer on mahogany, the peg holes being drilled into

small rectangles of ivory inlaid into the wood. The light veneer strip is probably sycamore or holly. The style of the board suggests a date anywhere between 1820 and 1880.

Bell and Hammer was introduced into England from Germany where it was known as Schimmel, at least as early as 1816 and was played as late as 1870. The cards, bone dice, hammer and dicing cup may well be replacements and are not helpful in dating. The workmanship of the box, the type of chessmen, the unbacked bone dominoes and the equipment for The Game of the Race suggest that the compendium was probably made about 1840.

(262) In the days before radio and television, home entertainment depended upon the members of the family, two favourite pastimes being the making of music and the playing of games. This compendium, *c.*1840, was designed for use in the home or for taking on journeys, either on land by coach, or by sea on a ship. The richly-marked mahogany box is strengthened at the corners with five brass angles and has a lock and key. The lid houses a leather-covered race-game in four sections, two of which have a chess board on the reverse and two form a backgammon board. The

top of the box held a tray containing a cribbage board, a set of backgammon pieces doubling as draughtsmen, cribbage markers and two dice. The front of the box opens in two halves, each carrying half a chess set. One white pawn is missing and another is damaged. Each piece has a small hole drilled into the base which fits on to brass sprig to hold it in position on the shelf during the swaying of a carriage or the rolling of a ship. The tablemen-cum-draughtsmen are of ebony and boxwood and can be seen in a trough in front of the cribbage board.

Beneath the cribbage board is a

GAMES TABLES
GEORGIAN CHESS TABLE

263

VICTORIAN WORK/GAMES TABLE

264

265

(263) Made about 1820, this Georgian, rosewood chess table has simple clean cut lines but is a mixed piece. About sixty years later an owner decided to protect the playing surface with a plate glass cover, mounted in a mahogany frame which clips on to the table with a single steel spring.

The playing surface is an 8 x 8 chequer of rosewood and satinwood, but at sometime it has been badly repaired and the replacement squares do not match the originals, indeed in two places the checkering has been lost.

The chessmen are from Zimbabwe and are of carved soapstone. The pieces may well portray tribal leaders. Note that the rooks are grass huts.

(264) A high Victorian Style table, veneered with burr walnut and made about 1850. The upper surface is embellished with a Tonbridge ware picture of Eridge Castle and a typical border. The top of the table hinges at the back and the opened leaves rotate through a right angle to lie across the length of the table (265). The new upper surface presents a fine chequered chess board, backgammon board and cribbage board, a nice choice for passing a wet afternoon, or a long winter evening when the light was too poor for needlework.   The chessboard chequering is of ebony and satinwood, as are the points of the backgammon board and the sections of the cribbage board. The peg holes of the last are in satinwood.

Below the playing surface is a drawer with twenty compartments of varying sizes for cottons, silks, buttons and other small items of haberdashery. Below the drawer is a veneered 'bag' with a single thin stringing of satinwood. The worktable is supported by two turned pedestals of walnut, each branching into two legs, the knees being covered by a stylized carving of a hanging branch. The legs terminate in small paw-shaped feet. A turned cross-strut joining the pedestals strengthens the design.

185

VICTORIAN LOO TABLE

266

VICTORIAN ENVELOPE CARD TABLE

(267) This late-Victorian card table is of a type once popular in middle class homes in the 1880s. Made of mahogany, some were of cheaper woods stained to look like mahogany, they were hand-crafted, but on a piece-work system that foreshadowed machine mass-production. The name 'envelope' is taken from the appearance of the four flaps when the table is closed. When open, each flap contains a shallow saucer for holding counters or money and below these flaps is a shelf with a dowel sliding in a slot in each leg, permitting the shelf to be lowered to hold a cup of tea or a slice of cake. The card playing area is covered with a silver-grey velvet cloth. The simple square sectioned legs swell out into knees carved with an acanthus leaf and the small 'pointed toe' feet are provided with brass castors. All the hinges and struts are of brass.

267

(266) The next table served a dual purpose. Originally designed for playing Loo, it doubled as a family breakfast table. The table is laid out ready for play, with a central pool of counters. The trump card is turned face-up alongside three cards dealt to each of six players and four ashtrays marked Hearts, Diamonds, Clubs and Spades, scattered around the table. There is one deal for 'MISS'.

The playing surface of the table is veneered with the scarce 'Prune-juice' mahogany. The robust pedestal terminates in a lotus bud and the triangular base, more correctly described as hyperboloid, has a narrow gadrooning along the upper edges. The scrolled feet have carved wings at either side. When not in use the top can be hinged into an upright position and locked there with two winged brass screws. Such tables were made from about

1820 to 1880. This table dates from the end of this period and is now probably a little over one hundred years old.

In Loo there is no limit to the numbers of players taking part, but six or seven make for a better game. A full pack of cards was used, the dealer placing an agreed number of counters, either three or a multiple of three into a pool, before dealing three cards face downwards to each player, plus an extra hand called 'MISS'. The next card is turned face up and fixes the trump suit. The dealer then asks each player in turn whether he will play or 'Take MISS'. The player has the choice of retaining his hand taking 'MISS' or throwing in his hand and retiring from the round. Further details of play are irrelevant here but can be obtained from books on card games.

ART DECO STYLE HALMA TABLE

268

JAPANESE GAMES TABLE

269

270

(269) This blue and gold games table is 27 inches (66cm) long, 13 inches (32cm) wide and 14 inches (34cm) high and is intended for use by players sitting on the ground. The sides and back are carved and gilded, the front gilded over deep blue paint. There are two small drawers for holding games paraphenalia and the legs fold into the underside of the table to permit easy storage when not in use. A set of *Hanafuda* cards is spread out on the playing surface.

(270) The upper surface of this table is a mosaic of ebony, ivory, coloured woods and mother-of-pearl. The heavy top hinges open and swivels through a right angle to rest upon the length of the table. When open the upper surface forms a card table with a central green baize area 23 inches (56cm) square. The whole area is 25 inches (61cm) square.

The card playing area lifts up in three hinged sections to expose a well 2 inches (5cm) deep in which is a backgammon board or, if only half the green baize surface is raised, an 8 x 8 checkered board for chess or draughts is ready for use. All the areas are decorated with the same high quality mosaic decoration.

Below the small apron is a shelf 5 inches above the floor and surrounded by a rail. The shelf is also decorated with mosaic. The apron and the legs are decorated and the lower 5 inches (12cm) of the legs bend in an outward-facing curve. The table was made in Damascus, Syria, about 1920 and belonged to a shipping family living in Wallsend. It was brought to Britain in one of the company's ships.

(268) This table is probably a relic of the British Raj in India. Made about 1920 in Art Deco style, it was used for playing Halma, a game invented in the United States of America by H. Monk, copyright 1885 and patented by the E.I.Horsman Company, 29 May 1888. The upper surface of the table is 20½ inches (50cm) square, and is 24½ inches (60cm) high. It is made of teak veneered with ebony, ivory and exotic oriental woods. On the underside of the playing surface is a box, sliding on runners, for holding the playing pieces.

The board consists of a checkered surface of 16 x 16 squares, half of ivory and half ebony. The four legs are decorated with an Art Deco design of ivory and ebony inlaid into the teak. A tray, some 4 inches (10cm) off the floor, is also inlaid and provides space for storing books and papers. The table's provenance has been lost, but it was bought from a furniture dealer in Low Fell on the south side of Gateshead, an area connected with shipping and the Far East. Produced in a native workshop, it has the charm of the village craftsman.

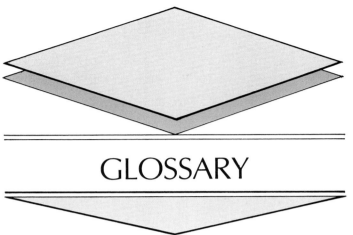

GLOSSARY

Approach See Capture.

Blockade To obstruct, therefore preventing pieces moving in any direction.

Capture To take a player's piece by trapping between two opposing pieces placed in a straight line on either side.

Dice Plural of die.

Die Cube used in game of chance.

Dress The laying out of cards on a board in a gambling game in readiness for placing of bets.

Elder The player going first in order of play.

En prise Piece being placed in a position which allows it to be taken.

File A line running vertically from top to bottom of the board at right angles to a rank.

Grace To be granted an extra turn.

Huff A piece is confiscated as penalty for infringing a rule.

Intervention See capture.

Jump Moving of one piece to an adjacent point by jumping over opposing piece.

Long Leap To capture by one piece jumping over another and landing beyond.

Orthogonal To move at right angles.

Point The point where lines cross on which pieces can be placed being neither on the squares or spaces between.

Pool A bank into which all players coins or counters are placed at beginning of, or during, play.

Rank A straight line running at right angles from one side across the board to a file.

Replacement See Capture.

Row See Rank.

Singleton A piece isolated from the others making it vulnerable to attack.

Teetotum A four-sided disc, each side inscribed with a letter or number, rotating on a central spindle. The disc is rotated and, on reaching end of spin, the uppermost letter decides player's move.

Trumps Every card in one suit chosen to rank temporarily above the others.

Younger The player going last in order of play.

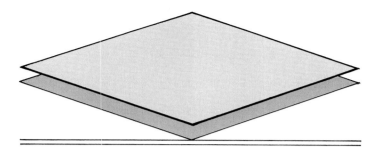

INDEX

A

Abalala'e	*59*
Aces	65
Aces in the pot	62
Achi	45
Advice to new collectors	161
Alea	18
All Fives	*118*
Alps	
Hoca	68
Alquerque	35
Aphelion	13, *78-79*
Asalto	*25, 26*
Asanti	54
Ascot	179
Ashtapada	27
Aviation	40

B

Backgammon	18, 175, 176
Bagatelle	142
Ballinderry board	25
Baré	60
Bezique markers	171
Blackjack	106-107, 138
Block Game	117
Blow Football	144
Bombay Inlaid Work	92, 182
Bonanza	137
Bone	171, 177
Bounce on the Stone	154
Bowl Game	154
British Columbia	
Slahal	151
Hand Game	151
Brother Jonathan	142
Brunei	
Pasang	52

Burma
Sittuyin	*33*
Burmese chess	33

C

Card games requiring boards or markers	132
Carpet Bowls	*147*
Carroms	140
Chaturanga	*27, 28*
Chess	29
Chi Chi Sticks	156
China	
Chi Chi Sticks	156
Chinese Chess	33
Chinese Dominoes	121
Disputing Tens	122
Four Numbers	71
Go	50, 98-101
Hoo, Hey, How	72
Poh Kam	159
Pong hau k'i	50
Shap luk kon tsu tseung kwan	26
Siang k'i	33
Sixteen Soldiers	26
Wei ch'i	50, 98-101
Chinese Checkers	48
Chinese Chess	33
Chinese Dominoes	121
Conquerors Castle	102-103
Continental Draughts	39, 80-81
Cows and Leopards	26, 90-91
Crown and Anchor	66
Cyprus	120
Cyprus	
Tavli	20

D

Dames	37
Dara	46
Darts	146
Diagonal Draughts	39
Dice and Spinners	62
Dice Game	152
Disputing Tens	122
Dominoes	116
Domino Pool	119
Double-nine dominoes	119
Double-twelve dominoes	120
Dover Patrol	40
Down the Kaiser	143
Draughts	37
Driedel	68
Duodecim Scriptorum	17

E

Egypt
Alquerque	35
Fanorona	36
Nine Men's Morris	45, 76-77
Quadruple *Alquerque*	36
Seega	23
Senat	16
Snake Game	11, 104-105
Sumerian Game	94-95
Tau	15
Tic-Tac-Toe	45
Eighty-one	146
Electric Derby	71
English Draughts	38
Ethiopia	
Santarij	34
Abalala'e	59
Baré	60

F

Fanorona	36
Five Field Kono	48
Fortune Teller	158
Fortune Telling	156
Fortune Telling Bagatelle	158
Four Balls	47
Four-handed chess	31
Four-handed cribbage	134
Four Numbers	71
Four Rank *Mancala*	60
Fox and Geese	25
France	
Continental Draughts	39, 80-81
French Solitaire	53
German Tactics	42
Jeu de Courses	70
Jeu Forcé	37
L'Attaque	39
Nain Jaune	137
Roulette	67
Shut the Box	65
Siege of Paris	43, 88-89
Solitaire	52
Tric Trac	18
Yellow Dwarf	137

G

Gambling Sticks	155
Game of the Pedlar	63
Game of the Race	14
Game for fifteen or more dice	65
Games of position	45
Games requiring manual dexterity	139
Games tables	185-187
Games using five dice	64
Games using one die	62

Games using three dice 64
Games using two dice 62
Games with six dice 65
Games with special dice 66, 67
Geographical Game
    Thro' Europe 13
German Tactics 42
Germany
    Poch 114-115, 136
Ghana
    Achi 45
    Wari 61
Go 50, 98-101
Go-moku 46
Gossima 144
Great Britain
    Aphelion 13, 78
    Asalto 25
    Conquerors Castle 102-103
    Cribbage 132
    Crown and Anchor 66
    Electric Derby 71
    English Draughts 38
    Four-handed Cribbage 134
    Game of the Pedlar 63
    Game of the Race 14
    Geographical Game
        Thro' Europe 13
    Journey to Crossroads 102-103
    Jubilee 13
    Ludo 10
    Officers and Sepoys 25, 92-93
    Pope Joan 135, 182
    Put and Take 67
    Race to the
        Gold Diggings 22, 96-97
    Reversi 49
    Roly Poly 69
    Shove-Ha'penny 139
    South Sea Adventures 108-109

Squails 140
Telepathic Spirit
    Communicator 156
Three-handed Cribbage 134
Tops 128
Ucca, see Ludo 27
Ups and Downs 82-83
Greece
    Pentalpha 53

H_____

Halatafl 25
Halma 48, 112-113
Hama-guri shells 168
Hand Game 151
Hasami Shogi I 47
Hasami Shogi II 41
Hei tiki 159
High Jump 24
Hnefatafl 24
Hoca 68
Hoo, Hey, How 72
How T'si Kong 166
Hyaku-nin-ishu 168

J_____

Japan
    Go 50, 98-101
    Go-moku 46
    Hama-guri shells 168
    Hasami Shogi I 47
    Hasami Shogi II 41
    Hyaku-nin-ishu 168
    I-go 50, 98-101
    Karuta Hiyaku-nin-Ishu 168
    Kyaku-min-itsusha 168
    Shogi 34
    Sugoruku 19
Japanese Chess 34

Jeu de Courses 70
Jeu Forcé 37
Journey to Crossroads 102-103
Jubilee 13

K_____

Karuta Hyaku-nin-Ishu 168
    Konane 42
Korea
    Five Field Kono 48
    Nyout 8
    O-pat-ko-no 48
    Tjyang Keui 34
    Korean Chess 34

L_____

Lacquer 180-182
Lam Turki 53, 90
L'Attaque 39
Lau Kati Kata 91
Liar Dice 66
Losing Draughts 39
Ludo 10
Ludus Latrunculorum 23, 84-85

M_____

Maharajah and the Sepoys 34
Mah-Jongg 122-128, *123, 124*
Making a Games Collection 160
Makruk 34
Mancala 54
Maori
    Hei Tiki 159
    Mu Torere 50
    Ti Rakau 149
Martinetti 64
Matador Game 119
Mexico
    Patolli 155

Ming Mang 42
Mu Torere 50

N_____

Nain Jaune 137
New Zealand
    Hei Tiki 159
    Mu Torere 50
    Ti Rakau 149
Nigeria
    Dara 46
Nine Men's Morris 45, 76-77
North American Indian
    Games 150
Nyout 8

O_____

Officers and Sepoys 25, 92-93
Ogura Hyakumin Issu 169
Olinda Keliya 57
One hundred and fifty one 146
Ogura Hyakumin Issu 169

P_____

Pachisi 9
Patolli 155
Pentalpha 3
Persia
    Shatranj 29
Ping Pong 144
Playable Games 73-115
Poch 114-115, 136
Poh Kam 159
Pong Hau K'i 50
Pope Joan 135, 182
Poker Dice 66
Put and Take 67

Q

Quadruple *Alquerque*   36

R

Race Games
Race to the
  Gold Diggings   22, 96-97
Ratti Chitti Bakri   37
Reversi   49
Roly Poly   69
Roman Empire
  Alea   18
  Duodecim Scriptorum   17
  Ludus Latrunculorum
    23, 84-85
  Tabula   18
Rotation   63
Roulette   68
Round the Clock   146
Royal Game of Billiard Bowls   148
Royal Game of Goose   11, 74-75
Royal Hurdle
  Race Game   86-87, 138

S

Saka   20
Salish Indians   151
Santarij   34
Scandinavia
  Hnefatafl   24
  Tafl   24
  Ballinderry board   25
Seega   16
Sequences   65
Se-tich-ch   154
Shap luk kon tsu tseung kwan   26
Shatranj   29
Shogi   34

Shove Ha'penny   139
Shut the Box   65
Siamese chess   33
Siang K'i   33
Siege of Paris   43, 88-89
Singapore
  Tams   39
Sittuyin   33
Sixteen Soldiers   26
Skittles with fifteen
  sliced spheres   143
Slahal   151
Snail Game   22
Snake Game   11, 104-105
Snakes and Ladders   14
Solitaire   52
Somalia
  High Jump   16
South East Asia
  Cows and Leopards   26, 90
South Sea Adventures   ·108-109
Spinners   67
Squails   140
Sri Lanka
  Pallanguli   55
  Olinda Keliya   57
Stave Game   154
Sugoruku   19
Sumerian Game   94-95
Sunka   55, 110-111

T

Tablan   26
Table Quoits   144
Table Skittles   144
Table Ten-Pins   143
Tabula   18
Tafl   24
Talismen, charms and
  good luck symbols   159

Tamilnadi   56
Tams   39
Tarot Cards   157
Tau   15
Tavli   20
Telepathic Spirit
  Communicator   156
Thailand
  Saka, see Backgammon   20
  Makruk, see Chess   34
Thiry-six   62
Three Dimensional
  Three in a Row   47
Three-handed Cribbage   134
Three rank Mancala   59
Tibet
  Ming Mang   42
Tic-Tac-Toe   45
Tiddle-a-Wink   120
Tiddley Winks   144
Tinware Games   178
Ti Rakau   149
Tjyan Keui   34
Tric Trac   18
Tri-Onimos   131
Tri Tactics   41
Tsolo   55
Twice Round the Board   146
Two-Handed Block Game   118

U

Ucca   11
United States
  Bonanza   137
  Bounce on the Stone   154
  Bowl Game   154
  Brother Jonathan   142
  Chinese Checkers   48
  Dice Game   152
  Fortune Teller   158

  Fortune Telling Bagatelle   158
  Gambling Sticks   155
  Halma   48, 112-113
  Se-tich-ch   154
  Stave Game   154
  Stockade   44
  Up to the Klondyke   22
  Wer-Lar-Da-Har-Mun-Gun
    154
Ups and Downs   82-83
Up to the Klondyke   22
Uta Karuta   168

W

War Games   23
Wari   61
Wei ch'i   50
Wer-Lar-Da-Har-Mun-Gun   154
West Africa
  Yoté   41
  Wari   60
  Whist markers   170

The games on pages 74/75,
102/103 and the Halma board on
page 112 were loaned by Donay
Antiques, Camden Passage,
London.
The games on pages 86/87 and
108/109 were loaned by Nicholas
Costa.
Snake Game photograph, page
105, Fitzwilliam Museum,
Cambridge.

ACKNOWLEDGEMENTS

The author wishes to thank John Strange and Megra Mitchell of Dunestyle Publishing for their help in the production of this book, Miss Kirsty McLaren for her photographic skill and patience in providing the attractive illustrations, and his wife for sharing her home for many years with a strange assortment of odds and ends from around the world.

ABOUT THE AUTHOR

After passing his seventieth birthday the author looks back over forty years of collecting games. The illustrations in this book are taken from items in the collection.

Born in Sudbury, Ontario, he came to England in 1928 to attend a boarding school in North Wales, and then Haileybury College, Hertfordshire. After five and a half years as a medical student at St. Bartholomew's Hospital, London, he qualified MRCS, LRCP. England; M.B., B.S. London, and then held a series of resident posts in London, Aberdeen and Hull before joining the R.C.A.F. in 1945 serving in England, Germany and Labrador, retiring in August 1948 as the Senior Medical Officer, R.C.A.F. Station, Goose Bay, Labrador.

After further surgical training and obtaining the FRCS England in 1949, he was appointed as a consultant Plastic Surgeon in 1952 working for the Newcastle Regional Hospital Board at Shotley Bridge General Hospital (Plastic Surgery Unit), and the Fleming Memorial Hospital for Children, Newcastle-upon-Tyne for thirty years, retiring in 1982. Since then he has had published *Maling and other Tyneside Pottery,* Shire Publications 1986; and *Political and Commemorative Places and Simulating Tradesmens' Tokens 1770-1802,* Schwer 1987. A prepublication copy of his first major work, *Board and Table Games from Many Civilizations,* Oxford University Press, 1960 won the Premier Award of the Doctors' Hobbies Exhibition in London, 1959.

The publishers would like to thank Donay Antiques of Camden Passage London whose shop and enthusiasm was the inspiration for this title, Nic Costa for his help and encouragement and Kirsty McLaren for her photography.